Dōgen's Pure Standards for the Zen Community

SUNY Series in Buddhist Studies
Matthew Kapstein, Editor

Painting of Dōgen Zenji

Dōgen's Pure Standards for the Zen Community

A Translation of the *Eihei Shingi*

Translated by
Taigen Daniel Leighton
and Shohaku Okumura

with forewords by
Ikkō Narasaki Rōshi
and
Jūsan Kainei Edward Brown

Edited with an introduction by
Taigen Daniel Leighton

STATE UNIVERSITY OF NEW YORK PRESS

Published by
State University of New York Press, Albany

© 1996 State University of New York

All rights reserved

Printed in the United States of America

No part of this book may be used or reproduced in any manner whatsoever without written permission. No part of this book may be stored in a retrieval system or transmitted in any form or by any means including electronic, electrostatic, magnetic tape, mechanical, photocopying, recording, or otherwise without the prior permission in writing of the publisher.

For information, address State University of New York Press, 90 State Street, Suite 700, Albany, NY 12207

Production by Bernadine Dawes • Marketing by Nancy Farrell

Library of Congress Cataloging-in-Publication Data

Dōgen, 1200–1253.
    [Eihei shingi. English]
    Dogen's pure standards for the Zen community : a translation of the Eihei shingi / translated by Taigen Daniel Leighton and Shohaku Okumura : edited with an introduction by Taigen Daniel Leighton.
       p. cm. — (SUNY series in Buddhist studies)
    Includes bibliographical references and indexes.
    ISBN 0-7914-2709-9 (alk. paper). — ISBN 0-7914-2710-2 (pbk. : alk. paper)
    1. Monasticism and religious orders, Zen—Rules—Early works to 1800. 2. Spiritual life—Sōtōshū—Early works to 1800.
I. Leighton, Taigen Daniel. II. Okumura, Shohaku, 1948– .
III. Title. IV. Series.
BQ9449.D6543513 1995
294.3'657—dc20
                                                95-24658
                                                      CIP

10 9 8 7 6 5 4 3 2

Contents

List of Illustrations	vii
Foreword by Ikkō Narasaki Rōshi	ix
Foreword by Jūsan Kainei Edward Brown	xiii
Acknowledgments	xix
Introduction by Taigen Daniel Leighton	1

Overview of Dōgen's Writings • 1
The Role of Community in Buddhism • 2
Alignment with Nature • 5
Cultural Adaptation and Expression • 6
Introductions to the Individual Essays • 8
Chan Stories and the Sōtō Use of Koans • 13
Significance of the Eihei Shingi
   in Dōgen's Teaching and Practice • 14
Contemporary Understandings
   of Dōgen's Historical Context • 17
Earlier Monastic Codes • 20
The Textual History of the Eihei Shingi *• 21*
Development of Standards for the Community
   in the Keizan Shingi *• 22*
Translation Issues: Gender and Pronouns • 23
Dōgen's Use of Language • 25
Glossaries and Notes • 25
Personal Experience of the Monastic Container • 27
Conclusion • 29

The Pure Standards of Eihei Dōgen Zenji
[Eihei Shingi]

Instructions for the Tenzo (Tenzokyōkun)	33
The Model for Engaging the Way (Bendōhō)	63
The Dharma for Taking Food (Fushukuhanpō)	83
Regulations for the Study Hall (Shuryō Shingi)	109
The Dharma when Meeting Senior Instructors of Five Summer Practice Periods (Taitaiko Gogejarihō)	121
Pure Standards for the Temple Administrators (Chiji Shingi)	127

Director [Kan'in] • 152
Inō [Supervisor of Monks] • 167
Tenzo [Chief Cook] • 170
Work Leader [Shissui] • 179

Appendix: Afterword to the Shohon Edition	205
Glossary of Japanese Terms	207
Glossary and Index of Names	235
Lineage Charts	251
Selected Bibliography	261
The Translators	271

List of Illustrations

Diagram of the Interior of the Monks' Hall	58
Diagram of the Eiheiji Building Layout	59
Exterior of Kuin: Kitchen and Temple Administrators' Office Building	60
Exterior of the Monks' Hall	60
Interior of the Study Hall	61
Exterior of the Dōgen Zenji Memorial Hall	61
Ōryōki Eating Bowls Wrapped Up	62
Ōryōki Eating Bowls Unwrapped and Set Out, with Food	62

Foreword

Ikkō Narasaki Rōshi

In the *Gakudō Yōjinshū* [Points to watch in studying the Way], Dōgen Zenji said, "The buddha way is right under your feet." The buddha way is not some special kind of way. It is simply the way in which you live completely.

With everything you encounter, without separating self and others, become one with that thing with your whole body and mind, dealing with it most thoroughly. Dōgen Zenji called this *jijuyū zammai* [samadhi or concentration of self-fulfillment]. This *jijuyū zammai* is the criterion of the correctly transmitted buddha way.

The shingi [pure standards] accurately show us how to carry out fully jijuyū zammai with our body and mind throughout all the activities of monastic life, including zazen and kinhin [walking meditation], as well as washing the face, using the toilet, putting on robes, eating meals, doing prostrations, reciting sutras, sleeping, waking up, and so on.

Since all of our activities within the twenty-four hours are practice of the buddha way, embodying this jijuyū zammai that is the criterion of the buddha way is truly difficult, and is the highest priority. So to live based on shingi is extremely important.

According to the *Goyuigon Kiroku* [Record of bequeathed sayings] written by Gikai on the second day of the second month of the seventh year of the Kenchō Period [1255], Zen Master Tettsu Gikai, the third abbot of Eiheiji, acknowledged the following to Zen Master Koun Ejō, the second abbot of Eiheiji:

> I had heard our late master [Dōgen Zenji] espouse the teaching that the manners and conduct we follow now in this monastery are nothing other than the affair of buddhas and the Buddha Dharma itself. Nevertheless, in my private thoughts I still believed that there was a true Buddha Dharma other than that.
>
> However, recently I revised my view. Now I understand that the manners and dignified actions in the monastery are exactly the true Buddha Dharma. Even though there are limitless forms of Buddha Dharma shown by buddhas and ancestors, they all are this one color of Buddha Dharma. Other than the present dignified decorum of buddha in raising our arms and moving our legs, there could be no principle of the profound buddha nature. I honestly believe this truth.

This statement by Gikai can confirm that the core of Dōgen Zenji's Buddha Dharma is, "Dignified manner is Buddha Dharma; decorum is the essential teaching."

According to Dōgen Zenji, a monastery is a community of people with bodhi mind who practice jijuyū zammai diligently in everything they encounter without an attitude of seeking gain. The inner reality of practice for such a community is described in the *Shōbōgenzō*, and the manner for carrying out this practice is shown in the *Eihei Shingi*. Therefore, Dōgen Zenji said that the pure standards are the body and mind of ancient buddhas.

It is not too much to say that Dōgen Zenji's Buddha Dharma lies solely in the practice of the *Eihei Shingi*. Moreover, as his descendants we must bear in mind that no matter how the style of Dōgen Zenji's successors develops and changes, it originates from the sitting platform in the monks' hall.

It is truly delightful that during the more than forty years since World War Two, Dōgen Zenji's Buddha Dharma has attracted many people's interest and has made an impression in Europe, America, and many other countries in the world. Intimate interchange and communication among many practice centers has been taking place, and zazen is being sincerely practiced.

For those earnest Way-seekers, barriers such as language, customs, and culture must be big obstacles. However, thoroughly engaging the Way at the monks' hall and sharing together all the community's activities during the twenty-four hours, based on the *Eihei Shingi*, are critical to the purpose of embodying Dōgen Zenji's Zen. I firmly believe that there is no way besides this to carry out fully the true dharma.

Fortunately, the six chapters of *Eihei Shingi* have now been translated into English by Rev. Shohaku Okumura, who has been guiding Westerners in zazen for a long time, and by one of his American dharma friends, Rev. Taigen Daniel Leighton. I think this is a fine project and admire their active vow.

I sincerely hope that by following the *Eihei Shingi*, practitioners will maintain the essential function of the buddha way and succeed to the living wisdom of the buddhas and ancestors.

I hereby recommend this translation of the *Eihei Shingi* not only to monks but also to lay practitioners overseas, and wish that the light of the Dharma treasure will grow endlessly.

On an auspicious spring day in the fifth year of Heisei (1993) at Zuiōji Monastery.

translated by
Taigen Leighton and Shohaku Okumura

Foreword

Jūsan Kainei Edward Brown

When I was starting out as the head cook at Tassajara Zen Mountain Center in May of 1967, I went to our teacher Suzuki Rōshi asking if he had any advice for me.

"When you wash the rice, wash the rice. When you cut the carrots, cut the carrots. When you stir the soup, stir the soup," was his answer. I did my best to actually put his words into practice, to really focus on what I was doing in the kitchen.

One thing it meant was putting my energy and awareness into the activities of cutting, cleaning, stirring, walking, and standing, instead of into the words, daydreams, preoccupations, and chitchat where my energy seemed to more naturally flow. This is stream-diverting, going against the current.

One needs not question whether the present moment's activity is worth doing; it is simply the one requiring attention at the present. There is no time for worry, regrets, wishes, complaints, demands. The world appears vivid with spinach, lettuces, black beans; with cutting boards, baking pans, and sponges. Where previously one had waited or looked for the world to provide entertainment or solace, here one enters into a world vibrant with the energy and devotion flowing out of one's being. "If you want to realize Suchness," as Dōgen Zenji's "Fukanzazengi" says, "practice Suchness without delay."

Later I was introduced to Dōgen Zenji's "Instructions for the Tenzo," one of the pieces translated here, and found a wonderfully resonant collection of sound advice. Words carefully given, taken to heart, and acted upon can be powerfully transformative. We can grow wise and compassionate instead of simply older. The words of Zen Master Dōgen in this book have the potential to awaken deep concentration and seeing into the nature of things. One shifts out of the mind-world of "What's in it for me?" into the world of mutual interdependence and interconnectedness. And this is not simply something to talk about but something to be done.

Implicit in our culture is the idea that we can have happiness, relief, and relaxation when we finish taking care of things, when we don't have to relate to anything. Dōgen Zenji's encouragement points out the Zen way: "All day and all night, things come to mind, and the mind attends to them; at one with them all, diligently carry on the Way." "Director, take care of the numerous affairs." Realization, awakening, liberation, patience, generosity, and well-being are in attending to things rather than avoiding or neglecting them. They are in activity in the world and not just the meditation hall. Further, Dōgen Zenji also has simple admonitions for how to attend to things.

"Do not comment on the quantity or make judgments about the quality of the ingredients you obtained . . . just sincerely prepare them." Work with what you have to work with. This is basic and most profound. We cannot control what comes our way, so we find out how to work with what comes: ingredients, body, mind, feelings, thoughts, time, place, season, flavors, tastes. This is counter to blaming one's parents, one's upbringing, society, others. This is no longer conceiving of oneself as a victim ("Why me?" "Why this?") or omnipotent ruler ("Get it together." "Grow up."). This is contrary to our cultural norm, which asks, "How do I get rid of anger (sorrow, grief, jealousy) without actually having to relate with it?" To actually relate with things, to move things and be moved by things, is the heart of intimacy, the way of growing in wisdom and compassion, peace and fulfillment.

For many months while I was the head cook, perhaps a year or more, Suzuki Rōshi gave me that same advice: "When you wash the rice, wash the rice. . . ." One day, though, the advice changed. I had come to him complaining that the people who worked with me in the kitchen didn't seem to be following his advice. To me they seemed to be talking excessively, coming to work late, taking long bathroom breaks, and not being particularly engaged in what they were doing in the kitchen. "What can I do?" I asked.

While I recounted all this, the rōshi seemed to be very understanding and supportive, seeming to agree that yes, good help is hard to find. When I finished, he paused briefly and then responded, "If you want to see virtue, you'll have to have a calm mind."

My first thought was, "That's not what I asked you! I asked you how to get these people to behave." But I kept my mouth shut and let his words settle into me. After a while I decided to practice "seeing virtue." Again this is not our Western way. We think the way to proceed is to keep pointing out our own and each other's faults, so we can work on them and become perfected. But the standards keep changing and we never measure up. The inherent, implicit virtue of things, of ourselves independent of performance, is overlooked.

Dōgen Zenji addresses this in many ways, "When you take care of things, do not see with your common eyes, do not think with your common sentiments. Pick a single blade of grass and erect a sanctuary for the jewel king." Common eyes do not see the virtue, the blessedness, of an apple being an apple, a human being being a human being. Common sentiments can criticize the cooking without appreciating all the hard work, effort, and intention that went into it.

"Never alter your state of mind based on materials." Just because we discard something does not mean we benefit ourselves or others by reviling it. It is simply that this goes here, that goes there. To dislike washing pots or scrubbing the floor is to denigrate the value of one's own awareness engaged with things. We "don't like" what? Having to handle dirt? Getting our hands wet? The pots? Having to move our body in some particular way? The lack of potential fame and fortune? The lack of "profit"? Virtue, preciousness, value is embedded in our attending to things. The effort to do this becomes effortless. We become whole and connected.

We also find in *Dōgen's Pure Standards for the Zen Community* "The Dharma for Taking Food," "Regulations for the Study Hall," "The Dharma when Meeting Senior Instructors." I am struck not so much by the specific regulations as by the general flavor of a culture permeated by order. These days we are "free," lacking order—we pride ourselves on it, suffer from it, yet find the prospect of order stifling.

While I was doing a Zen and Psychoanalysis workshop with André Patsalides, he pointed out that cultures with "eating rituals" have fewer eating disorders than cultures which are lacking in "eating rituals." Seemingly our preference is to be free to have our disorders rather than to work within the context of structure.

So it is rather marvelous to get a taste of Dōgen's sense of useful rules and regulations: those which contribute to the peace and harmony of the community, those which encourage us to look into the heart of the matter, those which promote "seeing virtue" by legislating respect and "not altering your state of mind" when meeting different seniors.

In this sense living within the context of structure in a meditation community is sometimes described as being inside a rock tumbler. Turning around and around in this world over time, one grows smooth and polished, refined and reflecting. The sharp edges of personal preference and personal freedom to "act out" have been worn down. One can accord with the nature of things. So it is understood that posture and activity embody attitude and thought that literally "shape" one's world. When you change your behavior, your posture or stance, you change the world as well.

Zen Master Shitou said, "Mind itself is Buddha. Mind, Buddha, sentient beings, enlightenment, affliction are all different words for the same thing" (Thomas Cleary, trans., *Timeless Spring*). Then what shall we do? How shall we handle things? We tend to think that we can control things in order to have a "better" life, but of course it never works out that way. Endlessly getting rid of afflictions, accumulating enlightenment, we end up in the same place. Dōgen Zenji's words remind us how to dwell and settle there in peace and harmony, benefiting ourselves and all beings.

One of our human tendencies is to create a "nest" or "den," where we can live in supposedly beautiful solitude apart from the messiness of actually having to relate with anything. We even think at times that if something powerful comes up that forces us to pay attention to it, then we are entitled to "blow it away." How dare it interrupt our sacred solitude! For Dōgen Zenji, however, awakening is not something that occurs in isolation, but is intimately related with our everyday activities and affairs. We awaken with all things.

So I am grateful to Dōgen Zenji, Shohaku Okumura, and Taigen Dan Leighton for bringing these words to us, words that offer the vision and practical admonitions for realization.

Acknowledgments

Many people helped to make this translation possible. The support of the late Rev. Kanzan Yūho Hosokawa, founder of the Kyoto Sōtō Zen Center, allowed us to use the facilities of the Shōrinji temple west of Kyoto, where most of the translation work was done.

We especially would like to acknowledge the generous assistance of Ikkō Narasaki Rōshi, abbot of the Zuiōji and Shōgoji monasteries, who since this translation was completed also has become the vice abbot of Eiheiji, the headquarters temple of Sōtō Zen founded by Dōgen Zenji. My experience of participating in the spring 1992 practice period led by Ikkō Narasaki Rōshi at Shōgoji Temple in Kyushu, during which the "Chiji Shingi" was used as a main text, was of great benefit to this translation process. Narasaki Rōshi's disciples Hōkan Saitō Sensei and Ekai Korematsu Sensei helped resolve some particularly difficult details in the *Eihei Shingi*. We are grateful to Kōki Suzuki Sensei for providing the text of Kōshō Chidō's afterword to the 1667 version and also for helping to clarify some of the historical background.

We also thank Ikkō Narasaki Rōshi for his kind foreword to this translation. It is informed by his deep warmth and dedication from nearly fifty years of training Japanese priests in the traditional monastic practice. His foreword discusses the importance of the teaching that "Dignified manner is itself the Buddha Dharma," a teaching that is upheld in Sōtō Zen as one of the primary teachings of Dōgen and is most fully expressed in *Pure Standards for the Zen Community*.

In addition to Narasaki Rōshi's Japanese perspective, I am very pleased to include a foreword with an American viewpoint by Edward Brown, a senior priest and teacher of the San Francisco Zen Center, which includes the Green Gulch Farm and Tassajara Zen Mountain temples. Edward is best known for his helpful and popular series of Zen baking and cooking books, which developed out of his long experience as tenzo. He thus has a unique perspective on the important essay in *Dōgen's Pure Standards for the Zen Community*, "The Instructions for the Tenzo."

Edward Brown's extensive experience of participating in and leading American Buddhist practice communities also provides a good vantage for commenting on the contemporary relevance of all of Dōgen's standards. Edward's foreword very clearly describes, in terms accessible to our Western psychological orientation, the value of these monastic standards and structures in developing positive attitudes, and how such practice can cut through our particular cultural obstacles and help us to engage fully in our own lives.

We were fortunate to have the generous cooperation of Daihonzan Eiheiji in providing photographs and the diagram of the layout of the Eiheiji buildings, with our special thanks to the Eiheiji International Department. The diagram of the inside of the Eiheiji monks' hall is by Shohaku Okumura.

ACKNOWLEDGMENTS

Andy Ferguson worked with great care, using his skillfulness with both Chinese language and computer graphics, to provide the lineage charts, which help clarify the times and relationships of the persons mentioned by Dōgen. Any mistakes that may have slipped into the charts are mine, not Andy's.

During the two years I was living in Kyoto working on this translation with Okumura Sensei, a great many people were very helpful and supportive. I particularly would like to acknowledge the extraordinary personal support and kindness of Norman Waddell, A. J. Dickinson, Dr. Keiji Toyoshima, Stephen Gibbs, Ann Overton, Preston and Michiyo Houser, and Shinkai Tanaka Rōshi. Thanks also to Hōyū Ishida, Kyoko Yamauchi, Tom Wright, Yasuo Deguchi, David and Elin Chadwick, Mugai Takano, Minoru Tada, Tom Kirchner, John Einarsen, and Robert MacClean. (In the interest of consistency, all modern Japanese names are given with the family name last, in the English mode.)

While I was finalizing preparations of this manuscript in California, my friend and past translation collaborator, Kazuaki Tanahashi, and Mel Weitsman Rōshi, abbot of the Berkeley and San Francisco Zen Centers, kindly provided me with a rough draft of a translation of "Chiji Shingi," which they had been working on together. Although it was received too late to review in full, I consulted their efforts on a few points in the text that had remained ambiguous. This work therefore now reflects and incorporates some of their understanding and interpretations.

Thanks to John Wright and the *Chicago Review* for publishing a brief excerpt from this work. Thanks to Rev. Meiya Wender of Green Gulch Farm for her careful reading and helpful suggestions. In the later stages of preparing this work, Ellen Randall also provided careful reading and suggestions, as well as support and inspiration.

I am unspeakably grateful to Tenshin Anderson Rōshi, former abbot of the San Francisco Zen Center, for his long-time guidance and subtle teaching, and also for first suggesting that Okumura Sensei and I work on translating the *Eihei Shingi*.

Finally, I want to express my deep gratitude to my translation collaborator, Shohaku Okumura Sensei, whose dedication, sincerity, and true humility is a constant inspiration. It has been a great privilege to study Dōgen's practice teachings with him, through the exacting demands of translation.

Rev. Taigen Daniel Leighton

Introduction

Taigen Daniel Leighton

Overview of Dōgen's Writings

This book presents a complete translation of the *Eihei Shingi*, one of the major writings of the Japanese Zen master Dōgen (1200–1253). Eihei Dōgen traveled to China and brought back the practice of Zen in 1227. He is considered the founder of the Sōtō branch of Japanese Zen, a continuation and development of the Caodong (pronounced "Tsow-dong") lineage of the Chan [Zen] tradition, the lineage that Dōgen inherited from his Chinese teacher. But Dōgen's teaching was not limited by any particular school of Buddhism, as he fully integrated the fundamental principles of Buddhist practice, philosophy, and community lifestyle as they had been expressed in China.

Dōgen's body of writings, especially his masterwork, the *Shōbōgenzō* [True dharma eye treasury], is generally esteemed today as one of the great summits of Japanese Buddhist philosophy. His essays include discussions on meditation practice, psychology, and poetic insight into the nature of reality. Although Dōgen is venerated as the founder of a major branch of Japanese Zen Buddhism, even within the Sōtō sect Dōgen's writings were largely unknown up until this century; they were studied by only a smattering of Sōtō scholars and monks. In this century Dōgen has finally gained wide acclaim as a spiritual thinker and philosopher, among secular as well as religious commentators in both Japan and the West. Contemporary attention to Dōgen's writings has focused on such themes as his expression of Buddha Nature teaching, his profound and dynamic view of time, his teachings on the practice and meaning of zazen (seated meditation), his creative and insightful use of language, and his radical nondualism, especially the nondualism of practice and enlightenment.

The work translated here, the *Eihei Shingi*, concerns community practice; it contains Dōgen's principal writings of guidelines and instructions for everyday life in the monastic training center he established. Some sections of this work are technical in nature and may be of interest primarily to Buddhist scholars and professional monastics. But many aspects of this work will also be of value to more general readers interested in the broad issue of the Zen tradition's attitude toward spiritual community life. These wider aspects are more apparent in the text's first essay, "Instructions for the Tenzo [Chief cook]," and in the many koans or Zen stories in the long final essay, "Pure Standards for the Temple Administrators."

The Role of Community in Buddhism

The communal institution has been an important aspect of Buddhism since the time of Shakyamuni Buddha twenty-five hundred years ago in Northern India. The fellowship of practitioners, or sangha, established then has often functioned since as a radical contrast to existing social conventions and conditioning. The Buddhist monastic order, despite its varying relationships and accommodations to the ruling powers throughout Asian history, has offered an alternative or counterculture to the status quo of societies based on exploitation and disregard for individual human potential. This spiritual institution has had, in fact, a civilizing effect on Asian societies, moderating the brutal tendencies of various rulers.

The common designation of Buddhist monks as "home-leavers" ideally implies the act of renouncing worldly ambition by joining the monastic community, and also the inner work of abandoning ensnarement from the bonds of social and personal psychological conditioning. Although the essential insight of Buddhist awakening affirms the fundamental rightness and interconnectedness of the whole of creation, just as it is, the sangha remains as a historical instrument to perform the long-term work of civilizing and developing the awareness of our species so as eventually to actualize and fulfill for all beings the vision of our world as a pure land, informed by wisdom and compassion.

The monastic enclosure was developed in Shakyamuni's time when the monks halted their peripatetic mendicant practice to abide together for a few months during the rainy season. Unlike the Catholic monkhood, which is usually entered for life, a major paradigm of Mahayana Buddhist monasticism has been oscillation between periods of training in the monastic enclosure and reentry into the marketplace. Monks test their practice by returning to interact with conventional society, and also help fulfill the developmental function of the Buddhist order by sharing with the ordinary world whatever they have learned of self-awareness, composure, and compassion during their monastic training. In Japan, from Dōgen's time to the present, monks finish a period of training and go out to function as temple priests, ministering to the laity. Some later return to the monastery for further development or to help train younger monks. Traditionally in China and Japan, monks would also leave their monastic community to wander around to other teachers and test their practice and understanding.

In accord with its purpose, monastic community life is seen as an opportunity for its participants to develop their capacity for enacting the universal principles of awakening in the concrete aspects of their lives. Great emphasis is given to taking care to perform each activity with a wholehearted, positive attitude. The monastic lifestyle, procedures, and forms are strong supports for the practitioners immersed in the process of deepening their personal experience of the nonalienated, integrated nature of reality. Each ordinary function is treated as a tool for enhancing mindfulness of one's state of awareness and innermost intention. Some contemporary Zen teachers in the West, such as the Vietnamese master Thich Nhat Hanh and Robert Aitken Rōshi, have given similar attention to presenting updated practices for mindfulness in everyday life. Such exercises are developments of the traditional monastic daily practices depicted here by Dōgen.

The *Eihei Shingi* includes regulations and procedural instructions for these monastic forms and activities, including such details as the manner of sleeping and of brushing teeth. But the context for all the particular forms is Dōgen's practical attitude of care and mindful attentiveness to the real stuff of our lives and to communal harmony. The experience of ultimate truth and of Buddhist teaching must be applied to our everyday activity and relationships in the phenomenal world. Since the highest realization is not at all separate or elsewhere from our ordinary activity, Dōgen's lofty poetic and philosophic expression often bursts through amidst his descriptions of mundane procedures.

No currently existing Zen temple or monastery exactly follows all of the routines described here, although a few in Japan come close and still use this work as a guide. And many Zen centers in the West, as well as training temples in Japan, follow a great many of the monastic forms described herein. These forms are tools to help us find appropriate community lifestyles and practices.

Alignment with Nature

These monastic guidelines and forms also serve the function of realignment and attunement with the harmonious order and flow of nature. For example, the schedule of activities in Dōgen's monastic community followed the natural cycles. Time was signaled by various bells, drums, and wooden sounding blocks not regulated by abstract hours and minutes but according with divisions of time based on the varying sunrise and sunset times. The bell for evening zazen and the signal for night's end (see "Model for Engaging the Way") are traditionally determined by such means as whether or not there is enough daylight for the signal person to see the lines in his hand at arm's length, or whether or not ants on the ground are distinctly visible. The purpose of Zen community, to embody fully the reality of buddha nature, is not at all separate from achieving harmony with the natural environment and its rhythms. The community practice forms reflect the ecological Buddhist worldview of mutual interdependence.

The value of nature in the Zen tradition is reflected in the fact that many monasteries in China and Japan were situated deep in the remote mountains, as was the case for Eiheiji, the monastery Dōgen established, and also for many of the temples in the stories Dōgen recounts in *Eihei Shingi*. However, many Buddhist monasteries have been essentially suburban. Temples have been located on the outskirts between the city and the wilderness, and have served as an interface for the harmony of nature with whatever may pass for civilization at the particular time.

Cultural Adaptation and Expression

The monastic forms—schedules, style of robes, or eating utensils—may vary and adapt slightly through different times and cultures, but these forms and practices are far more enduring than the forms of the artificial world of fashion and culture. Throughout decades and centuries the styles of the laypeople are ever shifting, while the monks, as they follow these traditional practices, all look and live essentially the same.

Dōgen carefully illustrates in the *Eihei Shingi* the fundamental spirit and attitudes for communities of practitioners dedicated to universal spiritual awakening and to the harmonious expression of its practice in the group. Such underlying considerations transcend different cultural manifestations, and may provide useful guidance not only to Zen centers, but to all spiritually based communities.

Inevitably over the coming generations, Zen communities that endure in the West will develop their own appropriate forms and rituals for group practice. The forms Dōgen discusses are closely based on Buddhist teaching from China and reach back directly to the historical Buddha's time in India. While it may be argued that some of these forms reflect the native Japanese (and Chinese) cultural talent for regimentation, Dōgen intersperses with procedural instructions many expressions of the underlying attitudes for communal practice of transcultural awakened mind. Despite the often wholesome Western emphasis on individual responsibility, initiative, and development, Westerners also will have to develop workable patterns for harmonization if they are to sustain engagement in communal practice of dharma. Dōgen's instructions clearly embody and exemplify principles of gratitude, sincerity, and harmony that are essential for any group spiritual practice.

Although Western communities will certainly make adaptations in ritual forms, historically this process has been an organic one over several generations, and cannot be artificially predetermined based on our conditioned intellectual views and opinions. Dōgen expresses his practical attitude to the process of cultural adaptation in "The Dharma for Taking Meals," the third essay in the *Eihei Shingi*, where he discusses the use of chopsticks in dharma communities in China and Japan. In India Shakyamuni Buddha and his disciples used their fingers for eating, as was customary in their society. But Dōgen does not imply that chopsticks are inherently superior to fingers or vice versa. Rather, he notes that practitioners in China and Japan, although they may want to follow Buddha's example exactly, simply lack cultural awareness and guidance in proper decorum for eating with hands.

A more significant instance of cultural relativity and adaptation appears in the "Pure Standards for Temple Administrators," where Dōgen quotes without comment the proscription in the Indian Vinaya (the rules for monks' conduct) against agriculture as a source of monks' livelihood. This was based on the Indian cultural priority of the sanctity of animal life, including earthworms and other small creatures imperiled by agrarian cultivation. However, slightly earlier in the same work Dōgen extols in detail the virtues of the diligent practice of the garden and field manager in the Chinese monastic model. In the Chinese cultural milieu the emphasis for Dharma communities had shifted radically from the earlier Indian monastic values to the priority on self-sufficient livelihood and integration of realization with everyday practical activities. In China it was more important to display the possibility of awakened conduct even amidst mundane circumstances, and this jibed with the developing principles of Mahayana Buddhist practice.

Introductions to the Individual Essays

The *Eihei Shingi* consists of six sections. A given reader may find one essay more interesting than another, and they need not be read in sequence. As mentioned at the outset of the introduction, the general reader might find most useful the opening essay and long closing one, as the middle essays deal more with monastic forms and procedures.

First is "Instructions for the Tenzo" ["Tenzokyōkun"], written in 1237 at Kōshōji, Dōgen's temple in Uji just south of Kyoto, where Dōgen began assembling a community in 1233. This essay details specific duties of the *tenzo* or chief cook, going through a whole day. Normally a day is considered to begin in the evening, but here the tenzo's job is delineated starting after lunch. Dōgen makes clear the paramount importance of the practice responsibilities of this position and that dedicated effort for the community well-being is as valuable a spiritual practice as meditation or as study of the sayings of the ancient masters. As elaborated in Edward Brown's foreword, the practice of attentive work with all the ingredients at hand, as experienced in kitchen work, is essential to Zen attitudes and development.

In his "Instructions for the Tenzo," Dōgen includes colorful examples of great Zen teachers and their doings while serving as tenzo, and also of his own rich encounters with tenzos while practicing in China. He elaborates the appropriate mental attitude for the tenzo, which must equal that of an abbot. Dōgen says of the tenzo position, "Since ancient times, masters with Way-seeking mind, lofty people who had awakened their hearts, were appointed to this job.... If you do not have the mind of the Way, then all of this hard work is meaningless and not beneficial."

The second essay, "Model for Engaging the Way" ["Bendōhō"] was written in 1246 at Daibutsuji [Great Buddha Temple]. Dōgen founded this temple far from Kyoto in the remote mountains of Echizen (now Fukui) on the north coast of Japan after moving there in 1243. Later in 1246 he renamed it Eiheiji [Eternal Peace Temple], after the era name from 58 to 75 C.E., when Buddhism and the first sutras officially entered China. It continues today as one of the two head temples of the Japanese Sōtō School.

"The Model for Engaging the Way" describes procedures and decorum for daily conduct (beginning with the evening) in the *sōdō* [monks' hall], where the monks sit zazen, eat meals, and sleep in assigned places. Dōgen asserts that just to maintain dignified demeanor while in accord with the daily community activities is exactly the practice of full awakening. This wholehearted engaging of the dharma at one with the community is itself, "the practice-enlightenment before the empty eon." So, he says, "do not be concerned with your actualization;" i.e., do not seek after some enlightenment later or elsewhere from this harmonious community practice.

As of this writing, few if any Zen centers in the West have traditional sōdōs where monks sleep in the same hall where they sit and eat. But in Japan, this sōdō-style practice is still very much the model for monastic training centers authorized by the Sōtō school.

The third essay, "The Dharma for Taking Food" ["Fushukuhanpō"] was written in 1246 at Eiheiji. Here Dōgen gives detailed instructions for the formal manners and procedures for serving, receiving, and eating food in the monks' hall using the traditional set of bowls and cloths, called *hau* or *ōryōki*. Dōgen uses eating to illustrate closely the dignity with which all daily activities should be conducted by dharma practitioners. This formal eating practice is a valuable mindfulness exercise, providing the opportunity to observe carefully and bring consciousness to one's conduct and interaction with an essential aspect of the phenomenal world. This practice also allows the monks to express deeply their respect for the teaching, each other, and the whole world.

Dōgen makes it clear near the beginning of the essay that there is no separation between food and spiritual teaching. "Dharma" in the following passage implies all of the meanings of the original Sanskrit word: primarily the teaching of reality, but also the truth of reality itself, the elements of that realm of reality, and this teaching as means or path to align with that reality. (Dharma as the teaching is meant as the dharma teaching of perfect truth rather than specifically as the Buddha Dharma of Buddhism, although all Buddhist teachers certainly would find the true dharma to be within the Buddha Dharma.) "Just let dharma be the same as food, and let food be the same as dharma.... If dharmas are the dharma nature, then food also is the dharma nature. If the dharma is suchness, food also is suchness.... Food is the dharma of all dharmas, which only a buddha together with a buddha exhaustively penetrate.... Dharma is itself food, food is itself dharma. This dharma is what is received and used by all buddhas in the past and future. This food is the fulfillment that is the joy of dharma and the delight of meditation."

These traditional procedures and attitudes for serving and eating food in Zen monasteries became the inspiration for the Japanese tea ceremony. Tea was first imported from China to Japan in the ninth century but achieved new heights of popularity in Dōgen's time as an aid for monks in maintaining their meditative wakefulness. Dōgen himself mentions drinking tea in the "Model for Engaging the Way." These dignified monastic manners were eventually transformed into a high art epitomizing the subtlety and range of Japanese aesthetics when the Way of Tea was formalized, a few centuries after Dōgen, in the Rinzai temples of Kyoto.

The fourth essay in the *Eihei Shingi*, "Regulations for the Study Hall" ["Shuryō Shingi"] was written at Eiheiji in 1249. Dōgen details the courteous and considerate conduct appropriate for monks committed to total enactment of the Way. The relationship between fellow practitioners is profoundly intimate. "Siblings in Buddha's family should be closer to each other than with their own selves." Dōgen's guidelines honor both the respect due to those with experience and the underlying equality of all community members. "You should know that temporarily we are guest and host, but for our whole lives we will be nothing other than buddhas and ancestors."

The fifth and shortest essay, "The Dharma when Meeting Senior Instructors" ["Taitaiko gogejarihō"] is from a talk given in 1244 at Yoshimine Temple, where Dōgen's assembly was awaiting completion of the nearby Eiheiji. Here Dōgen gives beginning novices sixty-two specific injunctions for the appropriate etiquette when in the presence of senior instructors, defined as those who have completed five of the annual three-month-long practice periods.

While such hierarchical attitudes may be disconcerting seen from Western views of egalitarianism, one might also see these instructions as guidance for newcomers in the respectful attitude most conducive to harmonious entry into the community. The instructions also strongly encourage nondiscrimination toward various seniors by the novices based on personal preference or judgment. Enacting these practices expresses the appreciation and respect due to the sustained experience of practice and to those who have taken on the responsibilities of instructing others in the spiritual life. At the end Dōgen clarifies that these deferential guidelines are not meant to be applied between senior instructors themselves. But then he concludes that "Seeing seniors is inexhaustible. The first summer practice period we see seniors; at the ultimate fulfillment [of attaining buddhahood] we see seniors." Within dharma community there is no end to embodying attitudes of appreciation and gratitude.

The sixth and final essay of the *Eihei Shingi*, "Pure Standards for the Temple Administrators" ["Chiji Shingi"], by far the longest, was written at Eiheiji in 1246 and gives instructions with examples for the conduct and commitment of those in the monastic administrative positions. The first half of the essay gives twenty-one koans (classical teaching stories of dialogues or actions of former great masters), all of which concern previous temple administrators. In retelling the stories themselves, Dōgen sometimes quotes directly from the Chinese Chan (Zen) literature, and sometimes gives his personal reading of the original incidents. All the cases are followed by his own commentaries, which we have identified by indenting them in the text.

As a koan collection, the "Pure Standards for the Temple Administrators" is unique in its focus on community practice. What becomes apparent in reading these examples is that its heroes are often very far from what would be considered exemplary by any conventional standard. Dōgen most highly praises some of his exemplars specifically for incidents in which they apparently violate precepts and regulations, or even are temporarily expelled from the community—for example Fushan Fayuan and Xuefeng Yicun as tenzos and Wuzu Fayan when he was mill manager. For Dōgen the purpose of the Zen community is not based on usual social, cultural, or psychological criteria, but solely on the unswerving devotion to universal awakening.

The second half of the "Chiji Shingi" expounds in turn the duties and careful attitudes of the main administrators: the director, the *inō* [monks' supervisor], the tenzo, and the work leader. Dōgen first quotes the instructions for each post from his primary sourcebook, the *Zen'en Shingi* (see below), and then adds his own comments including some further examples and colorful stories. This last section of "Pure Standards for the Temple Administrators" is replete with Chinese cultural and monastic lore, but one senses that Dōgen may have intended further editing and elaboration. Had he lived longer, perhaps the sections for the other three administrators might have been developed into separate texts parallel to "The Instructions for the Tenzo."

Chan Stories and the Sōtō Use of Koans

In addition to procedural instructions, in the *Eihei Shingi* Dōgen includes, with his own commentaries, many examples of stories and dialogues of the old masters that illustrate the appropriate attitudes and intention for communal practice. These especially appear in the first section, "Instructions for the Tenzo," and in the long final section, "Standards for Temple Administrators." Some of these stories appear as well in classic koan anthologies such as the *Book of Serenity* [Shōyōroku], *Blue Cliff Record* [Hekiganroku], and *Gateless Gate* [Mumonkan]. But many of the stories or koans [literally, "public cases"] that Dōgen offers here are not available in the major sources and comprise a valuable addition to Zen teaching lore.

A popular misconception holds that koans are only used in the Linji/Rinzai branch of Zen and not in the Caodong/Sōtō lineage that Dōgen transmitted. The Sōtō tradition dates back to such seminal Chan figures as Shitou Xiqian (700–790) and Dongshan Liangjie (807–869), and later its monastic community life had been strengthened by Furong Daokai (1043–1118) and its meditation praxis poetically articulated by Hongzhi Zhengjue (1091–1157). Many figures throughout the history of this lineage commented on the koan literature in detail in their teachings, although these stories were not used in a systematic program of meditation as they often have been in the Linji tradition. In fact, the two traditions frequently had a cooperative relationship. Dōgen's first teacher was from the Rinzai lineage, and a great many of the koans cited in "Standards for the Temple Administrators" involve figures in the Linji/Rinzai tradition, including Linji himself.

Dōgen compiled other collections of koans and commented on the classical stories frequently in his masterwork, the *Shōbōgenzō*. An aspect of Dōgen's use of koans can be seen from his teaching of *genjōkōan* [the koan manifesting], which emphasizes seeing one's own life experience and problems as koans to engage with. Conversely, he sees the classic stories of the old masters as intimate expressions of the existential issues of one's own life.

Most of the stories Dōgen includes in his *Pure Standards for the Zen Community* focus on the theme of the mutual cooperation, dedication, and kindheartedness necessary for those in responsible positions in the community. In the very beginning of the *Eihei Shingi*, at the start of "Instructions for the Tenzo," Dōgen says that the temple administrators "are all Buddha's children, and together they carry out Buddha's work." But in the sangha [or Dharma community] all members are considered Buddha's children, and all are doing the work of Buddha, i.e., bringing awakened compassion to the world so as eventually to actualize Shakyamuni's buddha field for all beings. Therefore, in the stories Dōgen cites as models for community leaders, the dedication and cooperative spirit exemplified are really guidance for all members of the spiritual community.

Significance of the *Eihei Shingi* in Dōgen's Teaching and Practice

The writings in the *Eihei Shingi* mark the beginning of the later phase of Dōgen's teaching career. From the time of his return to

Japan from China in 1227 until his departure from the Kyoto area to Echizen in 1243, the emphasis of Dōgen's writing might be said to encompass the extensive elaboration of the universality of the nondualistic buddha nature and the efficacy of zazen as its expression in practice. During this period, Dōgen was directing his teaching to all interested sincere practitioners, lay students as well as monks.

After 1243, as Eiheiji was being developed in the remote Echizen mountains, Dōgen's teaching was addressed more specifically to the community of monk disciples who gathered around him for concentrated training. As he sought to develop a core group of dedicated people who could carry on his work, his teaching emphasis naturally shifted to the value for them of precepts, discipline, and ordination, and of the intense "continuous practice" available in the setting of daily monastic training.

Dōgen's intention to carefully promulgate guidelines for monastic communities was clear even in his very early work. In "Talk on Wholehearted Practice of the Way" ["Bendōwa"], written in 1231 before he had established any community, Dōgen sought to convey the essential meaning of the zazen meditation practice he was introducing to Japan. But at the end of this work he added, with a feeling of regret, "I do not have a chance now also to present the standards for monasteries or regulations for temples, especially as they should not be treated carelessly."

Although much of his later work, including the *Eihei Shingi*, was focused on establishing clear standards for harmonious monastic communities, certainly zazen was still the core praxis. In the "Model for Engaging the Way" section of the *Eihei Shingi*, written in 1246, Dōgen presents detailed instructions for dignified conduct and procedures during the entire day in the monks' hall. As part of this, Dōgen includes both physical and attitudinal instructions for zazen, largely paraphrased (with some amplification) from Dōgen's first work, "Fukanzazengi." This work, the

"Way of Zazen Recommended to Everyone," first drafted in 1227 soon after Dōgen's return from China, is his basic instructions for zazen, to which "Bendowa" is a commentary.

The Zen monastic community that Dōgen depicts and encourages in the *Eihei Shingi* cannot be understood except as the expression of a harmonious lifestyle based on and emerging from the experience of zazen. Throughout his career, Dōgen advocated this nondualistic, objectless meditation practice, known also as "just sitting," which developed from the "serene illumination" meditation elaborated by Hongzhi Zhengjue in China in the previous century. This practice does not involve striving for gain or for manipulation of reality; it promotes active attentiveness to our present life experience just as it is. The self is seen as not estranged from the objective, phenomenal world. This "beyond-thinking" neither negates nor grasps at our thoughts and feelings, but attunes us to the deep harmony of reality that underlies the illusion of separation from the world that is created by discriminative consciousness.

All of Dōgen's suggestions for regulating everyday activities in the community are directed at helping practitioners together to embody and actualize this awareness in every aspect of ordinary life. The physical facilities and daily routines of the community also clearly revolve around the practice of zazen in the monks' hall.

Dōgen refers to this zazen as *jijuyū zammai*, the samadhi [concentrated awareness] of self-fulfillment or self-joyousness. The etymology of this term is relevant. The *ji* of jijuyū means self. The compound *juyu* means joyful or fulfilled, but separately the two characters mean to receive or accept one's function. So zazen, and self-fulfillment, is also by definition here the samadhi of the self accepting its function, or its job or position. The monastic community is based on this awareness. Each member is fulfilled, and their true nonalienated self is actualized, by each person fully accepting and carrying out their job or position in the monastic mandala. Thus Dōgen stresses wholehearted engagement in one's job, as seen in the "Pure Standards for the Temple Administrators," where the nature, practice, and importance of many monastic positions are specifically delineated. This self-realizing samadhi is itself simply the reality of life (and death), and is not limited to the sitting posture. The purpose of Zen training and community practice is not just to extend this zazen awareness into everyday life but actually to discover the deep satisfaction and joyfulness of jijuyū samadhi emerging in all of our daily activities and relationships.

Contemporary Understandings of Dōgen's Historical Context

Some contemporary academicians, both in Japan and the West, have made much of the shift in Dōgen's writing from the earlier emphasis on the universal value of zazen to the later monastic emphasis, and have imputed doctrinal contradictions, disputing extensively over which phase is the "true Dōgen." However, such scholastic deliberations completely fail to recognize the fundamental intention of Dōgen's work. While some of Dōgen's writings have rightfully earned him the modern reputation as a great philosopher, he never was concerned with producing a new, dogmatically consistent, philosophical doctrine along the lines of Western philosophical theories. Rather, his philosophy was always at the service of his main purpose: that of religious practitioner and spiritual guide.

The meaning of Dōgen's words must be realized in their context of practical teachings for particular students. From the viewpoint of sincere spiritual practice, rather than from the intellectual calculations and limited conceptualizations of consistency that are sharply criticized as obstacles throughout true Zen literature, Dōgen's work can be seen as simply the natural unfolding of one person's awakened mind/heart. He consistently promoted practice that he considered appropriate and beneficial to the purpose of introducing thoroughly his understanding of Buddhist life into his native country.

It is true that in Dōgen's early works he emphasizes that full personal realization is available to any practitioner with sincere aspiration, lay or monk; whereas in some of Dōgen's final writings after *Eihei Shingi*—for example "The Merit of Home-Leaving" ["Shukke Kudoku"]—Dōgen states that full buddhahood, including transmission of the teaching to others, requires ordination as a monk. Earlier he had said that thorough personal awakening experiences depend only on wholehearted diligence. This emphasis is repeated in his later work. But the point of the later teaching, addressed to his monk disciples, is that historically the teaching of awakening has been transmitted and maintained only by a lineage of ordained monks. Still the case to modern times, this certainly need not be viewed as a doctrinal "contradiction," or a denigration of the insights and efforts of sincere lay practitioners.

We must recognize the intended function of Dōgen's teachings to particular groups of students. The complicated question of the various degrees and understandings of ordination and their role in practice is already proving to be a rich and difficult issue that must be engaged in Buddhism's development in Western cultures.

Recent historians have made valuable contributions to our knowledge of the particular conditions Dōgen faced and the backgrounds of his audiences. The context of the Buddhism prevalent in the culture of his time emphasized magical, esoteric ceremonies conducted by priests for the upper classes, and veneration of nature spirits and buddha and bodhisattva figures. Dōgen responded by strongly encouraging active personal experience of practice and Buddhist truth through zazen and community life, not only available to the aristocracy. But this does not at all mean, as some modern interpreters have imagined, that Dōgen advocated a "pure," clinical meditation practice that abandoned the prevalent worldview of Japan and Mahayana Asia with its rich, devotional religiosity. Chinese and Japanese Buddhism incorporated the native shamanistic sense of the spirit world, and fully recognized sacred qualities of the natural environment. The *Pure Standards for the Zen Community* includes veneration of native spirits and chanting of dharanis [magical incantations] as well as sutras. Dōgen maintained a ritual practice and poetic sensitivity congruent with a mystical outlook of the sort that contemporary Western Buddhists more usually associate with Tibetan Buddhism.

Many of Dōgen's monk disciples came to him from the Daruma school, a slightly earlier, immature "Zen" movement in Japan that had some characteristics Dōgen strongly criticized. In parts of the *Shōbōgenzō* Dōgen used very harsh language to wean these disciples from their mistaken views of "natural" enlightenment, e.g., that the mere intellectual understanding that "Mind itself is buddha" is sufficient. These iconoclastic attitudes, perhaps analogous to the "Beat Zen" that preceded contemporary American Buddhist practice centers, misled these monks toward nihilistically ignoring the necessity for continued diligent practice and ethical conduct. As contemporary American Zennists have also learned, merely "going with the flow," without vigilant attention to the consequences of conduct, is not sufficient. Dōgen's commitment to ongoing practice, both to counter decadence and laxity and as the appropriate expression of genuine awakening, was a major concern in his standards for community life.

Awareness of this historical context can clarify specific aspects of Dōgen's teaching. However, in the name of demythologizing previous sectarian, overly sanctified images of Dōgen in the Sōtō school, some academic historians have imputed diverse, elaborate, and even self-serving motivations to Dōgen. For example, they explain his move to Eiheiji as akin to a political power play. Such allegations apparently are based on these historians' own projections, since no actual historical data can confirm Dōgen's motivation. Hopefully, with further study of his work, a balanced view of Dōgen as a person may emerge that will include acknowledgment of both his human fallibility and the possibility of deep Mahayana commitment and faith as his determining intention.

Earlier Monastic Codes

Dōgen's writings in the *Eihei Shingi* were all inspired by the legendary original code for Zen communities, the *Hyakujō Shingi*. This work, said to be written by the great early Chinese master Baizhang Huaihai (749–814; Hyakujō Ekai in Japanese), was already lost before Dōgen's time. Baizhang is considered the originator of the Zen work ethic, embodied in his famous saying, "A day of no work is a day of no food." The *Hyakujō Shingi* is referred to as the model for Dōgen's primary written source for Zen monastic standards, the *Zen'en Shingi* [*Pure Standards for the Zen Garden*; *Chanyuan Qingguei* in Chinese], which was written in 1103 by the Yunmen lineage master Changlu Zongze. The last section of the *Zen'en Shingi* is designated as an extract from the *Hyakujō Shingi*. However, as there is no record of the *Hyakujō Shingi* from Baizhang's own time, its existence is uncertain.

The *Eihei Shingi* frequently quotes the *Zen'en Shingi* verbatim, or in paraphrase, when giving procedural instructions or admonitions. We have noted many such passages. However, Dōgen also quotes, and some of the *Zen'en Shingi* passages also refer to, extracts from various Vinaya texts from India, which give the early Buddhist rules of discipline and community conduct.

Clearly Dōgen aimed at maintaining ancient monastic community standards dating back to Shakyamuni Buddha in India. But unlike other Zen collections of regulations, Dōgen focuses on beneficial attitudes for community practice, often merely quoting the earlier shingi collections for procedural descriptions while adding original personal anecdotes and discourses concerning attitudinal or psychological orientations.

The Textual History of the *Eihei Shingi*

Dōgen did not himself compile his six essays in *Eihei Shingi* into one volume. However, he may have intended them to become a single work but was unable to accomplish this before his death at age fifty-three. In any case, the six works in the *Eihei Shingi* comprise all of the materials on community practice written by Dōgen in Chinese. (The *Shōbōgenzō* was all in Japanese.) Chinese was the formal literati language in Japan, much as Latin functioned in medieval Europe. Dōgen's *Shōbōgenzō* was the first significant philosophical writing to use the native Japanese language. Some of the essays in the *Shōbōgenzō* written during the same period as the *Eihei Shingi* writings also dealt with monastic practice and procedures.

The first known compilation of the *Eihei Shingi* was by the fifteenth Eiheiji abbot Kōshū in 1502. It included only the "Tenzokyōkun" and "Chiji Shingi." All six essays were first published together in 1667 by the thirtieth abbot of Eiheiji, Kōshō Chidō (d. 1670) in what is known as the Shohon edition. A translation of Kōshō Chidō's afterword to his version is included in this book as an appendix. He emphasizes the value of these writings as a guide for monastic practice despite their lack of literary polish compared to some of Dōgen's other works. This supports the likely view that some of the material may have been unfinished, or at least unedited, before Dōgen's early death.

The Sōtō school in Kōshō Chidō's period was strongly influenced by the popularity of the new Ōbaku Zen school. This school was founded by the Chinese monk Yinyuan Longqi (1592–1673), who arrived in Japan in 1654. Although some Sōtō monks were initially impressed with the Chinese forms of the Ōbaku School, many of them, led by Gesshū Sōko (1618–1696), were moved to examine more closely the Sōtō school roots in Dōgen's teaching. They came to feel that the later Chinese teachings of the Ōbaku monks had lost the essence of the wisdom expressed by Dōgen, with his radical nondualism. Gesshū, who helped initiate a period of reform and renewal in Sōtō Zen, especially insisted that Dōgen's writings included his own model for monastic practice, or shingi. *Eihei Shingi* was compiled and published by Kōshō Chidō as part of this response to the Ōbaku School and especially to the Ōbaku version of the monastic regulations.

The currently accepted Rufubon edition was published in 1794 by Eiheiji's fiftieth abbot, Gentō Sokuchū (1729–1807), who also supervised the publication of a major edition of the *Shōbōgenzō*. Various short passages that are in the text of the Shohon edition appear only as footnotes in the later Rufubon version, suggesting that they may have been added by Kōshō Chidō to Dōgen's original texts as explanations in the Shohon version. We have included these in the text and marked them with parentheses, which will not be used otherwise in the text itself. See, for example, "The Model for Engaging the Way," note 11.

Development of Standards for the Community in the *Keizan Shingi*

Since its publication as a unified text in the seventeenth century, the Sōtō school has used the *Eihei Shingi* as a primary source for instructions on monastic forms and procedures. Another primary source has been the *Keizan Shingi*, written near the end of his life by Keizan Jokin (1264–1325). Keizan, a Dharma successor three generations after Dōgen, is credited, along with his successors, with widely popularizing the Sōtō school in Japan. Keizan actively developed forms for extending Zen practice to the general lay populace. He incorporated into the Sōtō tradition the earlier Japanese spiritual context and was personally strongly influenced by Shugendō, the mountain ascetic tradition, as well as the Shingon school of Vajrayana Buddhism. Much of the ritual Keizan developed, which is still used in Sōtō temples, was derived from the Shingon tradition.

Along with his work of disseminating Sōtō ritual practice among lay followers, Keizan also maintained strong concern for the thoroughness and strictness of the Zen monastic training institution. Keizan founded Sōjiji Monastery, still the head Sōtō temple along with Eiheiji, and he is revered as the school's cofounder. Keizan's shingi generally accords with Dōgen's writings, while further elaborating ceremonial patterns and practices and monastic schedules.

In modern times the *Gyojikihan*, compiled by the Sōtō school in 1889 based largely on Dōgen's and Keizan's shingi, has also become an important guidebook for Sōtō rules and ceremonies.

Translation Issues: Gender and Pronouns

In patriarchal East Asian culture, women were not generally in positions of power in the community, and the official histories rarely mention the many female adepts, although several of them are cited in the stories Dōgen includes in the "Pure Standards for Temple Administrators." There is nothing inherent in these monastic practices and procedures, however, that precludes women from carrying out the various positions and jobs that Dōgen describes. Thanks to the insights of feminism, this reality is already clearly reflected in the recent adaptations of the tradition in Western (especially North American) society. Many current Western Dharma teachers are women, and in most American Buddhist communities women and men practice together, with women in responsible positions.

Personal pronouns in the Chinese used by Dōgen in the *Eihei Shingi* (as well as in his native Japanese language) are not gender specific. One of the many limitations of English in the translation of this material is that, unlike Chinese or Japanese neuter pronouns, third-person singular pronouns and possessive pronouns in English require gender (i.e., he, she, his, hers). To avoid inaccurately implying gender specifications, we have tried to avoid "he or she" constructions, but this is occasionally very awkward. To aid comprehension in the detailed procedural descriptions, especially in the "Model for Engaging the Way" and "The Dharma for Taking Meals," we sometimes have used "he" or "his," e.g., "The abbot enters the hall, and after he bows, he takes his seat." This should not be misconstrued as a gender distinction.

English pronouns provide numerous other problems for translation into English. Frequently in the Chinese in which Dōgen wrote the *Eihei Shingi*, the subject is unstated. Usually the implied subject is clear in context, but sometimes there is intended ambiguity, suggesting multiple meanings. Occasionally such ambiguity can be retained in English, but for coherent translation one usually has to supply at least a limiting pronoun like "you," meaning the students Dōgen is addressing in his teaching. Sometimes the translators had to guess at the implied subject. In such cases we have bracketed our interpretations of implied subjects. Brackets have been used throughout to help clarify the meaning of the text. In some cases such bracketed phrases also may be our interpretations.

Dōgen's Use of Language

Dōgen is famous for his difficult and elaborate use of language. Compared to modern Japanese, the Japanese he uses is like Chaucerian English as it is related to modern English. Also he employs many technical Buddhist and Zen terms and expressions. These problems aside, Dōgen also frequently turns inside out conventional grammar and usage to elucidate the inner meaning of Buddhist teaching and point to the limitations of conventional thought patterns. Often in his writings Dōgen uses wordplay and puns to reinterpret traditional understandings of koans or of passages from sutras. He thereby dramatizes the deeper, radical nondualism of developed Mahayana understanding, which often confounds standard subject-object grammatical constructions.

In the face of his linguistic subtlety, we have strived in this translation to convey faithfully and intelligibly Dōgen's meaning. Some Dōgen translators have resorted to frequent interpretative paraphrase. As noted previously, parts of this work are less philosophical and literary than Dōgen's *Shōbōgenzō*. Nevertheless, there are numerous passages that required much discussion and contemplation to clarify. On a number of occasions, after some hours of detailed consideration of a single sentence, the meaning would become apparent when we returned to a very literal reading of Dōgen's original.

Glossaries and Notes

In the text we have used the Chinese names (using the modern pinyin transliteration) of the personages Dōgen cites in the teaching stories or otherwise in the text. A glossary of names is included at the end, arranged alphabetically by Chinese names and providing the person's dates (when available), the alternate Wade-Giles system of transliteration, the Chinese characters, and their Japanese pronunciations, with basic biographical information and all the pages in the text where they appear.

In the dialogues in the text, Dōgen's original often identifies the participants by titles such as teacher, master, or abbot, even when the title was given after the events of the story. In the interest of clarity, we have usually used the commonly known names in the dialogues rather than such titles.

Lineage charts are also added after the glossary of names. These may help clarify the interrelationships of the teachers mentioned, but it should be noted that many of these figures studied intently with other teachers besides the ones formally identified as their primary Dharma teachers. The actuality of the lineage of Zen teaching and experience is the interweaving of these lineages and the tangled causes and conditions of awakening. The lineage charts include names of some significant persons not mentioned elsewhere in *Dōgen's Pure Standards for the Zen Community*, and do not include some less important figures mentioned by Dōgen.

Also included as an appendix is a glossary of Japanese technical terms from Buddhist teaching or monastic practice, as well as some terms that may clarify ambiguities in the translations. These are given in the text or the notes in italics. The glossary provides the Chinese characters, definitions, background information, and the places in the text where the term is used, although relevant meanings of the terms are also identified in the notes. For commonly used terms italics may only be used for their first appearance in the text, and many of the terms are given in translation after they are first used or noted. (Such commonly used or translated terms may only have their first usage listed in the glossary.)

The endnotes, located immediately after each of the essays, also clarify historical or literary allusions, discuss relevant Buddhist and Zen doctrine and teaching methods, and mention parallel or related sources or texts. These hopefully will make the material Dōgen presents more accessible. When possible, we have tried to give the references to quotations or allusions from available English translations; otherwise, we cite original source materials. Ambiguous phrases or sentences are also discussed in the notes, with possible alternative readings described.

Personal Experience of the Monastic Container

Westerners sometimes view all regulations and rules as inherently restrictive and harsh. But Dōgen's attitude is not one of enforcing regimentation. Rather, all of these procedures are designed to support internal discipline and deepening self-awareness based on the practitioners' own inmost intention.

My own experience of monastic training has been both challenging and rewarding. I lived for almost three years at Tassajara Zen Mountain Center in the deep mountains of Monterey County, California, which follows a Western adaptation and modification of the forms in the *Eihei Shingi*. Residents sleep in individual cabins rather than in the monks' meditation hall, so the sleeping rituals described in "The Model for Engaging the Way" are unknown. Thus the day is formally considered to begin in the morning instead of the evening, with the abbot's jundō before morning zazen. Formal ōryōki eating also follows a slightly modified form from that of the *Eihei Shingi*.

Despite such differences, in the last twenty-five years many have benefited from the richness of practice periods at Tassajara. During my first three-month practice period, immersed in a life continuously governed by a prescribed monastic schedule, I felt that I had never before so totally experienced my own time. I was free to participate wholeheartedly in whatever activity came next, with no necessity to give mental energy to my own arrangements and agendas. The sense of space and openness that I had felt sometimes in zazen, and which had drawn me to stronger commitments to practice, were extended palpably into every part of the daily routine.

Of course, later, as I settled into the experience of numbers of practice periods, the subtleties of personal preference and agendas reasserted themselves, and I struggled with the need to face more thoroughly the obstructions of unconscious habits and tendencies; which required refining my own intentions. This aspect of the practice—rubbing against subtle resistances to the forms and to fellow practitioners—was perhaps more beneficial, although often less enjoyable, than my previous enthusiasm.

Some years later in Japan, I experienced traditional monks' hall practice that was extremely close to the forms described by Dōgen during several stays at the Saikōji temple outside Kyoto with Shinkai Tanaka Rōshi, now the tantō (head of practice) at Eiheiji. I also did a ten-week practice period at Shōgoji temple in Kyushu, which Ikkō Narasaki Rōshi and Dainin Katagiri Rōshi, the late abbot of the Minnesota Zen Meditation Center, established specifically to be a training temple for Japanese and Western monks to practice the traditional forms together. The thoroughness of sleeping as well as meditating and eating at the same place in the sōdō is a powerful and satisfying mode of practice.

The greatest distinction I noticed at Shōgoji between the Japanese monks and their Western counterparts was that whereas we Westerners were most intent on asking questions, endeavoring to understand the details of various new monastic forms, the Japanese concentrated on enacting these rituals impeccably. Our questioning was a little uncomfortable for some of the monks (although welcomed by the instructors). Rather than refining some understanding, the Japanese monks' effort was to embody fully the ritual movements and take care of monastic equipment, doing each activity "beautifully."

Later Shinkai Tanaka Rōshi said to me, "Understanding is not important; understanding is easy. The point is just to continue." An important value of monastic practice is simply that it provides a context in which to continue, to sustain attention to the details of one's own awareness and conduct. This sustained attention to oneself and to the world constantly arising before us is essential to the experience of Buddhist liberation.

Conclusion

Participation in communities based on Dōgen's standards may still perhaps be more natural for modern Japanese people, who so readily accept group identification and who seem to thrive amid group ego. Westerners, on the other hand, are recently experiencing the weaknesses as well as the value of a society based on ideals of individualism. In Western culture, where all the traditional guidelines for even the simplest interrelationships often seem to have become irrelevant, there is currently a great thirst for supportive community based on genuine spiritual value. Dōgen's detailed depiction of the attitudes of appreciation and commitment in his standards for the Zen community might be useful guidance for many now seeking to reestablish harmonious community life. May these teachings be helpful to all those seeking to live together informed by compassion and insight.

The Pure Standards of Eihei Dōgen Zenji
[*Eihei Shingi*]

Instructions for the Tenzo
(Tenzokyōkun)

compiled by Monk Dōgen at Kannon Dōri Kōshō Hōrin Zenji Temple[1]

From the beginning in Buddha's family there have been six temple administrators. They are all Buddha's children and together they carry out Buddha's work. Among them the tenzo [chief cook] has the job of taking care of the preparation of food for the community. The *Zen'en Shingi* says, "For serving the community there is the tenzo."[2] Since ancient times, masters with Way-seeking mind, lofty people who had awakened their hearts, were appointed to this job. After all, isn't this the single color of diligently engaging in the Way? If you do not have the mind of the Way, then all of this hard work is meaningless and not beneficial. The *Zen'en Shingi* says, "You must put to work the mind of the Way, offering appropriate variety [in the food served] so that the community can feel satisfied and at ease." In ancient times such people as Guishan and Dongshan filled this position; formerly various great Ancestors have worked at this job.[3] Therefore, isn't the tenzo different from both usual worldly cooks and even the imperial cooks?

When this mountain monk [Dōgen] was in Song China, during my spare time I made inquiries of former tenzos with long experience and they brought up some examples they had seen and heard and related them to me. This guidance is the marrow bequeathed since ancient times by buddhas and ancestors who had the mind of the Way. First of all, you must deeply study the *Zen'en Shingi*. After that, it is necessary to hear discussions about details of the job from former tenzos.

Here is how to fulfill the job for a whole day and night. First, after lunch, consult with the director and assistant director in their offices to get the provisions for the next day's breakfast and lunch. This includes rice, greens, and other items. After you receive them, carefully protect these ingredients as if taking care of your own eyes. Zen Master Baoming Renyong said, "Guard the temple properties as if they were your own eyes." Respect [the temple food] as if it were for the emperor. This attitude applies to both raw and cooked food.

Thereafter, all the temple administrators gather in their offices and discuss what combinations of flavors, which vegetables, and what breakfast gruel to prepare for the next day.[4] The *Zen'en Shingi* says, "Decide on the ingredients of the different courses for breakfast and lunch after discussions with all of the temple administrators." The [six] temple administrators [*roku chiji*] are: the director [*tsūsu*], assistant director [*kansu*], treasurer [*fūsu*], supervisor of the monks' conduct [*inō*], chief cook [*tenzo*], and work leader [*shissui*]. After agreeing on the different courses, write a menu and post it on the signboards at both the abbot's room and the monks' study hall.

Next, get ready the following morning's breakfast. Select the rice and prepare the vegetables by yourself with your own hands, watching closely with sincere diligence. You should not attend to some things and neglect or be slack with others for even one moment. Do not give away a single drop from within the ocean of virtues; you must not fail to add a single speck on top of the mountain of good deeds. The *Zen'en Shingi* says, "[If the food is] without the excellence of the six flavors and without the endowment of the three virtues, the tenzo is not serving the community."[5] While examining the rice, watch for sand; while examining the sand, watch for rice. If you minutely observe from different viewpoints without absentmindedness, then naturally the food will integrate the three virtues and include the six tastes.

Xuefeng was tenzo when he studied with Dongshan.[6] One day, while the rice was being cleaned, Dongshan asked, "Do you sift out the sand from the rice or do you sift out the rice from the sand?" Xuefeng said, "I throw out the sand and rice at the same time." Dongshan said, "Then what will the community eat?" Xuefeng overturned the bowl. Dongshan said, "Later you will meet somebody else."[7] In such a manner, lofty ancients of the Way have carefully practiced this job with their own hands. As their successors we must not be negligent. It has been said that, for the tenzo, rolling up the sleeves is the mind of the Way. If you have made a mistake cleaning rice and sand, correct it by yourself. The *Shingi* says, "When you cook food, if you intimately and personally look after it, it will naturally be pure."

Keep the white water that drains from washing the rice, not wastefully discarding it. Since ancient times, we take a bag and strain the leftover white water to use it in the rice gruel. After you have collected the ingredients in a pot you must be sure to protect it from old mice falling in by mistake; also do not allow whoever idly wanders by to examine or touch it.

After preparing the breakfast vegetables, get together the wooden rice container, pots, and utensils that were used at lunch for the rice and soup, and attentively wash them clean. For all the various things, put away in high places things that belong in high places, and put away in low places things that belong in low places. "A high place is high level and a low place is low level."[8] Tongs and ladles and other utensils should all be treated equally, viewed with a sincere mind, and picked up and put down with a light hand.

After that put together the materials for tomorrow's lunch. First, remove with great care all the bugs, small inedible beans, rice bran, sand, and stones from the rice. While the tenzo is preparing both the rice and vegetables, the tenzo's attendant chants a sutra and dedicates it to Zaogong [the guardian god of the oven].[9] Next, choose and take care of the ingredients for the soup greens. Do not comment on the quantity or make judgments about the quality of the ingredients you obtained from the director, just sincerely prepare them. Definitely avoid emotional disputes about the quantity of the ingredients. All day and all night, things come to mind and the mind attends to them; at one with them all, diligently carry on the Way.

Before midnight arrange things for breakfast; sometime after midnight take care of cooking the breakfast gruel.[10] The next day, after breakfast, wash the pots, steam the rice, and cook the soup. While the lunch rice is soaking, the tenzo should not leave the sink area. To wash the rice properly, carefully watch with clear eyes that not one grain is wasted; then put it in a pot, light the fire, and steam the rice. An ancient said, "When steaming rice, regard the pot as your own head; when washing rice, know that the water is your own life."

Soon after the rice is cooked, put it either in a bamboo basket or wooden container and place it on the table [for food that's ready].[11] You should also cook the vegetables and soup at the same time that the rice is steaming. The tenzo closely watches while the rice and soup are cooking, and has the attendant, kitchen workers, or oven person arrange the kitchen implements.

Recently at large monasteries there are rice cooks and soup cooks, but still they are supervised by the tenzo. In ancient times there were no rice cooks or soup cooks; the tenzo was the only worker.

When you take care of things, do not see with your common eyes, do not think with your common sentiments. Pick a single blade of grass and erect a sanctuary for the jewel king; enter a single atom and turn the great wheel of the teaching.[12] So even when you are making a broth of coarse greens, do not arouse an attitude of distaste or dismissal. Even when you are making a high-quality cream soup, do not arouse an attitude of rapture or dancing for joy. If you already have no attachments, how could you have any disgust? Therefore, although you may encounter inferior ingredients, do not be at all negligent; although you may come across delicacies, be all the more diligent. Never alter your state of mind based on materials. People who change their mind according to ingredients, or adjust their speech to [the status of] whoever they are talking to, are not people of the Way.

If you are resolute in your intention and are most sincere, you will vow to be more pure-hearted than the ancients and surpass even the elders in attentiveness. The appropriate manner of putting the mind of the Way to work on this is to decide that even if the old masters got three coins and made a broth of coarse greens, now with the same three coins you will make a high-quality cream soup. This is difficult to do. Why is that? The difference between the ancients and people of today is as remote as that between heaven and earth. How could we ever stand even with them? However, when we attentively undertake this job, we can definitely surpass the old masters. This principle is a certainty that you still do not yet clearly understand, only because your thinking scatters like wild birds and your emotions scamper around like monkeys in the forest.[13] If those monkeys and birds once took the backward step of inner illumination, naturally you would become integrated.[14] This is a means whereby, although you are turned around by things, you can also turn things around. Being harmonious and pure like this, do not lose either the eye of oneness or the eye that discerns differences.[15] Take one stalk of vegetable to make the six-foot body [of buddha]; invite the six-foot body to make one stalk of vegetable. This is the divine power that causes transformations and the buddha work that benefits beings.

When you have completely finished taking care [of the food], see what is there and place it here [where it belongs].[16] When the drum beats or the bell rings, follow the assembly and join the dharma meeting.[17] Do not miss even one morning or evening meeting.

When you return to the kitchen, right away you must close your eyes and clearly envision how many people are in the monks' hall; how many distinguished retired monks and other monks with high positions there are in private rooms; how many monks are in the infirmary, the elderly monks' residence, and the dormitory for recuperating monks; how many traveling monks are in the guest dorm; and what number of people are in hermitages. Carefully calculate in this way, and if you have the slightest uncertainty ask the inō [monks' supervisor], the heads of the various monastery departments, the managers of the different offices, and the head monk of each department.[18] When you have settled your questions [about the number of people to be fed], carefully determine [as follows] how to provide one grain of rice for each grain of rice that will be eaten.[19] If you divide one grain you will have two half-grains. [Sometimes divide it into] one third or one fourth, one half or two halves. If you put two separate half-grains of rice together, you will have one whole grain of rice. Also, if you give one ninth [to someone], see how many parts are left over; or, if you take back one ninth, see how many parts they still have.

If [the monks] get to eat one grain of Luling rice, they will see Monk Guishan; also if you get to offer one grain of Luling rice, you will see the water buffalo.[20] The water buffalo eats Monk Guishan; Monk Guishan tends the water buffalo. Have I determined it yet or not? Have you calculated it yet or not? After inspecting and clearly discerning these details, when you see an opportunity explain, when you face a person speak. After all, exertion like this, with the suchness of unity and the suchness of duality, whether for two days or three days, must not be forgotten even for a little while.

When a patron comes to the monastery and offers money for food, the temple administrators should discuss it together, as is the custom at Buddhist monasteries.[21] When donated materials are to be dispersed, also they discuss it together. Do not violate their authority and create a disturbance in the job.

After the lunch or breakfast has been properly prepared and placed on the table, the tenzo puts on the *okesa*, unfolds the *zagu*, and, facing the *sōdō*, offers incense and does nine prostrations.[22] Then the food is sent out.

Throughout the day and night, prepare lunch and breakfast without wasting time. If you sincerely arrange the implements and prepare the food, all of your conduct and performance becomes the activity for the sustained development of a womb of sages.[23] Taking the backward step of transforming the self is the way to bring ease to the community.

Now we in Japan already have heard the name Buddha Dharma for a long time. However, the venerable ones have not taught, and previous people have not recorded, the description of how to prepare monks' food respectfully.[24] How much more have they not seen, even in a dream, the observance of doing nine prostrations toward the monks' food? People in our country think that the way monks eat, and the way food is prepared in the community, is the same as the way birds and hairy beasts eat. Truly we must pity this, truly we must grieve. What a shame!

When this mountain monk [Dōgen] was at Tiantong Temple, a person named Yong from Qingyuan Prefecture had the job of tenzo.[25] I happened to be passing through the eastern corridor on my way to the Chaoran hut after lunch, when the tenzo was drying mushrooms in front of the buddha hall.[26] He carried a bamboo cane, but had no hat on his head. The sun beat down on the hot pavement and the sweat flowed down and drenched him as he resolutely dried the mushrooms. I saw he was struggling a bit. With his spine bent like a bow and his shaggy eyebrows, he looked like a crane.[27]

I approached and politely asked the tenzo his age. He said he was sixty-eight.

I asked, "Why do you not have an attendant or lay worker do this?"

The tenzo said, "Others are not me."

I said, "Esteemed sir, you are truly dedicated.[28] The sun is so hot. Why are you doing this now?"

The tenzo said, "What time should I wait for?"

I immediately withdrew. Thinking to myself as I walked away, I deeply appreciated that this job [expresses] the essential function.

Another time, in the fifth month of the sixteenth year of the Katei period [June or July 1223], I was on my ship at Qingyuan. While I was talking with the Japanese captain, an old monk arrived who looked about sixty years old. He came straight onto the boat and asked one of the crew if he could buy some Japanese shiitake mushrooms. I invited him to drink some tea and asked him where he lived. He was the tenzo at the monastery at Ayuwang Mountain.[29] He said, "I am from the western part of Sichuan, and left home forty years ago. This year I am sixty-one years old. I have spent time at many monasteries in various areas. In recent years I stayed with Guyun Daoquan. Then I went to practice at Ayuwang Monastery, where I have been kept very busy.[30] Last year, after the end of the summer practice period, I was appointed tenzo of the temple. Tomorrow is the fifth day celebration, and I do not have any special food to serve.[31] I want to make noodle soup, but I do not have any mushrooms. Therefore I came here to try to buy shiitake to offer the monks from the ten directions."

I asked him, "What time did you depart from there?"

The tenzo said, "After lunch."

I said, "How far distant from here is Ayuwang?"

The tenzo said, "Thirty-four or thirty-five *li*" [about twelve miles].

I said, "When are you going to return to the temple?"

The tenzo said, "As soon as I finish buying the mushrooms I will go."

I said, "Today unexpectedly we have met and also had a conversation on this ship. Is this not a truly fortunate opportunity? Allow Dōgen to offer food to you, Tenzo Zenji."

The tenzo said, "It is not possible. If I do not take care of tomorrow's offering it will be done badly."

I said, "In your temple aren't there some workers who know how to prepare meals the same as you? If only one person, the tenzo, is not there, will something be deficient?"

The tenzo said, "During my old age I am handling this job, so in senility I am doing this wholehearted practice. How could I possibly just give away [my responsibilities]? Also, when I came here, I did not ask permission to stay away overnight."

I then asked the tenzo, "Venerable tenzo, in your advanced years why do you not wholeheartedly engage the Way through zazen or penetrate the words and stories of the ancient masters, instead of troubling yourself by being tenzo and just working?[32] What is that good for?"

The tenzo laughed loudly and said, "Oh, good fellow from a foreign country, you have not yet understood wholeheartedly engaging in the Way, and you do not yet know what words and phrases are."

Hearing this, I suddenly felt ashamed and stunned, and then asked him, "What are words and phrases? What is wholeheartedly engaging the Way?"

The tenzo said, "If you do not stumble over this question you are really a true person."

I could not understand at that time. The tenzo said, "If you have not yet fully gotten it, sometime later come to Ayuwang Mountain. We will have a complete dialogue concerning the principle of words and phrases." After saying that, the tenzo got up and said, "It's getting dark and I am going now." Then he left to return home.

In the seventh month of the same year [August or September], I rested my monk's staff at Tiantong Monastery.[33] At that time, this tenzo came to visit me and said, "After the summer practice period was over I retired, and I'm returning to my home village. I happened to learn at my monastery that you were here. How could I not come to see you?"

I was deeply touched and overjoyed to welcome him, and during our conversation I brought up the issues that we had mentioned before on the ship concerning words and phrases and wholehearted engagement of the Way. The tenzo said, "People who study words and phrases should know the significance of words and phrases. People dedicated to wholehearted practice need to affirm the significance of engaging the Way."

I asked, "What are words and phrases?"

The tenzo said, "One, two, three, four, five."

Also I asked, "What is wholeheartedly engaging the Way?"

The tenzo said, "In the whole world it is never hidden."

Although we discussed many topics, I will not record the rest now. For whatever bit I know about words and phrases or slightly understand about wholeheartedly engaging the Way, I am grateful to that tenzo's kindness. I recounted this conversation to my late teacher Myōzen. He was delighted to hear about it. Later I saw a verse Xuedou wrote for a monk that goes:

> One character, three characters, five, and seven characters.
> Having thoroughly investigated the ten thousand things,
>   none have any foundation.
> At midnight the white moon sets into the dark ocean.
> When searching for the black dragon's pearl,
>   you will find they are numerous.[34]

What that tenzo had said in former years and what Xuedou had expressed naturally match each other. More and more I realize that this tenzo was a true person of the Way. Accordingly, what I previously saw of words and phrases is one, two, three, four, five. Today what I see of words and phrases is also six, seven, eight, nine, ten. My junior fellow-practitioners, completely see this in that, completely see that in this.[35] Making such an effort you can totally grasp one-flavor Zen through words and phrases. If you do not do this you will be influenced by the poison of the varieties of five-flavor Zen, and your preparation of the monks' food will not be appropriate.[36]

Certainly, there are ancient stories to hear and recent examples to see concerning this job. There are words and phrases, and principles to follow. Shouldn't this [work] be called the true core? Even if you have the honor of being appointed as abbot, you must also have this same mental attitude. The *Zen'en Shingi* says, "The food cooked for both breakfast and lunch should be refined and abundant. The four offerings [to monks] should have no shortage. The World-Honored One, in his compassion, bequeathed twenty years to protect his descendants. The merit and virtue of one beam of light from the white hair [on his forehead] is received and used without being exhausted."[37] Therefore, "Just serve the community and do not worry about poverty. If you do not have a limited heart you will have boundless fortune."[38] Apparently, serving the community like this is the crucial attitude of the abbot.

As for the attitude while preparing food, the essential point is deeply to arouse genuine mind and respectful mind without making judgments about the ingredients' fineness or coarseness. Have you not heard that by offering to Buddha one bowl of white water [left from rinsing rice], an old woman attained wondrous merit during her life; and that by presenting half a mango fruit to a temple, King Ashoka could generate his final great act of charity and thereby receive the prediction of buddhahood and enjoy the great result?[39] Although they create relationship to buddha, [donations that are] abundant but lacking [in heart] are not as good as those that are small but sincere.[40] This is the practice of a [true] person.

Cooking so-called rich, creamy food is not necessarily superior, cooking plain vegetable soup is not necessarily inferior. When you are given plain vegetables to prepare, you must treat them the same as rich, creamy food, with straightforward mind, sincere mind, and pure mind. The reason is that when they converge in the pure great ocean assembly of Buddha Dharma, you recognize neither rich, creamy tastes nor the taste of plain vegetables, but only the flavor of the one great ocean. Furthermore, in developing the buds of the Way and nurturing the womb of sages, rich cream and simple vegetables are the same, not different. There is an old saying that a monk's mouth is like an oven. We should understand this. Reflect that simple vegetables can nurture the womb of sages and develop the buds of the Way. Do

INSTRUCTIONS FOR THE TENZO

not see them as lowly or worthless. A guiding teacher of humans and celestial beings benefits them with plain vegetables.

One also should not see the assembled monks as good or bad, or consider them as elder or younger. Even the self does not know where the self will settle down; how could others determine where others will settle down? How could it not be a mistake to find others' faults with our own faults? Although there is a difference between the senior and junior and the wise and stupid, as members of sangha they are the same. Moreover, the wrong in the past may be right in the present, so who could distinguish the sage from the common person? The *Zen'en Shingi* says, "Without distinction of sage or common, monks meet together throughout the ten directions." If you have the spirit of not arranging everything into right and wrong, how could you not carry out conduct of the Way that directly proceeds to unsurpassed *bodhi*? If you take one false step, then you will stumble as you face what is before you. The bones and marrow of the ancients are found completely where this kind of constant effort is made. In later ages you fellow-practitioners will also get it for the first time by making this effort. Could the regulations of High Ancestor Baizhang have been in vain?[41]

After I returned to this country I stayed at Kenninji monastery for a few years.[42] That temple gave someone this position [of tenzo] in name only, without him really doing it at all. He did not yet discern that this was buddha's work. How could he possibly understand and comply with the Way? Sincerely we must have compassion for those who never meet a [true] person and recklessly tear apart the conduct of the Way. I saw that this monk never once supervised breakfast and lunch. He entrusted it to a servant without brains or feelings and ordered him to take charge of all matters, large or small. [The tenzo] never went to see whether things were done correctly or not. It was as if there was a woman next door, and if he went to visit it would be a shame or a fault.

He occupied an office, sometimes taking naps, sometimes having chats, sometimes reading sutras, and sometimes chanting, for many long moons not going near a pot. Moreover, he did not buy the utensils or carefully consider the various menus. How could he have known his job? Needless to say, he had never even dreamed of the two [daily] occasions for making nine prostrations. When it was time to train novices he did not know anything. How pitiful and sad! He was a person without a Way-seeking mind who never had the chance to see anyone with the virtue of the Way. Although he had entered the jewel mountain he had returned empty-handed; although he had arrived in the jewel ocean he came back with a worthless body. You should know that even though he had never aroused true mind, if he had met one example of an original person he could have practiced the Way. Even though he had never met a true person, if he had deeply aroused his mind he could have hit upon practice of the Way. Since both were missing, how could there have been any benefit?

As I observed the people who were devoting themselves for a year to the jobs of temple administrators or heads of monastic departments in the various temples of Song China, each of them maintained the three essential attitudes of an abbot whenever they performed their jobs, encouraging themselves to strive at their tasks.[43] Benefit others, which simultaneously gives abundant benefit to the self. Make the monastery thrive and renew its high standards. Aspire to stand shoulder to shoulder and respectfully follow in the heels [of our predecessors]. Clearly know that there are fools who treat themselves [as indifferently] as others, and there are honorable people who consider others as themselves. An ancient said:

> Two-thirds of a lifetime has swiftly gone.
> On the spiritual foundation not a single speck has been polished.

INSTRUCTIONS FOR THE TENZO

While indulging, life randomly passes day after day.
If you are called but do not turn around, what can be done?[44]

You should know that if you have not yet met a guiding example you will be overcome by human emotions. We must pity the foolish child who took the fortune handed down by his wealthy father and, in front of others, uselessly worked digging up filth and excrement.[45] So now, how could we be like this? Appreciate that people of the Way who did this job before naturally matched their conduct and their virtue. The great Guishan's realization of the Way happened when he was tenzo. Dongshan's [answer], "Three pounds of sesame," was also when he was tenzo.[46] If you value anything, value realization of the Way. If you value any time, value the time of realizing the Way. As for what remains from cherishing immersion in the Way, there is an emanation even from offering sand as if a treasure.[47] We see that often there is a resonance from copying the [Buddha's] figure and doing prostrations. Even more, this job is the same and it still has the same name [as what ancestors such as Guishan and Dongshan did]. If you can convey this attitude about this activity, how could the elegance of this Way not manifest?

On all occasions when the temple administrators, heads of monastic departments, and the tenzo are engaged in their work, they should maintain joyful mind, nurturing mind, and magnanimous mind.[48] What I call joyful mind is the happy heart. You must reflect that if you were born in heaven you would cling to ceaseless bliss and not give rise to Way-seeking mind. This would not be conducive to practice. What's more, how could you prepare food to offer to the three jewels?[49] Among the ten thousand dharmas, the most honored are the three jewels. Most excellent are the three jewels. Neither the lord of heaven or a wheel-turning king can compare to them.[50] The *Zen'en Shingi* says, "Respected by society, though peacefully apart, the sangha is most pure and unfabricated." Now I have the fortune to be born a human being and prepare food to be received by the three jewels. Is this not a great karmic affinity?[51] We must be very happy about this.

Moreover, consider that if you were born in the realms of hell, hungry ghosts, animals, fighting gods, or others of the eight difficult births, even if you desired refuge within the sangha's power, you would never actually be able to prepare pure food to offer the three treasures.[52] Because of suffering in these painful circumstances your body and mind would be fettered. However, in the present life you have already done this [cooking], so you should enjoy this life and this body resulting from incalculable ages of worthy activity. This merit can never fade.

You should engage in and carry out this work with the vow to include one thousand or ten thousand lives in one day or one time. This will allow you to unite with these virtuous karmic causes for ten million lives. The mind that has fully contemplated such fortune is joyful mind. Truly, even if you become a virtuous wheel-turning king but do not make food to offer the three treasures, after all there is no benefit. It would only be like a splash of water, a bubble, or a flickering flame.

As for what is called nurturing mind, it is the mind of mothers and fathers. For example, it is considering the three treasures as a mother and father think of their only child. Even impoverished, destitute people firmly love and raise an only child. What kind of determination is this? Other people cannot know it until they actually become mothers and fathers. Parents earnestly consider their child's growth without concern for their own wealth or poverty. They do not care if they are cold or hot but give their child covering or shade. In parents' thoughtfulness there is this intensity. People who have aroused this mind comprehend it well. Only people who are familiar with this mind are truly awake to it. Therefore, watching over water and over grain, shouldn't everyone maintain the affection and kindness of nourishing children?

Great Teacher Shakyamuni even gave up twenty years of a buddha's allotted lifespan to protect us all alike in these later times. What was his intention? It was simply to confer parental mind. Tathagatas could never wish for rewards or riches.

As for what is called magnanimous mind, this mind is like the great mountains or like the great ocean; it is not biased or contentious mind. Carrying half a pound, do not take it lightly; lifting forty pounds should not seem heavy.[53] Although drawn by the voices of spring, do not wander over spring meadows; viewing the fall colors, do not allow your heart to fall. The four seasons cooperate in a single scene; regard light and heavy with a single eye. On this single occasion you must write the word "great."[54] You must know the word "great." You must learn the word "great."

If the tenzo of Jiashan Monastery had not studied the word "great," he would not have saved Taiyuan with a spontaneous laugh.[55] If Zen Master Guishan had not written the word "great," he could not have taken a stick of firewood and blown on it three times.[56] If Venerable Dongshan had not known the word "great," he would not have picked "three pounds of sesame" to demonstrate to a monk. You should know that former great mentors all have been studying the "great" word, and right now freely make the great sound, expound the great meaning, clarify the great matter, guide a great person, and fulfill this one great cause [for buddhas appearing in the world].[57] How could abbots, temple administrators, heads of monastic departments, and monks ever forget these three kinds of minds?

Written in spring of the third year of Katei [1237] to instruct later wise people who study the Way.[58]

Written by Monk Dōgen who transmits the Way, abbot of the Kannon Dōri Kōshō Hōrin Zenji Temple.

Notes

1. This temple's name literally means "Kannon Bodhisattva beneficially guides the sacred to flourish in jeweled woods Zen temple." It is usually called Kōshōji, "make the sacred flourish temple." Dōgen lived there from 1233 to 1243. This temple, at Dōgen's time in Fukakusa in the southern part of Kyoto, burned soon after Dōgen left and was rebuilt further south in Uji in 1648.

2. *Zen'en Shingi*, literally "Zen Garden Pure Standards," [*Chanyuan Qingguei* in Chinese] was compiled by Changlu Zongze, a master in the Yunmen lineage, in 1103. This quotation is from chapter 8 of the ten-chapter work.

3. This is Dongshan Shouchu, the disciple of Yunmen, and is not Dongshan Liangjie, who founded the Caodong (Sōtō) lineage. Dates lived, Chinese characters, and Japanese pronunciations for all persons named in *Eihei Shingi* appear in the "Glossary of Names" in the appendix with biographical data and page numbers where they appear in the text.

The Ancestors, sometimes translated "patriarchs," are the great founder figures of a lineage who established or developed branches of the teaching. The original Chinese word does not imply a gender distinction.

4. Traditionally in Zen monasteries, the temple administrators' offices are in the *kuri* building (also called the *kuin*) to the right of the dharma hall, which also houses the kitchen and food storage areas. In China and Japan the breakfast gruel is watery cooked rice. Any other grain might be used. The temple administrator [*chiji*] positions (*tsūsu, kansu, fūsu, inō, tenzo,* and *shissui*) are discussed in detail in the last section of the *Eihei Shingi*, "Pure Standards for the Temple Administrators."

5. The six flavors are sweet, spicy, salty, bitter, sour, and simple. The three virtues refer to food that is soft, clean, and in accord with dharma (prepared appropriately).

6. This is Dongshan Liangjie, founder of the Caodong (Sōtō) lineage transmitted by Dōgen to Japan.

INSTRUCTIONS FOR THE TENZO   51

   7. Dongshan indicates here that Xuefeng has some understanding but will need to meet another teacher. Later Xuefeng became a successor of Deshan.

   8. This quote refers to a story about Guishan and his student Yangshan Huiji, founders of the Guiyang (Igyō) lineage. Yangshan was digging on a hillside to make a rice paddy. Yangshan said, "This place is so low, that place is so high." Guishan said, "Water makes things equal. Why don't you level it with water?" Yangshan said, "Water is not reliable, teacher. A high place is high level. A low place is low level." Guishan agreed. See Chang Chung-yuan, *Original Teachings of Ch'an Buddhism: Selected from "The Transmission of the Lamp"* (New York: Vintage Books, 1971), p. 210.

   9. Zaogong (Sōkō in Japanese) is the native Chinese guardian spirit of the oven. Before starting to cook lunch, the "Daihi Shin [Great Compassionate Heart] Dharani" is traditionally chanted by the tenzo and their attendant in front of this deity's altar in the kitchen.

   10. Dōgen here refers to the time period between midnight and roughly 2 a.m., before which breakfast preparations should be completed, and sometime after the beginning of which the gruel should be cooked. It is not clear from his description when the tenzo is expected to sleep.

   11. A bamboo basket is used in summer, a wooden container in winter.

   12. Jewel King is an epithet for a buddha. This sentence refers to the story related in case 4 of the *Book of Serenity*. "As the World Honored One was walking with the congregation, he pointed to the ground with his finger and said, 'This spot is good to build a sanctuary.' Indra, Emperor of the gods, took a blade of grass, stuck it in the ground, and said, 'The sanctuary is built.' The World Honored One smiled." See Thomas Cleary, trans., *Book of Serenity* (Hudson, N.Y.: Lindisfarne Press, 1990), pp. 17–19.

   13. Instead of "birds," the common Rufubon edition has "horses." However, the earliest Kōshū version, copied by the fifteenth Eiheiji abbot Kōshū in the early sixteenth century, has "birds," which is clearly correct in the poetic context of the characters for the whole phrase. The

characters for "bird" and "horse" are somewhat similar. The later "horse" is evidently a miscopy. There is no extant version of the *Eihei Shingi* in Dōgen's own handwriting.

14. "Take the backward step of inner illumination" is *taiho henshō*, another expression for *ekō henshō* or "learn to withdraw, turning the light inwards, illuminating the Self," which is described in Dōgen's "Fukanzazengi." See Norman Waddell and Masao Abe, trans. "Fukanzazengi and Shōbōgenzō Zazengi," *Eastern Buddhist* 4, no. 2 (Kyoto: 1973). "Become integrated" is *dajō ippen*, literally "completely become one piece."

15. Dōgen says literally "one eye or two eyes." This refers to the eye of nondiscriminating wisdom or oneness, and the eye that discerns how to function amid the details of the relative, dualistic aspect of our life.

16. The original sentence is complex. In addition to referring to the kitchen work, "there" is *nahen*, which sometimes indicates absolute reality, and "here" is *shahen*, which sometimes indicates the concrete reality here and now.

17. "Dharma meeting" is a translation for *san*, which is the community meeting with the teacher to receive instruction, sometimes with questions and responses. There are various different kinds of *san*, depending on where and when it is held, e.g. *chōsan* in the morning, *bansan* in the evening, *shōsan* in the abbot's room, and *daisan* in the dharma hall.

18. The heads of the different monastic departments are called *chōshū*. The six chōshū are the head monk (*shuso*), the head scribe/secretary (*shoki*), librarian (*zōsu*), guest manager (*shika*), bath attendant (*yokusu*), and buddha hall manager (*chiden*).

19. "Carefully determine" is a translation of *shōryō*, which is used both for merchants settling on a price and in Zen dialogues for investigating understanding of dharma. This passage, including the ensuing description of dividing a grain of rice, refers to the tenzo's job of appropriately apportioning the food to the various parts of the monastery, as well as to each monk individually, according to their differing and changing needs. This also refers, metaphorically, to the process of sharing one's own practice with all the various beings and situations. Zazen

INSTRUCTIONS FOR THE TENZO 53

practice usually emphasizes nondiscrimination. But this nondiscrimination also does not discriminate against the careful calculations and consideration necessary for attentive practice amid the diversity of ordinary everyday life.

20. "Luling" (Roryō in Japanese) is a region of Jiangxi Province famous for high-quality rice. This also refers to a story about Qingyuan Xingsi, who came from Luling and was one of the two main disciples of the Sixth Ancestor. A monk asked Qingyuan, "What is the essential meaning of Buddha Dharma?" Qingyuan answered, "What is the price of rice in Luling?" This story uses Luling rice as a symbol of Buddha Dharma, which is not abstract but concerns everyday life. Although rice is the most important substance, the staple food in traditional Chinese society, its price is always fluctuating. This story can be found in the *Book of Serenity*, case 5. See Cleary, trans., *Book of Serenity*.

Guishan Lingyou said to his assembly, "After I have passed away I shall become a water buffalo at the foot of the mountain. On the left side of the buffalo's chest five characters, 'Gui/shan/Monk/Ling/yu,' will be inscribed. At that time you may call me the monk of Guishan, but at the same time I shall also be the water buffalo. When you call me water buffalo, I am also the monk Guishan. What is my correct name?" From Chang, *Original Teachings of Ch'an Buddhism*, p. 208.

21. "Patron" (or donor) is *seshu*, referring to lay supporters of the temple.

22. *Okesa* is a monk's robe, a large, rectangular wrap. Since the time of Shakyamuni, monks have traditionally sewn them together, originally from uniformly dyed, discarded rags. The *zagu* is a cloth spread on the ground to protect the okesa when monks bow. The *sōdō* is the hall where monks meditate, eat, and sleep. The *sō* of sōdō is one of four terms for monk that Dōgen commonly uses in Eihei Shingi. The others are *shu*, *unsui*, and *biku*.

23. "Sustained development of a womb of sages" is *shōtai chōyō*. This term is used for practice after enlightenment.

24. "Respectfully" is a translation in this context for *nyohō*, according to the dharma.

25. "This mountain monk" is the phrase Dōgen usually uses in the

following passages to refer to himself. Tiantong (in Japanese, Tendō) is the name of the mountain where the temple stood at which Dōgen met his teacher Tiantong Rujing. Yong is Yō in Japanese.

26. Chaoran hut (*Chōnensai* in Japanese) was probably a subtemple in this monastery. It might perhaps be another name for *Ryōnenryō*, the subtemple where Dōgen's Japanese teacher and friend Myōzen was staying during the illness from which he eventually died.

27. "Shaggy eyebrows" is literally "dragon eyebrows," a common Chinese literary expression.

28. "Truly dedicated" is our translation in this context for *nyohō*, in accord with dharma.

29. Guangri Chanshi (Kōrizenji) Temple was on Ayuwang (Aikuō in Japanese) Mountain in the Ming region of Zhejiang Province in eastern China.

30. Guyun Daoquan was a disciple of Zhuoan Deguang, who was in turn a disciple of the famous Dahui. The latter two were abbots of Ayuwang Monastery, so Guyun Daoquan may have also been an abbot there, and this tenzo perhaps went there for that reason. "Went to practice" is *kata*, literally "hung my belongings" (monk's robes and bowls) at this temple.

31. The fifth day of the fifth month is a traditional celebration day in China and Japan.

32. "Wholeheartedly engage the Way," is *bendō*. "Words and stories," here are *watō*, also an important term in the practice of meditative concentration on koans in the Linji tradition.

33. "Rest my monk's staff" is an expression for stopping travel to be a resident monk at a monastery.

34. The word for "characters" used by Xuedou in this verse is the same as that used for "phrases" in the "words and phrases" discussed by Dōgen and the tenzo. The black dragon's pearl, said to be held in her jaw, represents truth and buddha nature. This poem is from the *Soei Shū*, a collection of Xuedou's poems.

35. "This and that" are *shatō* (individual, concrete phenomena) and *natō* (universal interdependence).

36. One-flavor Zen is genuine practice free from attachment to, or

INSTRUCTIONS FOR THE TENZO   55

desire for, fame and profit. This is contrasted to five-flavor Zen which is practice diluted by expectations and by confusion from diverse teachings. "Appropriate" here is *kōshu*, which includes skillfulness, attention to the whole field of activity, and wholesome attitude.

37. The providing of the four offerings to the monks—food, clothing, bedding, and medicine—is the responsibility of an abbot. The word used for "abbot" before the quote is *shukuhanjū*, literally, "provider of food." The "World-Honored One" is an epithet for Shakyamuni Buddha. It is believed he was to have lived one hundred years, but died twenty years early to leave some of his life for his descendants. Accordingly, his followers need not worry over food and clothing. The white hair on Buddha's forehead emitting radiance is one of the thirty-two marks of a buddha.

38. This entire quotation is from volume 8 of the *Zen'en Shingi*.

39. King Ashoka was so lavish in his contributions to the sangha that toward the end of his life his ministers forbade him to make any further donations, so all he had to give to a temple was a half mango he had been eating. This story is from *Aikuō Kyō* [The sutra of King Ashoka], chapter 5. Ashoka's name in Japanese is Aikuō (Ayuwang in Chinese). The temple of the tenzo who had visited Dōgen on his ship was named after King Ashoka. The "great result" (or fruit) is buddhahood.

40. "Abundant but lacking (literally, "vacant," as in emptyhearted) is not as good as small but sincere," is a saying of Yunmen.

41. Baizhang is said to have compiled the first regulations for a Zen community. The *Zen'en Shingi* was compiled in an attempt to continue Baizhang's standards, since this writing had been lost. High Ancestor is *kōso*, usually used only for great founders, such as Mahakashyapa, Dongshan Liangjie, and now Dōgen himself.

42. Kenninji Monastery in Kyoto, established by Eisai, was where Dōgen lived before he went to China. At Kenninji Dōgen had met his previous teacher Myōzen, who went with Dōgen to China and died there.

43. The "three essential attitudes of an abbot" have been interpreted as either to benefit others, cause the monastery to thrive, and fol-

low the predecessors; or the three minds: joyful, nurturing, and magnanimous minds.

44. This is a poem by Xuefeng.

45. This refers to the famous story of the prodigal son in the *Lotus Sutra*. See Leon Hurvitz, trans., *Scripture of the Lotus Blossom of the Fine Dharma* (New York: Columbia University Press, 1976), pp. 85–95.

46. Dongshan Shouchu answered "Three pounds of sesame" to a monk's question, "What is Buddha?" See KōunYamada, trans., *Gateless Gate* (Los Angeles: Center Publications, 1967), case 18; and Thomas Cleary and J. C. Cleary, trans., *The Blue Cliff Record* (Boston: Shambhala, 1977), case 12. Dongshan answered, literally, three *kin* of *ma* (or sesame), which actually equals about four pounds. This *ma* is often translated as flax, four pounds of which could produce about the amount of material needed to make one robe. However, this *ma* is also used for *goma* or sesame. So it is probable that Dongshan originally meant, "Four pounds of sesame," since he was tenzo then, and this seems to be how Dōgen understood it. Also, this story is cited in case 77 of the *Blue Cliff Record*, in which Dongshan's teacher Yunmen answers the question, "What talk goes beyond the buddhas and ancestors?" by saying, "Sesame cake."

47. "Offering sand" refers to a story about a past life of King Ashoka, when, as a young child, he respectfully offered sand to Shakyamuni Buddha. This is said to have resulted in his becoming a king in a future life (from *Aikuō Kyō*, chapter 1).

48. "Nurturing" is *ro*, literally "elders" or short for "grandmotherly." "Magnanimous" is *dai*, literally "big" or "great." These three "minds" are *shin*, which also means "heart."

49. The three jewels or treasures are the buddha, the dharma (or teaching), and the sangha (or community).

50. The "lord of heaven" is Indra, the Indian god adopted as a protector of Buddhism (see note 12 above), and a "wheel-turning king" is a *chakravartin*, a virtuous world ruler.

51. "Karmic affinity" is the consequences resulting from previous causes produced by our activity in this or previous life-streams.

52. The eight difficult births (where it is difficult to come to practice

of the Way) are in hell; among the hungry ghosts; in animal realms; in the heaven of longevity; in Uttarakuru, the continent north of Mt. Sumeru in Buddhist cosmology where everyone is always being entertained; in being deaf, blind, or mute; in being knowledgeable and eloquent about worldly affairs; or in living before or after a buddha's presence in the world. The realm of the asuras, "fighting gods," is one of the six realms of birth and death, along with the hell, hungry ghost, animal, human, and heavenly realms.

53. "Half a pound" and "forty pounds" are approximate equivalents for the Chinese measurements Dōgen mentions, *ryō* and *kin*.

54. The words "great" and "magnanimous" are translations of the character *dai*. This is one of the basic Chinese characters, and one of the first that children learn to write. It is commonly thought to resemble the shape of the human body.

55. The tenzo of Jiashan Monastery (Kassan in Japanese), who is otherwise unknown, attended a dharma talk of Taiyuan Fu. During the lecture the tenzo burst into laughter. Taiyuan questioned him and, as a result of this dialogue, awakened. This story is from *Goto Egon* (Five lamps merging at the source), chapter 7.

56. Guishan was working in the mountains with his teacher Baizhang. Baizhang asked Guishan to bring some fire. Guishan held out a dead stick. Baizhang asked, "Where is it?" Guishan blew on the stick three times, and Baizhang agreed, saying, "It's like a worm eating wood." This story is from *Keitoku Dentōroku* (The transmission of the lamp), chapter 6.

57. The "one great cause for buddhas appearing in the world," to help beings enter and manifest buddha's way, is a reference to the *Lotus Sutra*. See Hurvitz, *Scripture of the Lotus Blossom of the Fine Dharma*, p. 30.

58. The Japanese word *Katei* refers to a different era than the one in which Dōgen was on his ship in China and met the tenzo of Ayuwang. That was during the Chinese era Jiading, also pronounced Katei in Japanese, although with one different character.

Diagram of the Interior of the Monks' Hall

A. Shōsō Manjushri
B. Abbot's seat
C. Tantō seat
D. Godō seat
E. Seidō seat
F. Shuso seat
G. South outer-hall seats
H. North outer-hall seats
I. South "lower" side seats
J. North "upper" side seats

1. Kanki
2. Jōen
3. Tsui chin
4. Raiban (bowing mat)
5. Inner-hall bell
6. Hou (fish-shaped drums)
7. Sōdō han (sounding board)
8. Outer-hall bell
9. Drum
10. Front entrance
11. Front curtain
12. Back entrance and curtain
13. Hallway for kinhin (walking meditation)

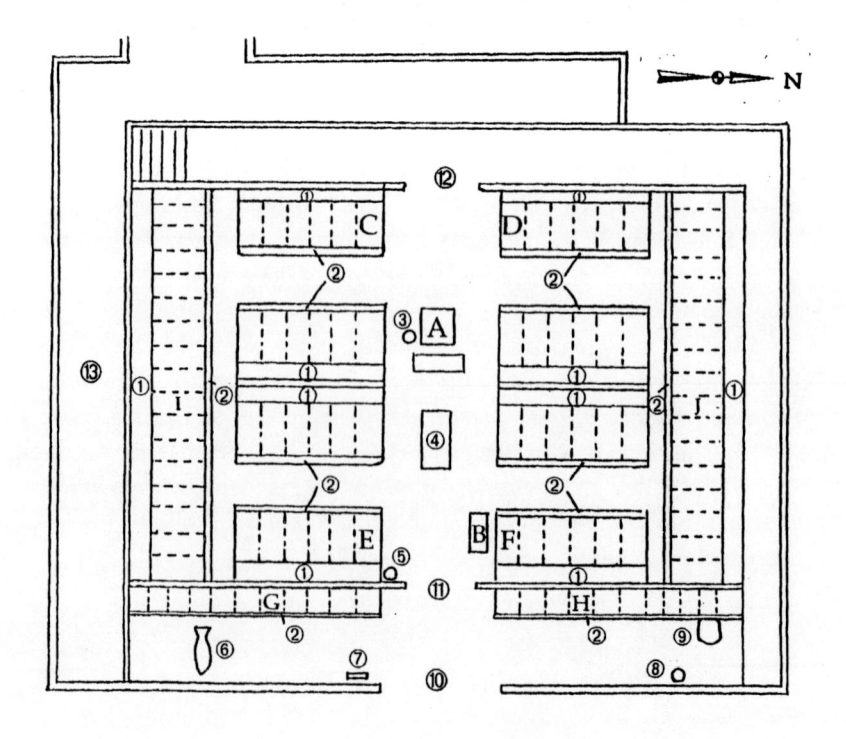

Diagram of the Eiheiji Building Layout

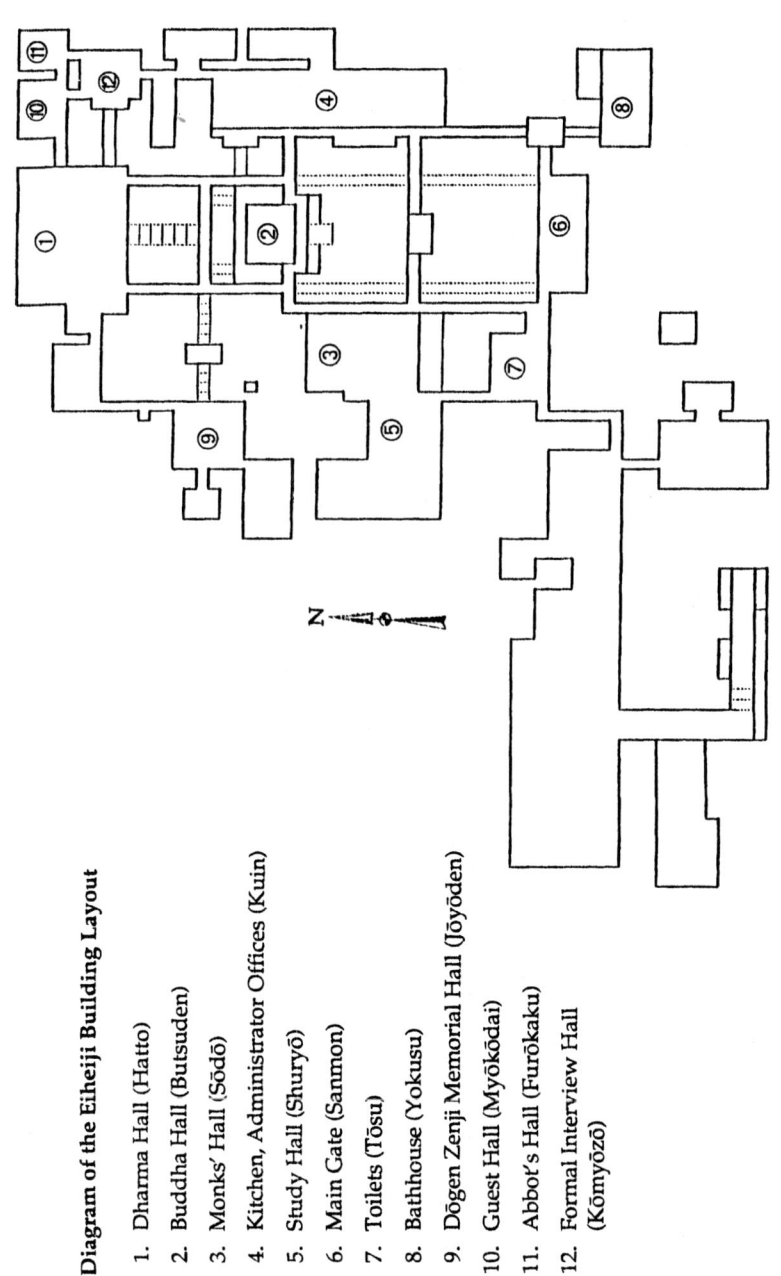

1. Dharma Hall (Hatto)
2. Buddha Hall (Butsuden)
3. Monks' Hall (Sōdō)
4. Kitchen, Administrator Offices (Kuin)
5. Study Hall (Shuryō)
6. Main Gate (Sanmon)
7. Toilets (Tōsu)
8. Bathhouse (Yokusu)
9. Dōgen Zenji Memorial Hall (Jōyōden)
10. Guest Hall (Myōkōdai)
11. Abbot's Hall (Furōkaku)
12. Formal Interview Hall (Kōmyōzō)

Courtesy of Daihonzan Eiheiji

Exterior of Kuin: Kitchen and Temple Administrators' Office Building. Courtesy of Daihonzan Eiheiji.

Exterior of the Monks' Hall. Courtesy of Daihonzan Eiheiji.

Interior of the Study Hall.
Courtesy of Daihonzan Eiheiji.

Exterior of the Dōgen Zenji Memorial Hall.
Courtesy of Daihonzan Eiheiji.

Ōryōki Eating Bowls Wrapped Up.
Courtesy of Daihonzan Eiheiji.

Ōryōki Eating Bowls Unwrapped and Set Out, with Food.
Courtesy of Daihonzan Eiheiji.

The Model for Engaging the Way (Bendōhō)

[written at] Daibutsuji[1]

All buddhas and all ancestors are within the Way and engage it; without the Way they would not engage it. The dharma exists and they appear; without the dharma they do not appear. Therefore, when the assembly is sitting, sit together with them; as the assembly [gradually] lies down, lie down also. In activity and stillness at one with the community, throughout deaths and rebirths do not separate from the monastery.[2] Standing out has no benefit; being different from others is not our conduct. This is the buddhas' and ancestors' skin, flesh, bones, and marrow, and also one's own body and mind dropped off.[3] Therefore, [engaging the Way] is the practice-enlightenment before the empty kalpa, so do not be concerned with your actualization. It is the koan before judgments, so do not wait for great realization.[4]

For evening zazen, when you hear the bell, put on your okesa, enter the monks' hall, settle into your place, and do zazen.[5] The abbot sits on the abbot's chair facing [the statue of] Manjushri and does zazen, the head monk faces the outer edge of the sitting platform and does zazen, and the other monks face the wall and do zazen.[6] While the abbot does zazen, a bench is set up behind a screen at the back of his chair, where either a *jisha* or *anja* may be in attendance on the abbot.[7]

When it is time for zazen, the abbot enters the hall from the north side of the front entrance, and goes in front of Manjushri, bowing and offering incense.[8] After greeting Manjushri, the abbot does one circumambulation of the hall with hands in *shashu*; returns and bows to Manjushri; goes and bows to the abbot's chair; turns clockwise and bows again toward Manjushri; tucks his robe sleeves under his arms; sits on the chair and takes off his slippers; and folds his legs and sits with legs crossed.[9] The jisha and anja keep standing inside the entrance to the south side, not accompanying the abbot during the circumambulation. After the abbot is sitting in his chair, the jisha and anja bow to Manjushri and quietly sit on the bench behind the chair. The jisha or anja keeps the abbot's [chip] incense container.

If the abbot is going to sleep in the monks' hall, a sleeping *tan* is set up between the shuso and the abbot's chair.[10] When it is time to wake up, [the abbot] returns to the chair and does zazen. (During morning zazen the rule is for monks not to wear their okesas. The abbot's okesa is hung over his chair.)[11] When evening zazen is supposed to end, during the second or third watch at either the first, second, or third portion according to the abbot's direction, the *han* is sounded.[12] When the han stops sounding, the monks gasshō, fold their okesas, wrap them in cloths, and place them above the cabinet [at their seats].[13] The abbot does not remove his okesa but gets up from the chair, goes before Manjushri and bows, and leaves through the north side of the front door. The jisha and anja both leave first and stay in front of the monks' hall, respectfully waiting for the abbot's departure.

One of them lifts up the curtain [in the entryway] to help [the abbot] leave. They also do this when the abbot enters the hall. If the abbot is sleeping in the hall, one or two anjas stay at the bench behind the abbot's chair, and one or two jishas sleep at the next place after Manjushri's jisha or next to the new monks' seats [in the outer hall].[14]

[After removing okesas] the monks continue zazen for a while. Slowly and deliberately they unroll their quilts [and bedding], place their pillows, and lie down when the others do.[15] Do not remain sitting when the other monks do not, or look around at the assembly. Do not arbitrarily leave your place and go where you should not. Just to go along with the community and lie down is the correct manner.

(*The Sutra of the Three Thousand Deportments* says that there are five kinds of manners for lying down. The first is for your head to be in the direction of the buddha. The second is not to look at the buddha while lying down. The third is not to stretch out your legs together [rather than keeping them bent]. The fourth is not to lie down on your back or front. The fifth is not to raise your knees.)[16] Definitely sleep lying on your right side and not on your left side. When you lie down your head should be towards buddha. Now [in the monks' hall] our heads are toward the jōen, so our heads are toward Manjushri. Do not sleep lying on your front. Do not raise both knees and lie on your back. Do not sleep on your back with your legs crossed. Do not stretch out your legs together. Sleep without taking off your robe.[17] Do not be shamelessly naked as in the manner of those from outside ways. Do not sleep with your belt untied. Lying down at night, remember the brightness.

Toward the end of night, hearing the sound of the han in front of the head monk's office (which is sounded at the fourth or fifth part of the third watch or the first, second, or third part of the fourth watch according to the abbot's decision), the assembly gets up gently, not rising precipitously. Do not still remain sleeping or lying down, which is rude to the assembly. Quietly take your pillow and place it in front of the cabinet, not making noise as you fold it. Be careful not to disturb the people on the neighboring tans.

Stay at your seat for a while, cover yourself with your quilt, and do zazen on your *zafu*.[18] Strictly avoid shutting your eyes, which will bring forth drowsiness. If you repeatedly open up [i.e., flutter] your eyes, a faint breeze will enter them and you will easily be aroused from your sluggishness. Never forget that passing away occurs swiftly and you have not yet clarified the conduct of the Way. Do not distract the assembly by stretching, yawning, sighing, or fanning yourself. In general, always arouse respect for the assembly. Never disdain or ridicule the great assembly. Do not cover your head with your quilt. As you become aware of sleepiness, remove the quilt and with a buoyant body do zazen.

Hearing an opportunity [from the sounds of people's movements], proceed to the washrooms and wash your face.[19] (Hearing an opportunity means when it is not crowded with other monks washing their faces.) Carry the *shukin* hanging over your left forearm with both ends either toward or away from you.[20] Let yourself down lightly from your seat; walk softly by a convenient route toward the back entrance; with both hands quietly pull aside the curtain; and leave.

If your place is in the upper [north] side of the hall, leave from the north side [of the back entrance], first stepping out with your right foot. If your place is in the lower part, leave from the south side, first stepping out with the left foot. Do not make noise dragging your slippers or stamping on the ground. While going to the washrooms through the back passageway and well shed, when you meet someone en route do not talk with each other.[21] Even if you do not meet anyone, how could you dare to sing or chant? Do not drop your hands down in your sleeves but hold them up in shashu and proceed. When you arrive at the sink area, wait for a place. Do not push aside the other monks. When you get a space, then wash your face.

The manner for washing your face is: hang the shukin over your neck with both ends hanging down in front of you, then with each hand grab one end, put them under the left and right armpits, and cross both ends over each other behind you. Again, bring them under both armpits to your front and tie them down on your chest. Your whole collar and both sleeves are tucked in tight above your elbows and below your shoulders as if fastened by a robe cord.[22] Next, hold your tooth stick, gasshō, and say:

> Holding the tooth stick,
> I vow with all beings
> that our minds will attain the true dharma,
> And naturally be pure and clean.

Then chew the tooth stick and chant:

> Chewing the tooth stick in the morning,
> I vow with all beings
> to care for the eyeteeth
> that bite through all afflictions.[23]

Buddha said not to chew more than a third of the tooth stick. Generally, you must clean your teeth and brush your tongue in accordance with dharma.[24] Do not brush your tongue more than three times. If your tongue gets red from irritation you should stop. In ancient times it was said, "For a pure mouth chew the tooth stick, rinse your mouth, and brush your tongue."[25] When you are doing this in front of others, cover your mouth so they will not see and become disgusted. Of course you should spit where others cannot watch. Temples in Song China do not have a place in their washrooms for chewing tooth sticks. Now at Daibutsuji we have a place for this in our washroom.

With both hands take your face basin to the front of the stove [in the washroom], put down the basin, and take a ladle and scoop hot water into it. Then return to the sink and lightly use your hands to wash your face carefully from the basin. Properly clean your eyes, your nostrils, around your ears, and your mouth until they are clean. Do not waste lots of hot water by using it immoderately. When rinsing your mouth, spit out the water outside of your basin. Wash your face with your body bent and head low, not standing straight, so that you do not splash water in your neighbor's basin. With both hands, scoop up hot water and wash your face, removing all grime. Next, use your right hand to untie the shukin and wipe your face. If there is a communal towel you may use it. Do not make noise with your ladle and basin or make sounds while gargling that may startle or disturb the pure assembly. In ancient times it was said, "Washing your face during the fifth watch is fundamentally for the sake of practice."[26] How could you spit loudly or rattle your basin to make noise in the hall and disturb the monks?

The dignified manner for returning to the hall corresponds to the way of exiting mentioned previously. Return to your place, cover yourself with your quilt, and do zazen in accord with dharma. If you wish, you need not use your quilt. Do not yet put on the okesa.

When you want to change your robe, do not leave your place but change there.[27] First cover yourself with your day robe, then quietly untie your sleeping robe and remove it from your shoulders, letting it fall around your back and knees so as to cover you like a blanket. When you have fastened your day robe, take your sleeping robe and store it in the cabinet at the back of your seat. To change from your day robe to your sleeping robe, of course do it the same way. Do not expose yourself while changing robes and do not stand on the platform and drag your clothes while folding them.

Do not scratch your head [scattering dandruff]. Also do not play with a *juzu* [rosary] making sounds that distract the assembly.[28] Do not chat with your neighbors on the platform, and when either sitting or lying down, line up evenly with each other. Getting on or off your seat, do not crawl around on the platform. Do not make noise by brushing off your seat.

During the fifth watch the han in front of the head monk's office is sounded three times. After the abbot and head monk are seated in the hall, the monks should not enter or leave through the front entrance. Do not fold up your sleeping mat and quilt, but wait for the signal of night's end, opening the great stillness, when the *unpan* in front of the kitchen and the hans before various halls are hit in sequence.[29] That is the time to fold up the sleeping mat and quilt, put them away with your pillow, and lift the curtain [in front of your cabinet where you place your bedding]. Then put on the okesa and sit facing each other. Also at the signal, the curtains at the windows and front and back entrances are raised, incense is prepared, and a candle is lit in front of Manjushri's altar.

The procedure for folding up the quilt is: when you hear the signal of night's end, take one corner of the quilt with each hand and fold it together vertically, making two layers. Then again fold it vertically into a long four-layer pile. Next fold it over the top horizontally and again a fourth time to make sixteen layers. Put it all the way back behind the sleeping mat and fold up the mat tight under the quilt with the pillow inserted in the quilt. Place the quilt with the folds toward you. Next gasshō and with both hands take the okesa and its wrapping cloth and place them both on the quilt. Then gasshō and open the wrapping cloth so it covers the quilt with both ends spread out and folded over the quilt to the left and right. Do not wrap it around the front and back of the quilt. Next, gasshō to the okesa; with both hands raise it up and place it on the top of your head. Gasshō and arouse your vow, uttering this verse:

> Magnificent robe of liberation,
> A formless field of blessing,
> I unfold and wear the Tathagata's teaching,
> Fully saving all beings.

After putting on the okesa, turn around to the right and sit facing the center. When you fold the quilt, do not stretch it out so that it reaches over onto the next tan, and do not do it abruptly, making an uproar. Simply comport yourself with decorum and respectfully accord with the assembly. After the signal of night's end, do not stretch out your futon and quilt and go back to sleep. After breakfast you may drink tea or hot water in the *shuryō*, or resume sitting at your place.[30]

The procedure for morning zazen is that, a short time after breakfast, the inō [monks' supervisor] hangs the "zazen" [lacquered] plaque in front of the sōdō and then sounds the han. The head monk and the assembly, wearing their okesas, enter the hall, and [the monks] do zazen facing the wall at their places. The head monk does not face the wall, but the chōshū [department heads] sit facing the wall like the other monks. The abbot does zazen at his chair.

Monks in zazen do not turn their heads to look and see who is entering or leaving. When you want to go out to the washrooms, before you leave your seat first take off the okesa and put it on the quilt. Then gasshō and get down off the tan, turning clockwise to face the edge of the tan. Put your feet in your slippers as you get down. Going in or out, do not look at the backs of the people doing zazen, but just lower your head and proceed.

Do not walk with long strides, but advance your body together with your feet. Look at the ground about six feet straight in front of you and take half-steps.[31] Walking with unhurried calm is exquisite, almost like standing still. Do not slide your slippers noisily so as rudely to distract the assembly. Keep your hands together in shashu inside your sleeves. Do not droop your sleeves down alongside your legs.

When you fold up your okesa, do not stand on your seat or hold the edge of the okesa in your mouth. Do not hold up the okesa and shake it vigorously. Also, when you fold it, do not step on the okesa or hold it under your chin. Do not touch the okesa with wet hands or leave it on Manjushri's altar or on the ends of the long platforms [toward the center of the monks' hall]. Do not sit with the edges of the okesa spread out and pressed down underneath you. Always watch to make sure that the okesa is arranged neatly. When you want to put on the okesa, first gasshō towards it. After you put down the okesa, the usual custom is to raise your hands in gasshō. You should know [these practices for taking care of the okesa]. During zazen, do not wear the okesa when you leave your place and go outside the hall.

When they hear the first lunch signal from the kitchen, the monks all gasshō and zazen is finished.[32] Then the monks leave the hall wearing their okesas. Zafus remain on the tans until after lunch, when they are stored. When the first lunch signal sounds, the inō has a *dōan* take down the zazen plaque.[33]

(During morning zazen, the zazen plaque is posted. For the other zazen times do not display the plaque. At *hōsan* times put up the hōsan plaque, and take it down when the evening bell sounds.[34] To signal zazen, in the morning a han is struck, in the evening the bell is rung. The monks enter the monks' hall wearing their okesas and do zazen facing the wall at their places. Before "end of night" [right after waking up] and during mid-afternoon [between about 3 and 5 P.M.] just do zazen without the okesa. At mid-afternoon go to your place in the hall carrying the okesa over your left forearm and take out your zafu for zazen. Do not yet stretch out your sleeping mat, or you may follow the old custom of spreading it out partway. Take your okesa from your arm, fold it up and put it on the quilt, and do zazen. For before-end-of-night zazen, put the okesa on the cabinet and do not move it.)

When you do zazen always use a zafu.[35] Sit in full-lotus position, which you do by first placing your right foot on your left thigh, and then putting your left foot on your right thigh. Or you can also sit in half-lotus, in which you simply press your left foot on your right thigh. Next put your right hand on your left foot and your left palm on your right palm facing upwards, with thumb tips lightly touching. Sit upright, with the back of your head straight above your spine, not leaning to the left or right, or to the front or back. Your ears should be in line with your shoulders and your nose in a line with your navel. Place your tongue against the roof of your mouth with teeth and lips closed. Keep your eyes open, not too wide or too narrow, without eyelids covering the pupils. Your neck should not bend forward from your back. Just breathe naturally through your nose, not loudly panting, neither [trying to breathe] long nor short, slow nor sharp. Arrange both body and mind, taking several deep breaths with your whole body so that you are relaxed inside and out, and sway left and right seven or eight times. Steady and immobile, settle into sitting and think of what is not thinking. How do you think of what is not thinking? Beyond-thinking.[36] This is the essential art of zazen.

When you get up from sitting, rise gradually.[37] When you get down from the platform, also descend gently. Do not lift your feet high or take long strides, hastily running ahead. Keep your hands in shashu in your sleeves, instead of dropping them down. Do not bob your head, but just look down ahead of you. Go carefully and slowly without making a commotion. When you attentively follow the assembly according to this dharma, it is exactly the criterion for engaging the Way.

The procedure for hōsan is as follows. Hōsan occurs after mid-afternoon zazen. When the great assembly finishes lunch in the monks' hall, put away your zafu, leave the hall, and rest at your study place in the shuryō. After a little while, at mid-afternoon (in worldy terms, at the end of the hour of the sheep [3 P.M.]), return to the monks' hall, take out your zafu, and do zazen. From then until the next day's lunch, the zafu stays out at your place.

Before hōsan, the head monk enters the monks' hall. The head monk's route for entering the hall is to go along the north walkway and enter the south side of the front entrance. After striking the han in front of the head monk's office three times, the head monk enters the hall and sits at his place after offering incense to Manjushri. Next the dōan announces to the monks in various offices that the head monk is sitting in the hall, or else the dōan may inform the monks by striking the han in front of the shuryō three times. Upon hearing the han, the monks enter the hall, put on their okesas, and sit facing each other at their places. At this time, people doing zazen facing the wall put on their okesas and turn to sit facing each other. After reporting to the abbot, the dōan displays the hōsan plaque [in front of the monks' hall].[38] After that, the dōan lifts the curtain in front of the hall and enters, bows to Manjushri, goes and faces the head monk in gasshō, and bows. Then, leaning over in shashu, the dōan says in a soft voice, "Oshō hōsan." [The abbot discharges the students from meeting.] The head monk listens silently in gasshō. Next the dōan returns to the front of Manjushri and, after properly bowing, stands straight in shashu and loudly calls out, "Hōsan." (This should be exclaimed very slowly.) Then the dōan leaves the hall and hits the bell three times for hōsan. (This is done, in worldly terms, about the middle of the hour of the rooster [6 P.M.].)

When the monks hear the bell they bow, as during meals, acknowledging the people next to them [by bowing straight ahead]. If still in the hall, the abbot gets up from sitting and bows; then after bowing in front of Manjushri, the abbot leaves the hall. The monks get down from their places, bow acknowledging their neighbors, unroll their sleeping mats, and lower the curtains [in front of their cabinets].

After returning to the shuryō, the monks bow to their neighbors and sit facing each other at their desks. They may have a hot drink if they wish. Sometimes hot drinks are served [formally], with the head monk of the shuryō sitting in his place. The shuryō manager offers incense before serving the drinks with the assembly all in gasshō.[39] The shuryō manager may offer incense wearing his okesa over his left arm or after putting on the okesa, depending on the instruction of the abbot or the custom of the particular temple.

The procedure for the shuryō manager to offer incense is, first, to go and bow [at the bowing mat] facing Avalokiteshvara.[40] Then he walks to the front of the incense burner and with his right hand offers [chip] incense; then turns clockwise, in shashu, and returns to the front [of the bowing mat] and bows. The shuryō manager walks in shashu to the upper [right] side of the shuryō, halfway between the first seat of both main platforms, and bows [towards the right end of the shuryō]. Then, after turning clockwise in shashu, he passes in front of Avalokiteshvara and walks to the lower [left] side of the shuryō, halfway between the first seat of both main platforms, and bows.[41] Then, after again turning clockwise in shashu, he goes back to face Avalokiteshvara and stands in shashu after bowing. After that, hot water or tea is served. When tea is finished, [the shuryō manager] again offers incense and bows, following the same procedure as before.

Notes

1. "Model for Engaging the Way" is "bendōhō," which also could be read, "Dharma for Practicing the Way." This was written at Daibutsuji, "Great Buddha Temple," founded by Dōgen in 1244 in the mountains of Echizen Province (now called Fukui) near the Japan Sea, away from Kyoto. The name was changed by Dōgen in 1246 to Eiheiji "Eternal Peace Temple," named after the Eihei era in Chinese history (58–75 C.E.) when the first Buddhist sutra was introduced to China.

In several places in this essay, Dōgen describes how a certain procedure should be done. What we have translated as the method, procedure, manner, or custom for doing something also could be read as the "dharma" for doing it.

2. "Not separating from the monastery" refers to a saying by the great Zhaozhou. Dōgen quotes it in the "Gyōji" ("Continuous Practice") essay in the *Shōbōgenzō*, "If you do not separate from the monastery for your whole life, even if you do not speak for five or ten years, nobody can call you mute. Thereafter, even buddhas cannot budge you." Whereas Zhaozhou says, "your whole life" or "one life," Dōgen says not to separate through "death and life [birth]," i.e., throughout many lifetimes. For an English version of *Shōbōgenzō Gyōji*, see Francis Cook, *How to Raise an Ox: Zen Practice as Taught in Zen Master Dōgen's "Shōbōgenzō"* (Los Angeles: Center Publications, 1978), pp. 175–203.

There is variation in Dōgen's writings, and also among contemporary Sōtō training centers, about doing late-night sitting practice after the designated bedtime. In some of his writings, e.g., his poetry, Dōgen extols such practice. The main point is to harmonize one's practice with that of the entire assembly. Practice is not to be conducted in a competitive manner or in a way that will disturb others.

3. "Skin, flesh, bones, and marrow" are terms used by Bodhidharma to characterize his different disciples. "Body and mind dropped off" (*datsuraku shinjin*) is an important term for Dōgen; it refers to complete awakening.

4. "Practice-enlightenment" here is *shushō*. *Shō* can also be translated as certification or authentication. The "empty kalpa" is the age

before the creation of the universe. "Actualization" here is *genjō*, which also means manifestation, or the present phenomena. "Kōan" (public cases) is used as a term for stories and dialogues of ancient masters that are sometimes used as meditation objects. Here it simply means the essential truth. "Genjōkōan" is the name of one of Dōgen's major essays. "Judgments" is *chinchō*, which also means omens or signs. "Great realization" is *daigo* or *dai satori*, which has sometimes been interpreted as a special experience resulting from practice—a view Dōgen is here refuting.

5. The monks' hall is called *undō* [cloud hall] here by Dōgen; it is also often called *sōdō*.

Although English grammar necessitates saying "do zazen," strictly speaking we could say zazen does you, or zazen does zazen.

6. The word for abbot is *jūji*, literally "[one who] resides in and maintains [the temple]." The abbot's chair, the *isu*, is traditionally a wooden armchair, separate from the monks' sitting platform. Its seat is large enough to sit cross-legged on, and it faces Manjushri. Manjushri (literally, *shosō* or "holy monk" throughout "Bendōhō") is the bodhisattva of wisdom, whose statue is traditionally on the central altar in the monks' hall. The head monk, the *shuso*, faces the center of the monks' hall, toward the *jōen*, the edge of the monks' platforms on which eating bowls are placed during meals.

7. A *jisha* is the abbot's attendant, usually a senior monk capable of fulfilling ceremonial and administrative needs. An *anja* acts as a personal assistant for monks in important positions.

The "Bendōhō" includes many technical Japanese terms commonly used in Zen monasteries. After the first italicized use of these terms in the text and notes we usually give them without italics.

8. The front entrance is usually on the east side of the monks' hall, so that Manjushri faces east; the north side of the front entrance, where the abbot's chair is, is to its right as one enters. This directional orientation may be changed based on topographical needs of individual temples. However, we shall designate as a standard the "north" side as to the right of Manjushri (when facing Manjushri). "Bowing" here is *monjin*, or greeting with a standing bow in *gasshō*, i.e., with palms joined

together, fingers outstretched. Hereafter, "bowing" means a standing bow in *gasshō* unless otherwise stated.

9. "Circumambulation" is *jundō*. During this jundō at the beginning of zazen, the abbot reviews the assembly, noticing attendance and posture. In modern Sōtō Zen, *Shashu* means hands folded at chest height with forearms parallel to the floor. The right hand covers the left hand, which is closed in a fist with thumb inside. Sometimes in "Bendōhō," this hand position is called *isshu* and "shashu" refers to holding the hands flat against the chest (not in a fist) with thumbs interlaced. It seems that Dōgen here intends the modern shashu hand position.

10. A *tan* is the long platform on which monks sit, eat, and sleep. Zazen is done facing the wall, while meals are taken facing out to the center of the room. The tan is also deep enough for the monks to sleep at their places, unlike the abbot's chair, which is only large enough for sitting.

11. The passage, "During morning zazen . . . over his chair." is not in the text of the popular Rufubon edition of the *Eihei Shingi*, which was published in 1794 by Gentō Sokuchū, the fiftieth abbot of Eiheiji, although it does appear in the footnotes. However, this passage does appear in the text of the Shohon edition of *Eihei Shingi* published by Kōshō Chidō, the thirtieth abbot of Eiheiji, in 1667. This is also true of many other passages to follow in the *Eihei Shingi*. We have placed these passages in parentheses.

12. A *han* is a hanging wooden block that is struck with a wooden mallet to signal events in the monastery. Traditionally Sōtō monasteries (including some to the present) divide the time between sunset and sunrise into five watches or *ko*. Each of these is also divided into five shorter periods called *ten*. The second and third *ko*, or watch, would be roughly between 10 P.M. and 2 A.M., varying seasonally with the length of the nighttime. The abbot's directions for the daily schedule might be made for an entire practice period.

13. At the foot of each tan is a wooden cabinet, *kanki*, with two large shelves for storing bedding and some personal items.

14. Manjushri's jisha (called the shosō jisha) takes care of the altar

and makes meal offerings to Manjushri. Manjushri's jisha, the new or visiting monks, monks who attend to guests, and the temple administrators all have their places in the outer hall [*gaitan* or *gaidō*], which is just outside the curtained entryway to the main or inner hall [*naitan* or *naidō*]. Both inner and outer halls are arranged with assigned places based on monks' positions and seniority. Generally, the monks with more important functions have their places closer to the altar, i.e., to the center of each hall.

15. "Quilt" is *hi*, a thick cloth used as a cover when lying down.

16. The number three thousand in the name of *The Sutra of the Three Thousand Deportments* derives from a bhikshu's approximately two hundred fifty regulations multiplied by four for the positions of walking, sitting, standing, and lying to make one thousand; and then multiplied by three for past, present, and future. This sutra was translated into Chinese by An Shigao, who came to China from Central Asia in 148 C.E.

17. "Robe" here is *sankun*, a Chinese-style robe worn beneath the okesa that had two separate top and bottom pieces. In the twelfth century, Chinese and Japanese monks adopted one-piece robes, *jikitotsu*, to wear under the okesa.

18. *Zafu* is the usual modern word for the round sitting cushion. Here and elsewhere in his writing, Dōgen instead usually uses the word *futon* for what we now call a zafu, as the *ton* of futon has the meaning "round." In contemporary Rinzai Zen, and possibly at Kenninji when Dōgen was there, flat cushions are used for zazen. In modern Japan a "futon" is a thick sleeping mattress. The word Dōgen uses for a sleeping mat is *mintan*. *Zabuton*, the word often used in the West for the square mat the zafu is placed on during zazen, is literally "sitting futon." In Japan the square mat upon which a zafu is sometimes placed is called *zaniku*, and the word *zabuton* is used for smaller, everyday sitting mats.

19. The "washrooms" or *kōka*, literally "back shelves," are the toilets and separate washroom at the back of the sōdō, off the back passageway.

20. *Shukin* is a piece of material, traditionally cotton or linen and off-white or gray colored, about fifteen inches by four yards in size. It is

used while washing in order to tie up the long sleeves of a monk's sitting robe.

21. The "back passageway" between the sōdō and the washrooms is the *shōdō* [illuminated hall], so-named because it had a skylight in the roof.

22. "Robe cord" is *tasuki*, a sash or cord used for tying up robe sleeves.

23. "Tooth stick" is *yōji*, a willow twig whose end was chewed and softened so as to be used like a modern toothbrush. Its length was between four and sixteen fingers' width. Both these gathas are adopted from the *Avatamsaka* [*Flower Ornament*] *Sutra* chapter entitled "Purifying Practice." See Thomas Cleary, trans., *The Flower Ornament Scripture* (Boulder, Colo.: Shambhala, 1984) 1: 318.

24. Up to recent times in China and Japan, many people brushed their tongues clean. According to contemporary dental hygiene standards, we might appropriately substitute "floss your gums." In the "Senmen" [Washing the face] chapter of the *Shōbōgenzō*, Dōgen makes clear that after it is chewed and softened, the tooth stick should be used to brush the gums as well as the front and back of teeth. In modern Japanese monasteries, Western-style toothbrushes are used, and tongue-brushing is not practiced. The ritual dental care and face washing that Dōgen introduced were significant innovations that have spread and been influential in Japanese society at large.

25. This quote, as well as the instruction not to chew more than one third of the tooth stick, is from *The Sutra of the Three Thousand Deportments*.

26. Also quoted in "The Daily Life in the Assembly" compiled in 1209 by Wuliang Congzhou. See the translation by Griffith Foulk in *Ten Directions* (Los Angeles) 12, no. 1 (1991).

27. "Robe" here is *jikitotsu*, literally "sewed together." It is the long one-piece robe as opposed to the earlier two-piece, top and bottom robes (see note 17 above). In the following description Dōgen refers to the day robe, *nichiri jikitotsu*, and the sleeping robe, *tamin jikitotsu*.

28. *Juzu* is a rosary or string of beads used by Buddhists, originally to count the number of chants or prostrations. See E. Dale Saunders,

Mudra: A Study of Symbolic Gesture in Japanese Buddhist Sculpture (Princeton: Princeton University Press, 1960), pp. 174–77.

29. "The signal of night's end" is called *kaidaijō*, or often *daikaijō*, literally "opening the great stillness." The *unpan* is a cloud-shaped flat metal gong in front of the kitchen that is struck with a wooden mallet.

30. The *shuryō* is the building behind the *sōdō* where the monks each have a place for study or rest breaks. The regulations for the shuryō compose a later section of *Eihei Shingi*.

31. "About six feet" is one *jin*, which is literally the length of both arms outstretched to the sides. The effect is of looking down at a forty-five degree angle, just as in zazen.

32. "First lunch signal" is *kahan*, literally "fire han." Three strikes of the unpan, done when the fire is extinguished under the rice, signal that food will be ready soon.

33. As indicated near the end of "The Dharma for Taking Food," zafus were stored after lunch under the sitting platforms. "*Dōan* " here is short for *dōsu kuka anja*. *Dōsu*, another word for *inō*, is literally "hall manager." The dōans, who are literally the inō's anjas or attendants, strike instruments during chanting and make some offerings (flowers, incense, etc.) to altars. The *dosu kuka anja* was perhaps a dōan who made offerings.

34. *Hōsan*, "release from study," means there is no meeting with the teacher that day.

35. As elsewhere, the word Dōgen uses here for zafu is *futon* (see note 18 above). He occasionally also uses the word *futon* for other cushions or blankets, so this might perhaps denote using some "cushion" rather than a round zafu.

36. This refers to a dialogue, quoted by Dōgen in several essays, between a monk and Yaoshan. The monk asked Yaoshan what he thought of while engaged in immobile sitting. When he responded that he thought of not thinking, or of that which does not think [*fushiryō*], the monk asked *how* he did that. Yaoshan responded, "beyond-thinking" [*hishiryō*], sometimes translated as "nonthinking." This beyond-thinking refers to a state of active awareness that includes both thinking and not thinking, but does not grasp, or get caught by, either thinking or not thinking.

When we are sitting, we do not follow or get involved in our thoughts, nor do we stop them. We just let them come and go freely. We cannot call it simply thinking, because the thoughts are not pursued or grasped. We cannot call zazen not thinking either, because thoughts are coming and going like clouds floating in the sky. When we are sitting, our brain does not stop functioning, just as our stomach is always digesting. Sometimes our minds are busy; sometimes calm. Just sitting without worrying about the conditions of our mind is the most important point of zazen. When we sit in this way, we are one with Reality, which is "beyond-thinking."

37. Much of the preceding passage, "Sit in full-lotus position ... rise gradually." is identical with a part of Dōgen's *Fukanzazengi* [The way of zazen recommended to everyone], although there are some slight variations and additions. See Waddell and Abe, *Fukanzazengi*.

38. The word for "abbot" here is *Dōchō* [head of the hall].

39. According to the *Zen'en Shingi*, there may be a head monk (shuso) for the shuryō, different from the head monk for the monks' hall, during each practice period. The shuryō manager, the *ryōshu*, fills a separate position rotated at weekly to monthly intervals between all of the monks. This person cleans and cares for the shuryō facilities, requests supplies when needed, and settles disputes within the shuryō.

40. Avalokiteshvara, the bodhisattva of compassion, is the figure on the altar in the center of the shuryō, just as Manjushri is the figure on the altar in the monks' hall. *Shosō* [holy monk] is the term used here for Avalokiteshvara, just as it was the term for Manjushri in the monks' hall.

41. Like the monks' hall (sōdō), the shuryō has an "upper" and "lower" side. The four first seats are those closest to the altar.

The Dharma for Taking Food
(Fushukuhanpō)

[written in 1246 at] Eiheiji

A sutra says, "If you can remain the same with food, all dharmas also remain the same; if all dharmas are the same, then also with food you will remain the same."[1] Just let dharma be the same as food, and let food be the same as dharma. For this reason, if dharmas are the dharma nature, then food also is the dharma nature. If the dharma is suchness, food also is suchness. If the dharma is the single mind, food also is the single mind. If the dharma is bodhi, food also is bodhi. They are named the same and their significance is the same, so it is said that they are the same. A sutra says, "Named the same and significance the same, each and every one is the same, consistent with nothing extra."[2] Mazu said, "If the dharma realm is established, everything is entirely the dharma realm. If suchness is established, everything is entirely suchness. If the principle is established, everything is entirely the principle. If phenomena is established, all dharmas are entirely phenomena."[3] Therefore, this "same" is not the sameness of parity or equality, but the sameness of awakening to the true sameness [*anuttara samyak sambodhi*].[4] Awakening to the true sameness is the ultimate identity [of all the suchnesses] from beginning to end.[5] The suchness of the ultimate identity from beginning to end is the genuine form of all dharmas, which only a buddha together with a buddha can exhaustively penetrate. Therefore, food is the dharma of all dharmas, which only a buddha together with a buddha exhaustively penetrate. Just at such a time, there are the genuine marks, nature, substance, power, function, causes, and conditions. For this reason, dharma is itself food, food is itself dharma. This dharma is what is received and used by all buddhas in the past and future. This food is the fulfillment that is the joy of dharma and the delight of meditation.

At breakfast time after the night's end signal *kaidaijō*, and at lunchtime before the drum is struck three times, sit at your meal place. At lunchtime after the three drum beats, the large bell is sounded to announce lunch. [At a temple] in the city the lunch bell is first; in the mountains or woods the three drum beats are first. At this time, if there are people sitting facing the wall they must turn and sit facing the center. If there are people outside the hall, they must then take a break from their duties and wash their hands. In formal bearing and attire they proceed to the hall. Next, three roll-downs are sounded on the han, and the monks enter the hall together.[6] When entering the hall, go silently, not nodding or talking and laughing. Either entering the hall or while inside, do not have conversations, just be silent.

The procedure for entering the hall is: raise your hands in gasshō in front of your face as you enter.[7] In gasshō your fingertips are even with the tip of your nose and when your head is bowed low, or upright, or slightly inclined, your fingertips follow at the same angle. Your arms are not held touching your chest, and your elbows are out from your sides. When going in the front entrance, monks from either side of the hall enter through the south [left] side, first with their left foot and then with their right. The reason for not entering through the north side or the center is out of reverence for the abbot. The abbot enters through either the north [right] side or the center, and the proper form for entering through the center is to step first with the right foot. After bowing to Manjushri, the abbot turns to the right and takes his place. The route for the head monk is to go along the north walkway of the monks' hall and come in through the front entrance on the south [left] side. (For people coming in the back entrance, if their place is on the upper-side platforms [the north half of the monks' hall] they enter the north [left] side of the back entrance by first stepping in with their left foot. People on the lower-side platforms [the south half] enter the south [right] side of the back entrance by first stepping in with their right foot. Since they are behind Manjushri, they proceed to their places after bowing to the east [toward the front entrance]). Their sitting place for meals depends on the number of years since ordination or the time spent in that monastery.[8] However, during the monastic practice period the seating always depends on time of ordination.[9]

The manner for getting up on the platform is: bow to those at the neighboring places. This is done by bowing to your seat, which is understood as a bow to those on both sides. Then turn around clockwise, and bow to the seat across from yours.[10] Next take your left sleeve with your right hand and tuck it back under your arm, and then with your left hand tuck your right sleeve under your arm. Then with both hands lift the front of your okesa and hold it up in your left hand. With feet together, stand on the ground next to the platform and leave your slippers in front of your place, as you steady yourself with your right hand and bend your left leg up onto the seat. Next, lift your right leg up underneath you and arrange yourself so you are sitting upright. Now it is also said to place your right hand on the platform and first pull your right leg up; then lift your left leg and sit upright. Sit pressing your left leg on top of your right thigh [always in half lotus during meals]. Next spread the okesa so it covers your knees without the robe underneath it showing. Your robes should not hang down onto the jōen [the edge of the platform where bowls are placed]; your body should be away from the edge by one bowl's width. Clearly maintain the purity of the jōen (called the triple purity because it is, first, where we place the okesa, second, where we spread out our eating bowls, and third, where our heads point [when sleeping]).

The director, the inō [monks' supervisor], the tenzo [chief cook], and the work leader all sit on the upper [right] side of the outer hall; while the guest manager, the bath attendant, the infirmary manager, the fire and fuel manager, and the supplies provider all sit on the lower [left] side of the outer hall.[11] Then the *mokugyō* is hit [with three roll-downs] and the monks quietly gather inside. Those who arrive after it is sounded are not allowed to enter the hall.[12] When they hear the sound of the unpan in front of the kitchen, the monks all take down their bowls.

The manner for taking down the bowls is as follows: moving calmly and carefully, stand up and turn around to the right to face the nameplate [at the back of your tan].[13] After a gasshō with your head lowered in a slight bow, take your bowls. Hold the bowls with your left hand as you unhook them with your right hand, and then carry them with both hands, not too high or too low but at chest height.[14] Turn around, then bend down and sit, placing your bowls behind your seat to the left. Do not poke your hips or elbows over into your neighbors. Be careful that your okesa does not brush against others.

At this time, Manjushri's jisha makes a meal offering to Manjushri. The *kasshiki anja* holds up the offering tray and the jisha

THE DHARMA FOR TAKING FOOD 87

proceeds ahead of the food in gasshō.[15] The jisha presents the food to Manjushri and, after returning and bowing at the front of the bowing mat, removes the cloth cover over the *tsui chin*.[16] After that the jisha walks in gasshō to the front of the bowing mat and bows, then turns to the right and goes to the outer hall, past the temple administrators' places, and sits at the jisha's place. When the third roll-down on the drum is almost finished, the small bell in front of the hall is rung.[17]

The abbot enters the hall and all the monks get down from the platforms. The abbot bows to Manjushri and then to the assembly; after the abbot takes his seat, the monks do likewise. The jishas who are attending to the abbot stand and wait in the outer hall, and then bow together when the monks sit down. A jisha brings a table [to the abbot] and bows and leaves. The abbot's bowls are placed on this table. The monks get back up on the platform, leaving their slippers below their seats, and sit upright on their zafus, aligned in an even row. Next they hold up their bowls and then place them down on the edge of their tans.[18] The inō [monks' supervisor] enters the hall and offers incense to Manjushri, bowing before and after. After bowing, he goes in gasshō to the tsui chin, bows, and hits it once, or sometimes does not hit it. The assembly unwraps and sets out their bowls.

The manner of setting out the bowls is: first gasshō and untie the knot on the wrapping cloths around the bowls.[19] Take the bowl wiping cloth and fold it up, once horizontally and into three layers vertically. Then place it horizontally behind the eating bowls [between the bowls and yourself], along with the utensil bag. The wiping cloth is about 1.2 feet long (one standard cloth width.)[20] Place the utensil bag above the wiping cloth and then stretch out the lap cloth over your knees. Next open up the wrapping cloth, with the corner that was toward you hanging out over the edge of the platform, and the corner that was facing out opened toward you and folded partly under itself [with the tip still showing].

Then the corners to the left and right should be folded under as far in as the bowl [with the corner tips still showing].

Next, with both hands open the place mat.[21] With your right hand holding the edge of the place mat that is toward you so that it is over the bowls, lift the bowls with the left hand and place them down on the left side of the place mat [which is set down on the open wrapping cloth]. Then remove each bowl using both thumbs, starting with the smallest and setting them out in sequence, without making noise. If your seat is a little too narrow, only put out three bowls.[22]

Next open the utensil bag and take out the spoon and chopsticks. In removing them, remove the chopsticks first; in inserting them, insert the spoon first. The bowl cleaning stick also is kept in the utensil bag.[23] Remove the spoon and chopsticks and place them horizontally behind the bowls with the points to the left. Then take the cleaning stick and place it vertically between the second and third bowls with the handle away from you, where a food offering can be placed. Next fold up the utensil bag and insert it behind the bowls horizontally together with the wiping cloth, under or behind the place mat.

Upon an occasion of a memorial meal being provided, [the donor] circumambulates and then gets down on one knee before an incense burner.[24] During this ceremony, remain in gasshō and do not talk, laugh, nod your head, or move around, but just sit silently. Then the inō hits the tsui chin once and says,

> We give homage to the Bhagavat,
> the perfect sutras,
> and the Mahayana bodhisattva sangha,
> with merit and virtue inconceivable.[25]

> This morning [a special meal] has been provided, and on behalf of the donor I would respectfully like to announce their dedication to the monks' hall. We humbly wish for great compassion to be manifested.

THE DHARMA FOR TAKING FOOD

(After announcing the dedication [the inō] says,) "This dedication statement has been opened and completely announced.[26] May the impartial divine eye actually bestow clear illumination. Humbly, together with the esteemed assembly we chant."

At this time the monks gasshō and in a loud voice mindfully chant with the inō,

> The pure Dharmakaya Vairochana Buddha,
> the complete Sambhogakaya Rushana Buddha,
> the ten trillion forms Nirmanakaya Shakyamuni Buddha,
> the future Maitreya Buddha,
> all buddhas, ten directions, three times,
> the Mahayana, *Wondrous Dharma Lotus Flower Sutra*,
> the great wisdom Manjushri Bodhisattva,
> the Mahayana Samantabhadra Bodhisattva,
> the great compassion Avalokiteshvara Bodhisattva,
> all venerable bodhisattva mahasattvas,
> maha prajna paramita.[27]

If the tsui chin [which sounds before each name] is struck too quickly it hits the [previous] buddha's foot; if struck too slowly it hits the [next] buddha's head.

When a regular meal is served [instead of one given by a donor; rather than the dedication for the donor, and before the names of buddha, the inō] hits the tsui chin and says, "Humbly we consider the three treasures, may they acknowledge us." At that time, the homage to the Buddha, [and dharma and sangha] is not chanted.[28]

After the ten names of buddha are chanted, the tsui chin is struck and the head monk chants the meal offering verse.[29] At breakfast time is recited:

> The ten benefits of this morning meal
> abundantly nourish practitioners
> with unlimited rewards,
> fulfilling eternal joy.

(The ten benefits are first, [healthy] color; second, strength; third, longevity; fourth, comfort; fifth, wholesome speech; sixth, good digestion; seventh, preventing colds; eighth, relieving hunger; ninth, relieving thirst; and tenth, suitable excretions: according to the Mahasanghika Vinaya.)[30]

At lunchtime [the head monk] recites:

The three virtues and six tastes [of this meal]
we offer to buddha, sangha,
and all beings in the phenomenal world,
giving nourishment equally to everyone.

(The three virtues are first, soft; second, pure; and third, made according to dharma. The six tastes are first, bitter; second, sour; third, sweet; fourth, spicy; fifth, salty; and sixth, mild: according to the *Nirvana Sutra*.)[31] The head monk, in gasshō, extends each tone during this chanting. If the head monk is not in attendance for the meal, [the *shoki* at] the next seat does the chanting.[32]

After the offering verses, the anja who announces the meal comes in the front entrance.[33] After bowing in front of Manjushri, the abbot, and then the head monk, the meal announcer anja goes to the south [left] side, inside the front entrance, next to the head of the platform.[34] After bowing in front of Manjushri, the anja then stands in shashu and announces the meal. The words must be announced clearly with the names correct. If there is any discrepancy the dharma of receiving food is not complete, and it must be announced again.

(When everyone is served, the inō proclaims it with one hit of the tsui chin. Then the head monk bows to the food and after the contemplations, the assembly begins to eat.)[35] The inō goes around behind the Manjushri altar, bows to the head monk, and asks him to say the donation verse. Then the inō returns to the tsui chin and strikes it once, and the head monk says:

THE DHARMA FOR TAKING FOOD

> Material gifts and teaching are the two offerings
> with immeasurable merit and virtue.
> The perfection of generosity
> is completely fulfilled.[36]

This is the manner for serving food. If the serving is overly quick, those receiving it will feel rushed; if the serving is very slow, those sitting for a long time will be bothered. The servers use their own hands and do not let the monks take the food themselves.[37] Servers offer food beginning with the head monk, and go in order until they finish by serving the abbot. The servers should bow humbly.

When serving soup or gruel, give the ladle two or three shakes and pause a little so as not to dirty the monks' hands or the edge of their bowls. Do this bending over, holding your other hand [in a fist] against your chest. Follow each monk's wishes as to the quantity of food. Do not drop down your hands when carrying seasoning containers. If it feels like you will have to sneeze or cough when serving, turn your back. People who carry the serving pots should do so according to this dharma.

The manner for receiving food is to accept it respectfully. Buddha said, "Receive food with reverence." We should study this. If food has not yet come, do not hold out your bowl in advance in supplication. With both hands, lift your bowl up from the place mat and hold it out low. Keeping the bowl level and straight, accept your food. Take a satisfying amount that you will not have to leave unfinished, and whether it is a lot or a little, signal with your hand when to stop.[38] Generally, when receiving food, do not grab the utensils from the server's hands and pick out whatever you want. Do not take food by putting your utensils into the community food container, or giving them to the server to do so. An ancient said, "Receive food with right intention, accepting soup and rice with level bowls. Eat soup and rice together, alternating with each other."[39] Do not receive food while supporting your arms on your knees. If a server is rushed and drops some grains or crumbs, or splashes some vegetable soup into your bowls, you must of course accept it. When the inō has not yet struck the tsui chin to announce that all have been served, do not make the offering [to the spirits]. When you hear the tsui chin, gasshō and bow to the food, and do the five contemplations:[40]

> First, regarding how great an effort [brought us this food], we consider where it has come from.
> Second, we reflect on whether our virtue and practice are worthy of receiving this offering.
> Third, to protect the mind, abandoning our mistakes from greed, hate, and delusion is essential.
> Fourth, truly this good medicine is for healing our fragile bodies.
> Fifth, now we receive this food for the sake of accomplishing Buddha's Way.[41]

After that, end the contemplations. Until you have done the contemplations, do not put out [food offerings] for the beings.[42] For the spirit offerings, take seven grains of rice with the thumb and first finger of your right hand and place them on the tip of the handle of the bowl-cleaning stick, or on the edge of the place mat. Generally, when putting out spirit offerings, do not exceed seven grains of rice, or for things like rice cakes or noodles, do not exceed [the size of] half a large coin. (Now at breakfast we do not give spirit offerings, although they did so in ancient times. Do not put out spirit offerings with your spoon or chopsticks.) After the offerings to the spirits gasshō and remain still.

The manner for eating the early morning gruel is: receive the gruel in the first bowl and place it on its bowl stand. When it is time [after the five contemplations], take the second bowl with the right hand, and place it level on your left hand, fingertips bent a little to support the bowl.[43] Next, with the right hand, take the spoon and scoop gruel from the first bowl into the second bowl. When doing this, hold the second bowl just to the left of the first bowl and then bring the second bowl near your mouth and eat the gruel with the spoon. Do so several times until the gruel is almost finished. After that, when the gruel in the first bowl is nearly gone, put the second bowl back on the place mat, pick up the first bowl, and finish eating the gruel. Then, after using the cleaning stick, put the first bowl down on its stand. Take the second bowl, finish the gruel still left in it, and use the cleaning stick for it also. Then wait for the water for washing the bowls.

The manner for eating at lunchtime is: raise the bowls near your mouth to eat. Do not eat by leaving your bowls on the place mat and putting your mouth over them. Buddha said, "Do not be arrogant while eating, but eat with reverence. If you express arrogance to each other you are just like a small child or even an indecent person."[44] The top half of the outside of the bowl is considered pure and the lower half considered impure. Place your thumb on the part of the bowl toward you and your first and second fingers touching the part of the bowl away from you, not using your last two fingers.[45] Follow this whether you take the bowls with your palm up or palm down.

Looking back to the decorum of Buddha in ancient India, the Tathagata and his disciples ate by rolling their rice into balls with their right hands. They did not use spoons or chopsticks. Buddha's children should know this. Emperors, sage wheel-turning kings, and rulers of nations also ate by using their hands to roll rice into balls. We should know this was the respectable manner. In India monks who were ill used spoons, but everyone else used their hands. They had not yet heard the name or seen the shape of chopsticks. We can see that chopsticks are used solely in countries this side of China. Now we use them in accord with the style of the land and the customs of the region. Although we are already descendants of the buddhas and ancestors and want to follow the decorum of Buddha, the deportment for eating with our hands long ago became obsolete, and so we do not have a teacher to show us the ancient Way. Therefore, for a while we have been using spoons and chopsticks and many bowls.[46]

When taking up or putting down bowls, and also when picking up your spoon or chopsticks, do not make any noise. Do not dig out rice from the middle of the bowl when you eat [to rush or make it appear that you need more]. Unless you are sick, do not seek after extra soup or rice for yourself. Do not cover the soup with rice hoping to get more [by making it appear less]. Do not look into other monks' bowls, arousing envy. Just eat with your attention focused on your bowls. Do not try to eat balls [or mouthfuls] of rice that are too big. Do not throw balls of rice into your mouth. Do not take food and then leave it uneaten to be thrown away. Do not make noise when chewing your food. Do not [loudly] slurp up your food. Do not lick your food.[47] Buddha said, "We should not stick out our tongue or lick our lips when we eat." We must study this. Do not wave your hands around when you eat.[48] Do not support your elbows on your knees when you eat. Do not scatter your food [or play with it.][49] Buddha said, "While eating do not scatter your bread or rice like a chicken." Do not pick up [or eat] your food with dirty hands.[50] Do not make noise while eating by stirring up or sipping your food.[51] Buddha said, "Do not heap up your food like a stupa."

Do not fill your bowls to overflowing. Do not mix soup into the rice in your first bowl. Do not stir side dishes into the first bowl to mix with your rice before eating it. Do not eat great mouthfuls, like a monkey storing up food in its cheek and gnawing on it. Generally, whether you are on the left or right side of the hall, do not eat your food too hurriedly or too leisurely. Def-

THE DHARMA FOR TAKING FOOD   95

initely you must never rush your eating and then fold your arms and look around the assembly. When seconds have not yet been announced, do not wipe your bowls clean or salivate, thinking of eating more. Do not crudely leave over some food, waiting for more rice or soup to eat it with.

Do not scratch your head and let dandruff fall into your bowls. You should keep your hands clean. Do not shake your body, hold your knees, sit crouching over, yawn, or sniffle loudly. If you have to sneeze, cover your nose. If you have to remove something from between your teeth, you should cover your mouth. Place inedible scraps or fruit pits out of sight behind your bowls, where they cannot provoke your neighbors' distaste. If there is leftover food or fruit in your neighbor's bowl, do not accept it even if it is offered to you.[52]

When it is hot in the hall, do not ask the serving monks to fan you. If your neighbor is someone who avoids breezes, do not use a fan [yourself]. If you yourself fear drafts, tell the inō and eat your meal in the outer hall. If there is something you need, point it out rather than calling out in a loud voice. After eating, if there is anything left in the bowls, wipe it up with the cleaning stick and eat it.[53]

Do not open your mouth wide and try to eat huge spoonfuls so that the extra food falls down into your bowls or leaves a mess on your spoon. Buddha said, "While waiting to eat, do not open up your mouth. Also, do not speak while food is in your mouth."[54] Buddha said, "Do not cover your rice with soup, vegetables, or other side dishes hoping to get more." This should be studied. Buddha said, "When eating do not cluck your tongue or audibly clear your throat. Do not puff on your food to warm it, or blow on your food to cool it off." Please also study this. (At breakfast time, after you eat your gruel, wipe your bowls with your cleaning stick.)

Generally, take three small scoops of rice for each mouthful. Buddha said, "Do not eat an extremely small or extremely large portion, but a moderate portion of food." Eat with the spoon pointed straight into your mouth, with nothing falling off it. Do not let bits of miso [or other seasonings] or grains of rice fall onto your lap cloth. If some food does fall onto your cloth, put it together in a place where you can give it to a server. If there are still husks covering your rice, remove them with your fingers before eating. Do not throw away the rice, but do not eat it before removing the husks.

The Sutra of the Three Thousand Deportments says, "If you see something that was not meant [to be eaten], do not eat it. But do not let your neighbors know about it. Also, do not spit in your food."[55] If there is extra food remaining in the bowls of reverend monks, it should not be stored for later but must be given to the servers.[56] After meals, dismiss that mind which thinks of food.[57] In general, during meals, just fully appreciate and contemplate the dharma of the principle of the Way not to waste a single grain.[58] This is exactly the manifesting of the sameness of dharma and food.

Do not make noise scraping your spoon or chopsticks on your bowls, or thereby damage the bowls' shine. If a bowl's surface is chipped, grime will stick in it, making it difficult to clean. When you drink the hot water you had received in the first bowl, do not slosh it around in your mouth and make sounds. Do not spit it out into the bowls or elsewhere. Do not use your lap cloth to wipe your face, head, or hands.

The manner for cleaning bowls is: first, do not touch your bowls with your robe sleeves. Receive water in your first bowl. (Now we use hot water). Use the bowl cleaning stick, and turning the bowl clockwise, attentively wash away the grime until it is clean. Then pour the water into the second bowl and turn the first bowl with the left hand, while the right hand washes both

THE DHARMA FOR TAKING FOOD   97

the inside and outside of the first bowl with the cleaning stick. After you have washed it in this manner, take the bowl in your left hand, and taking the wiping cloth with your right hand, unfold it over the bowl. Wipe and dry the first bowl by rotating it clockwise in both hands. Then put the wiping cloth into the bowl without any of it hanging out of the bowl.

Put the first bowl on its stand, wash the spoon and chopsticks in the second bowl, and wipe them with the wiping cloth. While doing this, do not let any of the wiping cloth stick out of the bowl. Insert the dried spoon and chopsticks into the utensil bag and place it horizontally between yourself and the bowls. In order to wash the second bowl in the third bowl, pick up the second bowl and cleaning stick in the left hand, and with the right hand move the third bowl to where the second bowl had been. Then pour out the water [into the third bowl] and wash the second bowl. Similarly wash the third and fourth bowls.

Do not wash the spoon and chopsticks and other bowls in the first bowl. First wash the first bowl, then the spoon and chopsticks, and then the second, third, and fourth bowls. Wipe the bowls completely dry and put them in the first bowl [in the same order] as they were [originally]. Then dry the cleaning stick and put it in the utensil bag.

Until you have poured out the cleaning water [into the servers' buckets], do not fold your lap cloth. Do not pour the leftover water on the floor.[59] Buddha said, "Do not leave extra food in the bowl cleaning water." We should study this. When the water bucket comes, first gasshō and then pour your water into the bucket. Do not pour the water on the robe sleeves of the server. Do not wash your hands in the water. The water should not be discarded on bare ground.[60]

The bowls after the first bowl should be placed inside the bigger bowls with both thumbs [and index fingers].[61] Next, take the bowls with the left hand palm up [and thumb on top] and place them in the center of the wrapping cloths. With the right hand palm down, take the near edge of the place mat and then, with both hands, fold it above the bowls and set it on top of them. Next, fold the corner of the wrapping cloth that is toward you out over the bowls, and then fold the corner hanging over the edge of the platform back over towards yourself.[62]

Next, put the utensil holder on the lap cloth [which has been folded and placed on top of the wrapping cloth]. In older times the cleaning stick was put above the wrapping cloth, but now it is inserted in the utensil holder.[63] Then unfold the wiping cloth above the utensil holder. [The wiping cloth had been held folded up in the left hand while the bowls were stacked together.] With your hands take the left and right corners of the wrapping cloth and tie them together over the center of the bowls. Tie the corners so that both ends point to the right. One reason for this is to indicate which side of the bowls should be towards yourself; another is to make it easy to untie the cloths.

After wrapping up the bowls, gasshō and sit silently, listening for the signal to leave the hall, which is the tsui chin being struck (by Manjushri's jisha). Manjushri's jisha sits in the outer hall in the place after the abbot's jisha. When it is time for [Manjushri's] jisha to hit the tsui chin, first he gets down from his seat and bows, then enters the inner hall in gasshō and bows in front of Manjushri. Then he passes to the south side of the incense stand, goes to the west side [or rear] of the tsui chin, and bows. The jisha waits in shashu for the abbot and the whole assembly to finish wrapping up their bowls, goes to the tsui chin, and hits it. Then the jisha gasshōs, covers the tsui chin with its cloth wrapper, and bows again.

(Now, in the case of Eiheiji,) hearing the tsui chin, the inō chants the "Existing in the World" verse. This is the traditional ritual of Bishop Yōjō [Eisai], so we are following it for now.[64] After this the abbot leaves the hall. As the abbot gets down from his chair, Manjushri's jisha withdraws from the tsui chin to behind the curtain around Manjushri, so as not to be visible when the abbot bows to Manjushri.

Next the assembly rises and hangs up their eating bowls. First, with both hands raise the bowls, then stand and turn toward the *katatan* nameplate at the back of the platform. With the left hand supporting the bowls, hook them onto the hanger with your right hand. Then gasshō and turn toward the front of your place and get down from the platform. Deliberately lower your feet, put on your sandals, and bow to your neighbors [by bowing to your seat], the same procedure as when tea is offered in the monks' hall, when entering or leaving the hall, or when getting up or down from the seats.[65] Then put your zafu down under the platform and leave the hall.

When there is no meeting after breakfast, the hōsan bell is struck three times. If there will be a morning meeting [*chōsan*] the bell is not struck. If there was a donor for the meal, then also after three hits of the hōsan bell [releasing the monks], the abbot goes up to the dharma hall [to give a lecture for donors]. Also, after tea offered in the monks' hall, the abbot bows before Manjushri and leaves, and then the hōsan bell is hit three times.

When the director or head monk has offered tea in the hall, after escorting the abbot out they return to the front of Manjushri and bow to the monks on both sides of the hall. Then the cups are taken out and the bell is hit three times for leaving the hall. Then the monks get down from their seats and leave the hall in the same dignified manner as they entered.[66] Taking a half-step with each breath is the dharma of walking for people emerging from meditation.

Notes

1. "Food" in the title is, literally, breakfast and lunch. In Sōtō monasteries from Dōgen's time to the present, optional evening food was available, called *yakuseki* [medicine stone]. It is served informally, not in the monks' hall, and is considered medicine, not a meal.

The initial quotation is from the *Vimalakirti Sutra*. Shakyamuni asked his disciples to call on the enlightened layman Vimalakirti during the latter's illness. They all declined because of being embarrassed during previous encounters with Vimalakirti. Subhuti, who was known for the deepest understanding of emptiness, declined because of an episode during which Vimalakirti questioned Subhuti's understanding of equanimity while begging for food and made the above statement. See Robert A. F. Thurman, trans., *The Holy Teaching of Vimalakirti: A Mahayana Scripture* (University Park: Pennsylvania State University Press, 1976), p. 27.

2. This is a quotation from the *Lankavatara Sutra*, chapter 3. See D. T. Suzuki, trans., *The Lankavatara Sutra: A Mahayana Text* (London: Routledge & Kegan Paul, 1932).

3. Principle is *ri*, a technical term in Buddhism contrasted to phenomena, *ji*. Ri refers to the fundamental source or universal reality beyond discrimination. These meanings of these terms derive from Huayan Buddhist philosophy and dialectics, derived from the *Avatamsaka Sutra*, which were a great influence on Mazu and other early Chan masters. Mazu made this statement immediately after giving the preceding quote from the *Lankavatara Sutra*. See Cheng Chien Bhikshu, trans., *Sun-Face Buddha: The Teachings of Ma-tsu and the Hung-chou School of Ch'an* (Berkeley: Asian Humanities Press, 1992), p. 66.

4. "Parity" here is *tōkin*, which is the equivalence of two separate things. "Equality" is *tōryō*, which is the equal measure of two different quantities. "Awakening to the true sameness [of all things]" is *shōtōkaku*, the usual Chinese translation for *samyak sambodhi*, the true nondualistic enlightenment of a buddha. This is the impartial attitude towards all distinct things as essentially the same, not having any inherent existence separate from the one interdependent reality.

THE DHARMA FOR TAKING FOOD 101

5. "The ultimate identity of all the suchnesses from beginning to end" is itself the last of the ten suchnesses in the *Lotus Sutra*, and is the sameness of all ten. This is from the "Expedient Devices" chapter of the *Lotus Sutra*, which Dōgen refers to in the rest of this paragraph. The *Lotus Sutra* says, "Concerning the prime, rare, hard-to-understand dharmas, which the Buddha has perfected, only a Buddha and a Buddha can exhaust their reality, namely, the suchness of the dharmas, the suchness of their marks, the suchness of their nature, the suchness of their substance, the suchness of their powers, the suchness of their functions, the suchness of their causes, the suchness of their conditions, the suchness of their effects, the suchness of their retributions, and the absolute identity of their beginning and end." From Leon Hurvitz, trans. (from the Chinese of Kumarajiva), *Scripture of the Lotus Blossom of the Fine Dharma* (New York: Columbia University Press, 1976), pp. 23–24.

6. Three roll-downs are *san'e*, a common signal in the monastery with seven, then five, then three slowly and evenly spaced hits, each followed by a series of rapidly accelerating hits that culminate with one, two, and then three hits.

7. "Procedure" is the translation of the same character *hō* that is used for dharma. (See also "Model for Engaging the Way," note 1.) This character also is used in Japanese for ordinary meanings such as method, procedure, model, or manner. But since Dōgen states that "food is itself dharma," this usage implies that these manners for taking meals are also dharma, or teachings.

8. The places for meals are usually the same as for sitting and sleeping. Years since ordination, or ordination age, is *kairo*, literally, "the end of the year that precepts [were received]."

9. "Monastic practice period" is *ango*, literally "peaceful abiding." These are ninety-day training periods of concentrated practice without traveling; they date back to the summer rainy season retreats of Shakyamuni's time. In Japan they have been held twice a year, in summer and winter.

10. "Turn around," *junten*, always means turning clockwise. "Clockwise" here is *jōken*, which is literally "the left shoulder." A clockwise turn, "to the right" as we would say in English, is leading *from* the

left shoulder, not turning *toward* the left. In the text of the Shohon (but not the Rufubon) version the phrase "jōken is with the left" is inserted after the first "jōken," although we have not included it in our translation to avoid confusion.

11. "Director" here is *kan'in*, which is the name formerly given to the one person who did the work that was later divided between the director (tsūsu), assistant director (kansu), and treasurer (fūsu), the first three of the six temple administrators, *chiji*, who sit together on the outer hall's upper side. Smaller temples still have just one kan'in position. Some larger temples have an additional kan'in administrator, whose job includes receiving important guests. On the lower side of the outer hall are two of the monastic department heads or *chōshū*: the guest manager and the bath attendant. Also sitting there are the infirmary manager, *dōsu*; the fire and fuel manager, *tanjū*, who is responsible for tending the fire for warmth and maintaining fuel supplies; and the supply provider, *gaibō keshu*, responsible for soliciting donations and acquiring food provisions.

12. At Dōgen's time the *mokugyō*, literally "wooden fish," was a long, hollow, fish-shaped wooden drum hanging in the outer hall that was struck with a long wooden pole. Now this instrument is called the *hou*, "fish drum." Mokugyō currently refers to a spherical wooden drum used during chanting. It is often painted red, and has the stylized image of two fishes with dragon heads, together holding a round jewel in their mouths. This spherical mokugyō was introduced to Japan by the Chinese monk Yinyuan (1592–1673), founder of the Japanese Ōbaku School.

Presumably those who were too late to enter the sōdō for meals ate either in the outer hall [gaidō] or in the kitchen offices.

13. "Nameplate" is *katatan*, literally "the tan where you hang your belongings," at the back of which is hung a nameplate for the monk staying there. In modern Sōtō Zen, a black lacquer plaque is used with white ink that is easily erasable.

14. When not in use, the eating bowls are hung from long hooks hanging down from a horizontal rod above the cabinets at the back of the platform.

15. This *kasshiki anja* later calls out the courses as they are served.

THE DHARMA FOR TAKING FOOD   103

During the offering, the anja carries the meal tray with small portions of that meal's food in miniature monk's bowls. This is carried around behind Manjushri to the jisha, who offers the food.

16. *Tsui chin* is a wooden sounding block used in rituals. It usually consists of a thin, eight-sided block a few feet high, with a small block, a few inches high, set on top of it to be used as a mallet. It stays to the left of the Manjushri altar, and when not in use the smaller block is covered by a cloth (in modern times usually purple).

17. Usually in modern Sōtō Zen, at this point the bell is rung seven times.

18. "Hold up bowls" is *takuhatsu*, which means to hold up the bowls at nose height with the thumb and first two fingers of both hands. Takuhatsu also refers to the customary monks' begging rounds, in which the bowls are also held in this way to receive donations.

19. "Bowls" here is *hatsu-u* (sometimes pronounced *hau*), a set of five eating bowls with wrapping cloth, wiping cloth, lap cloth, utensil bag with utensils, and lacquered paper place mat. It is also called *ōryōki*, literally, "container for the appropriate amount," a word used for the whole set or just for the largest bowl (although Dōgen does not use the word *ōryōki* in "Fushukuhanpō"). Ōryōki is more commonly used today than the word *hatsu-u*. There are different terms used in "Fushukuhanpō" for the various bowls. The largest bowl is *zuhatsu* [head bowl], which has rounded edges and is currently referred to in the West as the "buddha bowl." The tiny bowl stand on which the zuhatsu sits (which is slightly concave and made of black lacquered wood, as all the bowls are in modern times), is called *hatettsu*. All the other bowls are referred to as *kunsu*, and the largest of these is called *zukun*.

20. The original measurement is one *shaku*, almost exactly one foot, and two *sun*, one-tenth of a shaku.

21. "Place mat" is the *hattan*, a lacquered piece of paper on which the bowls are set to protect the cloth from water. Between meals it is folded up and sits on the bowls inside the wrapping cloth.

22. "Both thumbs" might also be interpreted as "[some] finger tips from both hands." The method using both thumbs is to lift each bowl with the thumbs on opposite inside edges. The meaning of the sentence

about putting out three bowls is unclear. Dōgen quotes it exactly from *Zen'en Shingi*, chapter 1, the "Taking Meals" section. It seems to refer to crowded sitting platforms and the space to one's sides, but this would not affect the width of the place mat. Sometimes only three bowls are put out, depending on the number of courses served.

23. "Bowl cleaning stick" is *hassetsu*, or *setsu* for short. It is a wooden stick about seven inches long with a changeable cloth tip and is used for wiping the bowls after meals.

24. "Memorial meal" is, literally, "fortune food," which may be either good or bad fortune, e.g., offered by the donor to commemorate someone's birthday or someone's death day.

25. "Give homage" is, literally, "make prostration." "Bhagavat" is Sanskrit, meaning "World-Honored One," an epithet for a buddha.

26. The dedication statement, including the name of the person memorialized, is written on a paper, which is physically opened and read.

27. The Dharmakaya *hosshin* is the universally pervading, dharma or reality body of buddha. The Sambhogakaya, *hōshin*, is the meditative bliss, reward body of buddha. The transliterated name for the Sambhogakaya, *Rushana*, is another version of Vairochana, which is transliterated as *Birushana* for the Dharmakaya. Although there is no distinction in the original Sanskrit, the Dharmakaya and Sambhogakaya were considered as two different aspects of Vairochana in the East Asian Tendai tradition (in which Dōgen had begun his monkhood and studies). The Nirmanakaya, *keshin*, is the transformation body of buddha, appearing in numerous useful historical manifestations. The name Manjushri is transliterated in Japanese as Monju. Samantabhadra, the bodhisattva of beneficial activity in the world, is translated into Japanese as *Fugen*, meaning "Universally Worthy." The bodhisattva of compassion, Avalokiteshvara, is translated into Japanese as *Kanzeon*, meaning "Regarder of the Sounds of the World."

28. "Homage to the Buddha" here is *tanbutsu*, the previous four-line verse praising the three treasures.

29. "Meal offering" here is *sejiki*, short for *sejikige* or meal-offering verse.

THE DHARMA FOR TAKING FOOD 105

30. The list of ten benefits is from the twenty-ninth chapter of the Vinaya (or disciplinary regulations) of the Mahasanghika school, an early Indian precursor of the Mahayana.

31. The list of three virtues and six tastes is from the first chapter of the *Mahaparinirvana Sutra*.

32. The shoki, or scribe, who is one of the six monastic department managers, *chōshū*, always sits next to the head monk in the sōdō, and also assists the head monk in various other ways.

33. "Anja who announces the meal" is *kasshiki anja*. As servers enter, this anja bows in shashu and announces the names of the courses at breakfast and lunch, i.e., "gruel" and "vegetables" at breakfast, and "rice," "soup," and "vegetables" at lunch. The anja also announces when servers enter to provide second helpings, to collect lunch spirit offerings [*saba*], to distribute water for cleaning bowls, and to provide buckets for collecting the water.

34. The four heads of the platform are the occupants of the seats closest to the altar and entrances. The head of the platform where the kasshiki anja stands, by the south, at the left "lower" side of the monks' hall, is the *seido* [west hall], originally a former abbot of another temple, now used for any highly respected visiting teacher. The head of the platform opposite this, by the back entrance on the south, lower side of the hall, is the *tantō* [head of the tan], the godō's assistant. In the upper, north side of the hall, the heads of the platform are the head monk [*shuso*] by the front entrance, and the *godō* [back hall], who is the head of training and sits by the back entrance. As described in "The Model for Engaging the Way," the abbot's chair is between the head monk and the front entrance.

35. For "contemplations," see the five contemplations below.

36. "Teaching" here is "dharma." Traditionally, laypeople offer material donations; monks offer teaching. In this essay, of course, Dōgen emphasizes that material food and the forms for giving and receiving it are also dharma. "The perfection of generosity" is written with the Japanese transliteration for the Sanskrit *dana paramita*, one of the six perfections or transcendent practices in Mahayana Buddhism. This same verse commonly is chanted now also in response to dona-

tions during takuhatsu begging rounds, with the additional line, "In the limitless dharma realm it reaches everywhere."

37. "Servers" are *jōnin*, literally, "pure people."

38. In modern Sōtō Zen, the usual signal to stop serving is to raise one's extended hand with palm up.

39. "Receive food with right intention . . . ," along with the previous quotation, is from the "Hyaku Shugaku" ["The hundred dharmas for monks to study"] in volumes 20 and 21 of the *Shibun Ritsu* [*The four-part Vinaya* (Rules of discipline)] of the Dharmaguptaka school of Indian Buddhism. This was the most popular version of the Vinaya in China.

40. "Do the five contemplations" (or reflections) and "end the contemplations," below, suggest that these possibly may have been done silently and not chanted, as they commonly are today.

41. "Accomplishing Buddha's Way" is *jōdō* [achieve the Way], used for Shakyamuni's enlightenment.

42. The "offerings for the beings," also called spirit offerings, is *saba* [beings' food]. They are for beings in the unfortunate realms, especially the hungry ghosts or spirits. They are usually put outside after lunch for animal "spirits" to eat.

43. "First bowl" is *zuhatsu*; the "second bowl" is *zukun*.

44. "Indecent person" is our somewhat interpretive translation here for *innyo*, literally, a licentious woman, commonly used to translate the Sanskrit word for "prostitute."

45. "The top half of the outside . . . using your last two fingers" is a direct quote by Dōgen from *Zen'en Shingi*. The meaning of the first sentence, about the top and bottom halves of the bowls, is unclear.

46. "Many bowls" is *kunsu*, all the bowls besides the largest. In India and South Asia monks only used one large bowl.

47. "Do not dig out rice" to "Do not lick your food." is all quoted verbatim from *Zen'en Shingi*, which in turn is extracted directly, with attribution, from volumes 20 and 21 of the *Shibun Ritsu*, the section called "The Hundred Dharmas for Monks to Study." The rules quoted up to here are numbers thirty-one to thirty-six and thirty-nine to forty-four. More continue, as noted, in the following passage, interspersed

THE DHARMA FOR TAKING FOOD   107

with other instructions by Dōgen. The *Zen'en Shingi* only gives the rules themselves, omitting the *Shibun Ritsu* anecdotes that necessitated each rule, and the examples of exceptions to each rule. Although Dōgen is here applying these rules to meals in the monks' hall, they were originally invoked for Indian monks who were eating in different contexts, e.g., being served by laypeople during begging rounds.

48. "Do not wave . . ." is number forty-five of the "hundred dharmas" of the *Shibun Ritsu*.

49. "Do not scatter . . ." is number forty-six of the "hundred dharmas" of the *Shibun Ritsu*.

50. "Do not pick up . . ." is number forty-seven of the "hundred dharmas" of the *Shibun Ritsu*.

51. "Do not make noise . . . sipping your food" is quoted from *Kyōkai Ritsugi* [Teachings on rules and forms], chapter 44, "The Dharma for Eating."

52. "Do not scratch your head . . . even if it is offered to you" is quoted from the part of the *Zen'en Shingi* immediately following the quoted extracts from the *Shibun Ritsu*.

53. "If your neighbor is someone who avoids . . . cleaning stick and eat it" is an exact quote of what follows immediately in the *Zen'en Shingi* after the previous quote.

54. "While waiting to eat . . . food is in your mouth" is a direct quote from *Zen'en Shingi*.

55. For *The Sutra of the Three Thousand Deportments*, see note 16 of "The Model for Engaging the Way."

56. "Reverend monks" is *jōza*, a translation for *thera*, the Sanskrit word for "elders" in the old Theravada tradition. Jōza originally meant senior monks who had been ordained over twenty years. Gradually it has come to refer to increasingly junior monks, and in Sōtō and Dōgen's usage, refers to those who have not yet been head monk.

57. "Thinks of food" is, literally, "salivate."

58. This is a difficult sentence, which perhaps also suggests "fully to appreciate and contemplate the dharma of not wasting a single grain of the principle of the Way."

59. "Do not pour . . . on the floor," is from the *Zen'en Shingi*.

60. "Bare" ground is, literally, "unclean" or "impure" ground. Unless this is a repetition of the instruction not to pour the water on the sōdō floor, it likely refers to the servers' disposing of the water after the meal, which is usually done where it can be used by plants.

61. For the method of handling bowls using both thumbs, see note 22. "Thumbs" here may also refer to index fingers, which should be used as well if needed for steadiness. The point is to do this carefully and quietly, as with all eating activities.

62. "The bowls after the first bowl should be placed ... back over towards yourself" is quoted almost verbatim from the *Zen'en Shingi*, with just a few conjunctive characters added by Dōgen.

63. The practice of putting the cleaning stick in the utensil holder was a change made since the *Zen'en Shingi*, which says to place it above the wrapping cloth.

64. Eiheiji here is called Kichijō [Auspicious Fortune], which is the *sangō* or mountain name of Eiheiji. East Asian Buddhist temples traditionally have both a mountain name and a temple name, *jigō*.

The "existing in the world" verse goes: "Existing in the world like vast space, like a lotus flower not attached to [muddy] water, the Mind's purity goes beyond. We prostrate ourselves to the unsurpassed World-Honored One." It is from the *Transcendent Sunlight Samadhi Sutra*.

Dōgen's statement here indicates his great respect for Myōan [Yōjō] Eisai. "Bishop" here is *sōjō*, traditionally the highest rank in the hierarchy of monks' supervisors in Japanese temples.

65. "Tea offered in the monks' hall" is *daiza chato*, a ceremony in which tea is offered to the assembly by the abbot or director four times a year: the winter solstice, New Year's day, and the beginning and ending of the summer practice period. "The same procedure ... down from the seats" is a quote from *Zen'en Shingi*.

66. The long passage, "When there is no meeting after breakfast, the hōsan bell is struck three times. ... leave the hall in the same dignified manner as they entered" is a quote from *Zen'en Shingi*.

Regulations for the Study Hall
(Shuryō Shingi)

for Kichijōsan Eiheiji Temple

Decorum in the study hall should respect the precepts of the buddhas and ancestors, follow the [instructions for] deportment of the large and small vehicles, and match the *Pure Standards of Baizhang*.[1] The *Zen'en Shingi* says, "All matters, whether large or small, should be in accordance with regulations." Therefore you should study the *Brahma Net Sutra*, the *Jewel Ornament Sutra*, and also the *Sutra of the Three Thousand Deportments*.[2]

In the study hall, read the Mahayana sutras and also the sayings of our ancestors, and naturally accord with the instructions of our tradition to illuminate the mind with the ancient teachings. My late teacher [Tiantong Rujing] said in a lecture, "Have you ever studied the *Sutra of the Last Instructions*?"[3] The whole pure assembly should abide in mindfulness that everyone in the study hall is each other's parent, sibling, relative, teacher, and good friend. With mutual affection take care of each other sympathetically, and if you harbor some idea that it is very difficult to encounter each other like this, nevertheless display an expression of harmony and accommodation.

If there is errant speech, it should be admonished. If you are given instruction, you should accept it. These are greatly beneficial experiences. Can't this be considered the great advantage of intimate relations? Gratefully we associate with good friends with abundant wholesome qualities, and are fortunate to take refuge in the three treasures that have been maintained.[4] Isn't this also a great joy? [The relations of] even worldly siblings are not matched by [those of] people from other families. Siblings in Buddha's family should be closer to each other than with their own selves.

High Priest Huanglong Huinan said, "Even making a crossing together in the same boat comes from relationship in previous lives, so don't we have even more previous connection if we are staying together for a ninety-day summer training period?"[5] You should know that temporarily we are guest and host, but for our whole lives we will be nothing other than buddhas and ancestors.[6]

In the study hall we should not read sutras with loud voices or intone poems, noisily disturbing the pure assembly. Do not boisterously raise your voice to chant dharani. Also, it is impolite to use a *juzu* in front of others.[7] All things should be done calmly.

Do not invite visitors into the study hall to meet for laughing chatter. Also, do not carry on dialogues with tradesmen, doctors, fortune-tellers, or other such business people. When you have discussions with tradesmen, avoid the area of the study hall.

In the study hall do not gather together for conversation, and do not shamelessly indulge in foolish joking. Even if we come upon a situation for laughter, we should stay with the four abodes of mindfulness and rely on the three refuges.[8] Like a fish in a dwindling pool of water, what pleasure can there be? Generally, do not talk or laugh with the people next to you. If you can be like this, staying in the assembly is like being in the [serene] mountains.

In the study hall, do not go to other people's desks and examine what they are reading, thus obstructing the conduct of the Way of self and others. [Such obstruction] is what is most painful for monks.

When something happens against the rules in the study hall, for small matters the study hall head monk or a virtuous senior monk should make admonishments. Larger matters should be reported to the inō for disposition. Beginners and mature newcomers should be corrected with harmonious respect and sensitivity.[9] Whether or not they accept it will clearly show whether they have the mind of the Way. The *Zen'en Shingi* says, "Speech, activity, routines, and deportment should be governed by the criteria of the assembly. Everything should be explained in detail." We should compassionately look after our juniors as if they were newborn babies. This is the unwavering mind of experienced practitioners.

In the study hall do not have conversations about worldly affairs, matters of fame and profit, the political intrigues of the land, or the rough or feeble quality of offerings to the assembly.[10] This is called speech that is meaningless, unbeneficial, disgraceful, and shameless, and should be staunchly restrained. Moreover, we are distant from the time of the sage [Shakyamuni] and have not yet accomplished the conduct of the Way. Our body is impermanent, our time difficult to hold on to. Therefore, patch-robed monks in the ten directions only treasure their time and must be diligent as if saving their heads from fire. Fully exert yourself, and do not vainly pass this time in leisurely chatting.

High Priest Shitou said, "I sincerely say to those who study the profundity, do not pass your time vainly."[11]

Do not disturb the dignified decorum in the study hall. Gasshō and bow according to the dharma. Do not slight them. In general, at all times do not neglect the dharma.

In the pure great ocean assembly of the study hall, who can be estimated as ordinary or sage? That would be as exceedingly foolish as gauging the person from seeing their appearance. When the World-Honored One was in the world, in his assembly were a blind monk and a monk who chewed his cud like a cow.[12] Even more, in the Semblance or Latter Age of Dharma with its declining circumstances, we should value only our affinity with the Dharma.[13] How could we dismiss our fellow practitioners? Even if their robes are worn and shabby and their equipment is old and damaged, we should not consider them with ordinary eyes. Do not disregard them. From ancient times, people of the Way have not had flowery robes and only use simple implements. We should not disparage those from humble families or laugh at beginning students. Even if you are laughed at, do not get angry and resent it. Furthermore, the humblest person may have the highest wisdom, and the highest-ranking person may be lacking in intention and wisdom.[14] Simply recall the Buddha's words, "When the four rivers enter the ocean they do not keep their original names; when those from the four castes leave home [to become monks], they are all alike called the Shakya clan."[15]

It is impolite for each person in the study hall to put a buddha or bodhisattva image at their own desk. Also do not hang any pictures.

When fellow monks in the study hall visit each other's places, they should always do so with decorum, either wearing their okesa or with it hanging over their left arm depending on the occasion. If they come to visit without decorum, not wearing their okesa or hanging it over their left arm, do not meet with them.

When you are at your desk in the study hall and you see a fellow monk approaching, first get down and stand by the platform. Corresponding with the style of the person arriving, either wear the okesa or hang it over your left arm, and either bow or do an informal full prostration.[16] Meeting together should be done with dignified deportment according to this manner.

Fellow monks in the study hall should not walk randomly between the left and right sides of the hall. Also, do not discuss whether others are present or not. Do not look around in sequence at each person's desk.

At your place in the study hall, do not offend the assembly by indulgently lying down or leaning against the boards at the end of the platform, or exposing your legs or body. You should think of the example of ancient sages and former worthies who sat under trees or on the open ground.

In the study hall the pure assembly does not save gold or silver coins, silk, or any such impure treasure. This is the dying admonition of the ancient Buddha. When the First Ancestor in India, Venerable Mahakashyapa, was still living at home, his family was a thousand times more wealthy than King Bimbisara. In the sixteen great nations [of India], nobody could match him [in wealth]. However, once he abandoned his home for practice of the Way, he grew his hair and beard long and his clothes were tattered and made from old discarded rags.[17] He never altered [this style] until he departed the world. A person with the mind of the Way should not be ignorant of this. Even High Ancestor [kōso] Mahakashyapa was like this, so how could ordinary students of recent times not themselves maintain [this spirit of practice]?

In the study hall any conversation should always be in a low voice. Do not make sounds with your slippers. Also do not make a disturbance by spitting or coughing. Do not become absorbed in the magnificence and splendor of Japanese [i.e., secular] literature. You should become familiar with the simple and true sayings of the buddhas and ancestors. If you discuss the expressions of the buddhas and ancestors, do not use a resounding voice. Such things are impolite to the assembly.

In the study hall, even seniors of long experience should not be impolite to other monks. If they break the decorum of the assembly, the inō should clearly correct them.

In the study hall, if you cannot find your robes or bowls or any other belongings, first post a notice. This sign should indicate: "In this study hall, such and such monk at a certain time lost a certain object. If anyone finds it, please put up a sign that you have it." Judgments [about theft] should conform with the pure standards. Do not arbitrarily attack someone. Also, we should be familiar with the words of Zen Master Daixiao.[18]

If you find something in the study hall, post a sign that you have it.

In the study hall do not keep secular books, writings on astrology or geomancy, scriptures from any other religions, or volumes of Chinese or Japanese poetry.[19]

In the study hall, do not keep such things as bows and arrows, spears and clubs, swords, or helmets and armor. Generally do not keep any military equipment. If someone stores short swords and the like, they must be expelled from the temple right away. Implements that violate prohibitions should never be brought into the study hall.

Do not keep string or wind instruments or instruments for court music in the study hall.

Do not bring into the study hall alcohol, meat, or any of the five pungent foods.[20] Generally, any kind of meat, garlic, onions, or strong-smelling vegetables should not be brought near the study hall.

When you are sitting together in place in the study hall, if some unpleasant task needs to be done, those in junior positions should [gladly] do it first. This is the decorum of monks. Students who are young should not stay at their place watching seniors do painful tasks, as this would be rude. If there is something pleasant [to do], offer it to your senior. This [attitude] is buddha's true dharma.

If practitioners in the study hall must do some sewing, they should take it to the sewing table [in the corridor behind the study hall]. When sewing, do not gather together for gossip or talk much with loud voices. You should keep in mind the steadfast practice of the buddhas and ancestors.

This study hall is a public space of the *dōjō*.[21] Even if he has his head and beard shaved, a fellow without the comportment of a monk should not be allowed to pass through or around the study hall, or stay the night inside it. Even if he is a dignified monk, if he is just traveling the monk should not be allowed to stay the night in the study hall. Do not let him wander around inside the study hall, as it would disturb the pure assembly.

In the study hall, do not engage in worldly activities.

The above-stated regulations are examples bequeathed by the ancient buddhas. May they be followed at this monastery for all time.

Written in the first month of the third year of Hōji [i.e., 1249].

Notes

1. "Regulations" in the title of this essay is *shingi*, pronounced the same as the *Shingi* [pure standards] of *Eihei Shingi*. The *gi* [standard or measure] is the same in both terms. The *shin* of *Eihei Shingi* means pure, while the *shin* of *Shuryō Shingi* means accupuncture needle or admonition. This is the same *shin* as in Dōgen's essay *Zazenshin* in the *Shōbōgenzō*.

The *shuryō* [assembly hall] is used by the monks for study and during breaks. It is structured like the sōdō [monks' hall], where the monks do zazen, eat, and sleep. Whereas the sōdō has Manjushri enshrined in the central altar, the shuryō has Avalokiteshvara. Instead of cabinets for bedding, as in the sōdō, at the end of each monk's platform in the shuryō is a small desk. For the procedure for serving tea in the shuryō, see the final section of "The Model for Engaging the Way." Kichijōsan is the *sangō* and Eiheiji the *jigō* for the monastery Dōgen established.

The Pure Standards of Baizhang, Hyakujō Shingi, is considered the original writing in Zen of standards for the monastic community. Attributed to Baizhang Huaihai, this text was already lost before Dōgen's time, and some modern scholars question if it ever existed. The last section of *Zen'en Shingi* is called "Verses from Hyakujō Shingi."

2. *The Brahma Net Sutra* discusses the ten major and forty-eight minor Mahayana precepts. See *Buddha Speaks the Brahma Net Sutra* (Talmage, Calif.: Dharma Realm Buddhist University, Buddhist Text Translation Society, 1982). The *Bodhisattva Jewel Ornament Original Conduct Sutra* discusses the three pure precepts. For the *Sutra of the Three Thousand Deportments*, see note 16 of "The Model for Engaging the Way."

3. *The Sutra of the Last Instructions, Yuikyōgyo*, is Shakyamuni's teaching on his deathbed, including admonitions and precepts. It is considered a Mahayana sutra, while the *Sutra on Three Thousand Deportments* is a Theravada sutra. It was translated into Chinese by Kumarajiva. See Phillip Karl Eidmann, trans., *The Sutra of the Teachings Left by the Buddha* (Osaka: Koyata Yamamoto, 1952).

4. "Wholesome qualities" is good roots, i.e., resulting from past actions. The "three treasures that have been maintained" is one of the three categories of three treasures (buddha, dharma, sangha). These are *itai sanbō*, the universal, omnipresent, unified body as the three treasures; *genzen sanbō*, the three treasures of the historical Shakyamuni Buddha; and *jūji sanbō*, the three treasures upheld and maintained after Shakyamuni, i.e., buddha images, printed sutras, and the community of fellow practitioners. *Jūji* [reside and maintain or uphold] is the word also used for the abbot of a temple.

5. "High Priest" is *oshō*, originally used for the Sanskrit *upadhyaya*,

one's ordination master. Today in China and Japan it refers to all fully trained, ordained monks.

6. "You should know that temporarily we are guest and host, but for our whole lives we will be nothing other than buddhas and ancestors," is a quote from *Zen'en Shingi*, except with the interesting change by Dōgen to "buddhas and ancestors" from the *Zen'en Shingi* "teachers and disciples."

7. Dharani, which here include mantras, are chants that have some special power or positive effect. *Juzu* rosary beads are sometimes used to count recitations of mantra or dharani.

8. The four abodes of mindfulness, *shinenju*, are remembrance of the impurity of the body, the suffering inherent in sensation, the impermanence of mind, and the insubstantiality of all entities. The three refuges are in buddha, dharma, and sangha.

9. "Mature newcomers" is *bangaku* [late students], those who first come to practice at a late age.

10. "Political intrigues" is literally "peace or disorder" of the land. In Dōgen's time, and through much of the history of East Asian Buddhism, the order of the nation was subject to the fortunes of competing warlords. For monks to side with the various factions was to court disaster when the tides changed. However, Mahayana Buddhism naturally includes concern for the well-being of the common people.

11. This quote is the end of the long poem "Sandōkai" [Unifying of sameness and difference], "Cantongqi" in Chinese, by Shitou. Shitou and the "Sandōkai" are important in the Sōtō tradition; the "Sandōkai" is still chanted daily in Sōtō training temples. See Thomas Cleary, *Timeless Spring: A Soto Zen Anthology* (Tokyo: Weatherhill, 1980), pp. 36–39.

12. The blind monk was Aniruddha. After once falling asleep during Shakyamuni's lecture, he vowed never to sleep again. He fulfilled this vow at the cost of ruining his eyesight but also developed the heavenly eye with its supernatural power to see past and future. Buddha's disciple, Cavampati, in his past life ridiculed a monk, so in this life he was always moving his mouth like a cow chewing its cud. However, he became the foremost in understanding of the Vinaya.

13. The Semblance and Latter Ages are *zōhō* and *mappō*, the two

ages said to follow the initial Age of True Dharma, *shōbō*, in which enlightenment, practice, and teaching all exist. According to this theory, which was popular in Dōgen's time, in the Semblance Age only practice and teaching are available, and in the Latter Age (considered to have already arrived) only the teaching occurs. Although Dōgen refers to this theory of Buddhist history as an encouragement in this case, elsewhere he discounts its validity, affirming that the whole of buddha's practice and enlightenment is always available.

14. "The humblest person . . . lacking in intention and wisdom" is a quote from the *Platform Sutra* of the Sixth Ancestor, Dajian Huineng, spoken by the future Sixth Ancestor to the person whom he asked to write his famous gatha on the wall. The Sixth Ancestor is a primary example in Zen lore of a humble, illiterate person with complete wisdom. The historical reliability of the story in the *Platform Sutra* is now questioned, but it has had great influence in the tradition. See Philip B. Yampolsky, ed. and trans., *The Platform Sutra of the Sixth Patriarch* (New York: Columbia University Press, 1967).

15. This quote of Buddha is from the Pali Suttas, chapter 21 on "Suffering and Pleasure," in the Agama corresponding to the Anguttara Nikaya. There are four great rivers of India and four rivers, somewhat differently named, in Indian cosmology. The four major castes in ancient India are brahman, kshatriya, vaishya, and shudra (nobles, warriors, common people, and slaves). Shakyamuni's monastic order was highly radical for its time in India, as he accepted equally those from all the castes.

16. "Informal full prostration" is *sokurei*, which is done with the *zagu* folded up and placed horizontally on the ground in front of the monk bowing rather than spread out on the ground.

17. "Old discarded rags" is *funzō'e* [literally, "robe from garbage or excrement"] a traditional term for okesa, which was originally sewn together from discarded scraps and rags.

18. Daixiao was a disciple of the Sixth Ancestor who later cared for the Sixth Ancestor's memorial stupa (which included his mummy). Someone tried to cut off the head of the mummy so he could enshrine it elsewhere, but he was apprehended. When the authorities asked

Daixiao what to do with him, he said, "According to the national law he should be executed, but in the compassion of Buddhism enemies and friends are [treated] the same. Furthermore, he tried to get the head to enshrine it and make offerings. His crime should be forgiven." This story is from Jingde record of the transmission of the lamp [*Keitoku Dentōroku*], chapter 5.

19. "Chinese and Japanese poetry" here is literally *shifu* and *waka*, particular poetic forms.

20. The "five pungent foods" are garlic, leeks, scallions, rocambole onions, and "wasabi" horseradish. This is the fourth of the forty-eight minor precepts in the *Brahma Net Sutra*, and is based on Indian dietary restrictions. See Buddhist Text Translation Society, *Buddha Speaks the Brahma Net Sutra*.

21. *Dōjō* is a place for practice/realization of the Way; it is used for the Sanskrit *bodhimandala*, originally the site of Buddha's enlightenment.

The Dharma when Meeting Senior Instructors of Five Summer Practice Periods (Taitaiko Gogejarihō)

1. When meeting senior instructors who have trained for five summer practice periods, you should wear your okesa and carry your zagu.[1]

2. Do not wear the okesa covering [both] shoulders. A sutra says, "When monks meet the Buddha, or other monks or seniors, they should not wear the okesa over both shoulders. [If they do], when they die they will enter the Iron Shackle Hell."[2]

3. Do not stand and look at a senior while leaning against something with your legs crossed.

4. Do not stand and look at a senior with your arms dangling.

5. Never laugh raucously without shame or embarrassment.

6. Stand according to the "Dharma of Serving your Teacher."[3]

7. If you are admonished, bow politely and listen and accept it, and, in accord with dharma, contemplate and reflect on it.

8. Always arouse a humble mind.

9. Do not scratch or pick at lice while meeting a senior.

10. Do not spit in front of a senior.

11. Do not chew your tooth stick [*yōji*] or rinse your mouth while facing a senior.

12. If the senior has not yet asked you to sit down [when you are with them], do not sit down casually.

13. When sitting on the same platform alongside a senior of five summers, do not [accidentally] poke them.

14. Do not sit at the place where a senior of five summers usually sits or lies down.

15. You should know that someone who has done five summer practice periods or more has the position of *ajari* [instructor]; someone with ten summers or more has the position of *oshō* [high priest]. This is nothing other than the sweet dew of the unstained dharma.

16. When a respected person of five summer practice periods asks you to sit down, gasshō and bow, and then sit down. Courteously sitting upright, do not lean against a wall.

17. When sitting do not be rude and indulgently lean against any furniture.

18. If there is discussion you should remain humble and not try to gain the superior position.

19. Do not open your mouth wide when yawning but cover it with your hand.

20. When you are before a senior, do not rub your face, stroke your head with your hands, or play with your legs or arms.

21. Before a senior do not make great sighing sounds. Be respectful in accord with dharma.

22. When you are before a senior, keep your body upright and settled.

23. If you see a senior coming to where you are with another senior, give them your seat and bow your head, waiting a while for the senior's instruction.

24. When you are across the wall from a senior's room, do not chant scriptures in a loud voice.

25. Unless a senior has directed you to do so, do not expound the dharma to people.

26. If a senior questions you, you should offer an appropriate answer.

27. Always observe the senior's expression, and do not cause the senior disappointment or serious distress.

28. While you are before a senior, do not exchange bows with your peers.

29. In front of a senior, do not accept prostrations from others.

30. If there is something burdensome to be done where a senior is, do it first yourself. If there is something enjoyable, offer it to the senior.

31. If you meet with a senior of five summer practice periods, you should revere the senior as an elder. Do not lose your enthusiasm.

32. If you are intimate with seniors who have done either five or ten summer practice periods, you should [still] inquire of them about the meaning of the sutras and precepts. Do not become negligent or lazy.

33. When you see that a senior is sick, you should respectfully nurture them and help them recover according to dharma.

34. When you are before a senior or near their room, do not utter unbeneficial or meaningless talk.

35. When before a senior, do not discuss the good and bad points or strengths and weaknesses of honored masters from other temples.[4]

36. You should not ignore a senior and engage in pointless argument or inquiry.

37. Do not shave your head, clip your nails, or change your underrobes when in front of a senior.

38. When a senior is not yet asleep, do not go to sleep first.

39. When a senior has not yet started eating, do not eat first.

40. When a senior has not yet bathed, do not bathe first.

41. When a senior has not yet sat down, do not seat yourself first.

42. If you meet a senior on the path, bow with inclined body, and then follow behind the senior. If you receive some instruction from the senior, simply obey it and then return [to what you were doing].

43. If you see a senior has forgotten something by mistake, point it out courteously.

44. If you see a senior making a mistake, do not laugh loudly.

45. When you visit a senior's room, first snap your fingers three times outside the door before entering.

46. If you enter a senior's room, enter through the side of the doorway. Do not go through the center of the doorway.[5]

47. When you enter or leave the chamber of either a five-summer or ten-summer senior, you should use the guest stairs, not the host stairs.[6]

48. If a senior has not yet finished the meal, do not finish eating first.

49. When a senior has not yet stood up, do not stand up first.

50. If a senior is expounding the sutras to a donor, sit upright and listen carefully. Do not get up hurriedly and leave.[7]

51. Do not scold someone you are supposed to scold while you are in front of a senior.

52. Before a senior do not call to someone from a distance with a raised voice.

53. Do not untie your okesa, set it down in a senior's room, and then leave.

54. When a senior is lecturing about a sutra, do not correct their mistakes from a lower seat.

55. Before a senior do not raise your knees and hold them with your arms.

56. When a senior is in a low place and you are in a high place, you should not bow to each other.

57. Do not bow to a senior from up on your seat.

58. When you are at your place and see a senior standing on the ground, do not bow to them in shashu.

59. You should be aware when a senior's teacher is present.

60. When a senior's disciple is present, you should be aware of their manners to their teacher and not disturb the senior.

61. When a senior meets together with a senior, both need not [follow these instructions for meeting] a senior.

62. Seeing seniors is inexhaustible. The first summer practice period we see seniors; at the ultimate fulfillment we see seniors.[8]

The above dharma for meeting a senior of five or ten summer practice periods is exactly the body and mind of the buddhas and ancestors. Do not fail to study this. If you do not study this, the ancestral teachers' Way will degenerate, and the sweet dew of the dharma will be extinguished. In the vast sky of the dharma realm, this is rare and difficult to encounter. Only people who have been developing wholesome faculties throughout previous lifetimes can hear this. Truly it is the ultimate summit of the Mahayana.

Taught to the assembly the second year of Kangen [i.e., 1244], the third month, the twenty-first day, in Echizen Province at Yoshimine Temple.[9]

Notes

1. "Senior" is *taiko* [greater than oneself]. "Instructor" is *ajari*, used for the Sanskrit *acharya*, any senior monk qualified to have disciples. In Dōgen's time, training periods of three months were held once a year during the summer. Dharma in the essay title refers to the "teaching" of the proper attitude towards practice with others, but it also obviously denotes the "manners" and even "etiquette" for meeting seniors.

2. In modern Sōtō Zen, the okesa is usually worn only over the left shoulder, as is done by all Buddhist monks. When bestowing ordination or during the twice-monthly repentance ceremony, the presiding priest wears the okesa over both shoulders. "Senior" here and in some other places in this essay is *jōza*, which seems to be used interchangeably with *taiko*.

3. The "Dharma of Serving your Teacher" is either a text attributed to the Indian Ancestor Ashvaghosha or another text by the same name by Daoxuan.

4. "Honored masters" is *sonshuku* [venerable elders].

5. The instructions for entering the senior's room recall the instructions for entering the monks' hall. See the third paragraph of "The Dharma for Taking Food."

6. "Guest and host stairs" is unclear. It may refer to left and right sides of the stairs to a senior's room.

7. "Donor" is *danotsu*, derived from the Sanskrit *danapati*. *Dana*, generosity, is the first of the six perfections in Mahayana Buddhism. The system of supporters for individual Japanese Buddhist temples since the seventeenth century is called *danka*.

8. "Ultimate fulfillment" is *gokuka* [final result], which refers to the fruit of practice and is equated with buddhahood.

9. Yoshimine Temple is a small temple near Eiheiji where Dōgen's community stayed for about a year during Eiheiji's construction.

Pure Standards for the Temple Administrators (Chiji Shingi)

for Eiheiji in Echizen, Japan

The temple administrator positions are esteemed and honorable, so they must be filled by experienced, virtuous people of the Way. Here are some examples.

The Tathagata [Shakyamuni's] younger brother Nanda was in the position of temple administrator and also became an actualized arhat.[1] The *Womb Treasury Sutra* tells that the World-Honored One was in Kapilavastu.[2] Buddha knew it was time for Nanda to be ordained as a monk, and so in the gate of [Nanda's] residence emitted a shining radiance.[3] Nanda said, "This is certainly the World-Honored One." He dispatched a servant to see if this was indeed the World-Honored One. Then Nanda wanted to see [Buddha] for himself.

His wife said, "If I let you go see him, certainly he will make you into a home-leaving monk." Then she pulled him back by his clothing.

Nanda said, "I'll be back shortly."

She said, "You should return before my face [i.e., cosmetics] has dried."

He replied, "I will do as you ask."

Buddha had [Nanda] take his begging bowl to fill with food. He returned with the full bowl, but Buddha had already gone. He gave it to Ananda, who asked, "From whom did you get this bowl?"

He answered, "This bowl is from Buddha."

Ananda said, "[You should] give it back to Buddha."

Nanda thereupon went to take the bowl to give to Buddha. Buddha had someone shave Nanda's head. Nanda said to the monk shaving his head, "Do not hold a blade to the head of a king of Jambudvipa."[4] Also he thought to himself, "In the morning I will follow the World-Honored One, but in the evening I will return home."

Buddha knew his thoughts and magically created a large pit [in front of Nanda. So Nanda thought that] even to the end of his life, how could he return home? Buddha told Ananda to make Nanda a temple administrator. Ananda conveyed Buddha's request.

Nanda asked, "What is a temple administrator?"

Ananda said, "They check and take care of things inside the temple."

Nanda said, "What should I do?"

Ananda answered, "After the monks go to beg for food, you should sweep and moisten the ground, carry firewood, remove cow dung to clean the grounds, make sure that nothing has gotten lost, and close the gates after the monks. When evening comes, open the gates, sweep, and wash the toilets."

After the monks left, Nanda wanted to close the gates for the community. He closed the west gate and the east one opened; closed the east and the west one opened. He thought, "Even if something is lost, when I become king I will construct a hundred thousand times more good temples than there are today." Thereupon he headed back to his home.

He was afraid that going by a major road he might meet Buddha returning, and so went on a small road. However, there he did see Buddha coming back. Nanda hid behind some branches of a tree, but the wind blew them and he was visible.

Buddha asked, "Why have you come?"

He answered, "I missed my wife."

Buddha instead brought him from the city [Shravasti] to the Eastern Garden. Buddha asked, "Have you ever seen Gandha Madana Mountain?"[5]

Nanda answered, "Not yet."

Buddha threw Nanda into the sleeve of his robe and flew off, and in an instant they could see the mountain. On top of the mountain was a fruit tree, and beneath the tree was a large female ape, who had been scorched and had one eye missing. Finally Buddha asked, "How is this like heaven?"

Nanda answered, "In heaven there is nothing lacking. How could it be compared to this?"

Buddha asked, "Have you seen heaven or not?"

He answered, "I have not yet seen it."

Buddha threw Nanda into the sleeve of his robe and in a while reached the Heaven of the Thirty-Three, where they wandered around until they reached the Pleasure Garden where they saw many beautiful ladies, and the Recreation Garden with various musical sounds.[6] In one place there was a heavenly maiden without a husband. Nanda asked Buddha [about her], and Buddha had Nanda ask her himself. She answered, "Buddha's brother Nanda is maintaining the precepts, and will be born here and become my husband."

Buddha asked, "Nanda, how does she compare to [your wife] Sondari?"

He answered, "Sondari compared to this heavenly maiden is like the one-eyed ape compared to Sondari."

Buddha said, "Practicing pure conduct, you will have this benefit.[7] If you now uphold precepts, you will be born in this heaven."

Thereafter Buddha returned with him to Jetavana. Then Nanda yearned for the heavenly palace and practiced pure conduct. Buddha proclaimed to the monks that they all should not share any dharma activities together with Nanda. All of the monks did not stay when he sat with them but got up and left.

Nanda thought, "Ananda is my brother, so he will not dislike me." So he went and sat together with Ananda, but Ananda arose to leave.

Nanda asked, "How can you abandon your brother?"

Ananda said, "I only avoid you because your practice is different."

He asked, "What do you mean?"

Ananda answered, "Your longing is for a birth in heaven. My longing is for nirvana."[8]

After hearing this, Nanda felt even more grievously distressed.

Buddha also asked, "Have you seen hell yet?"

He answered, "I've not yet seen it."

Buddha threw him into the sleeve of his robe and soon they saw various hells. They all had people being tortured, but there was a place with no person. Nanda asked Buddha about it. Buddha had him ask the hell guardian.

The hell guardian answered saying, "Buddha's brother Nanda is practicing in order to be born in heaven. For a while he will be up in heaven, but then he will return down to here and receive torment."

Nanda was terrified and his tears fell like rain. He spoke to Buddha about this.

Buddha said, "If you practice pure conduct to get heavenly bliss you will have this punishment."

Buddha brought him back to Jetavana and widely expounded the womb form.[9] Because of this Nanda first aroused the Mind [of Awakening], maintaining precepts for the sake of liberation, and later attained the stage of arhathood.

> Venerable Nanda was from the Kshatriya [warrior] class, son of King Suddhodana and brother of the Tathagata.[10] He filled the position of temple administrator and finally became an arhat. Shouldn't we value and shouldn't we cherish the merit and virtue of seeing Buddha, and the traces of previously actualized liberation? Therefore, only people with the mind of the Way and who consider the ancients should be appointed [as temple administrators]. Those without the mind of the Way should not be appointed. The mental attitude of temple administrators is the same as the mental attitude of abbots. Benevolence must come first; gentleness must come first. With great compassion and great sympathy to the assembled monks, welcome and serve all from the ten directions, and simply help the monastery flourish. [These positions] have been filled by people who do not look for worldly benefit but only exert the conduct of the Way. Truly this is engaging the Way and perfuming refinement, and nothing is before this![11]

Here is an example of a temple administrator intimately meeting together [with a teacher].

The great Guishan one day called for the director.[12] The director came, and Guishan said, "I called for the director. Why did you come?" The director did not respond. Also Guishan had the jisha call for the head monk. The head monk came, and Guishan said, "I called for the head monk. Why did you come?" The head monk did not respond.

Caoshan [later] answered, on behalf of the director, "I know the teacher did not call me." On behalf of the head monk he answered, "If you had the jisha call, perhaps I would not have come." Fayan answered differently, "I just heard the jisha call." Turning over this single circumstance [of this story], you must directly investigate the bloodline of temple administrators and monastic department heads [*chōshū*].

Here are examples of those who brought forth and clarified the great matter when filling the position of director.[13]

Zen Master Xuanze of Baoen Temple in Jinling, a successor of Fayan, served as director in the assembly of Fayan. One day Fayan said, "Director, how long have you been here?"

Xuanze replied, "I have already been in the teacher's assembly for three years."

Fayan said, "You are a student, so why don't you ever ask me about things?"

Xuanze said, "I dare not deceive the teacher. When I was at Qingfeng's place, I realized the peace and joy."[14]

Fayan asked, "Through which words were you able to enter?"

Xuanze responded, "I once asked Qingfeng, 'What is the self of this student [i.e., my own self]?' Qingfeng said, 'The fire boy comes seeking fire.'"[15]

Fayan said, "Good words, only I'm afraid that you did not grasp them."

Xuanze said, "The fire boy belongs to fire. Already fire and seeking fire resembles being self and seeking self."

Fayan exclaimed, "Now I really know that you do not understand. If Buddha Dharma was like that it would not have lasted till today."

Xuanze was overwrought and jumped up. However, out on the path he thought, "He is the guiding teacher of five hundred people. His saying I'm not right certainly has some good point."

He returned and repented. Fayan said, "Just bring me the question."

Xuanze immediately asked, "What is the self of this student?"

Fayan said, "The fire boy comes seeking fire." With these words, Xuanze was greatly enlightened.[16]

Zen Master Yangqi Fanghui of Yuanzhou followed Ciming. As Ciming moved from Nanyuan to Daowu, and then Shishuang, Yangqi always helped supervise temple affairs. Although he had been with [Ciming] for a long time, Yangqi still had not yet aroused realization.[17] Whenever he made inquiries, Ciming said, "Director, go for now [and attend] to the profusion of affairs."[18] Another day Yangqi again asked. Ciming's reply was as before. He also added, "Director, some time your descendants will spread widely under heaven. What use is it to be in such a hurry?"

There was an old woman who resided near the temple. Nobody could fathom her [understanding]. She was called Old Lady Ciming.[19] Whenever Ciming could find the time, he would visit her. One day it began to rain. Knowing that Ciming was about to go out, Yangqi watched for him on a small trail. As soon as he appeared, [Yangqi] finally grabbed and held [Ciming] and said, "This old man today must reveal it for me. If it is not revealed I will beat you."

Ciming said, "Director, knowing this kind of affair, just take a rest."[20] Before he finished speaking, Yangqi was greatly enlightened and did a prostration in the muddy path.[21]

He arose and asked, "How is it when we encounter each other on the narrow path?"

Ciming said, "You should just step aside. I want to go over there."[22] Yangqi went back [to the monastery]. The next day with full ceremony, [Yangqi] visited the abbot's room and made prostrations with gratitude.

Ciming scolded him, saying, "Not yet."

One day there was a [scheduled] dharma meeting with the teacher [san]. For a long while after breakfast the drum signal was not heard. Yangqi asked [Ciming's] anja, "Why don't you hit the drum for today's meeting?"

The anja said, "The high priest [Ciming] left and has not yet returned."

Yangqi took the trail to the old woman's place, and saw Ciming tending the stove while the old lady was cooking gruel. Yangqi said, "Teacher, the great assembly has been waiting for a long time today for the dharma meeting. Why don't you come back?"

Ciming said, "If you can give me one turning word I'll return right away. If you cannot, then everyone there should leave east or west." Yangqi covered his head with his bamboo hat [for traveling] and took several steps [away]. Ciming was greatly delighted and, after all, they returned together.

After this, whenever Ciming went playing out in the mountain, Yangqi carefully watched him leave, and even if it was evening [when he returned], Yangqi would always hit the drum to gather the assembly. Ciming [having] suddenly returned, angrily said, "How did you get this regulation of giving a lecture in the evening at a small monastery?"[23]

Yangqi answered, "After Fenyang's evening meetings.[24] How can you say this is not the regulation?"

Now in monasteries, there are still dharma meetings after *nenju* ceremony on three and eight days, originating from this.[25]

> In ancient times there was only the *kansu*. These days, the title *tsūsu* [director] is used for the [former] *kansu*, [from which] also are the positions of *fūsu* [treasurer] and *kansu*

[assistant director]. In modern times, temples have a profusion of tasks and so appoint two or three *kansu* [administrators]. Jinling [Xuanze] and Yangqi clarified the great matter right when they were *kansu* [directors]. Know the reward for the effort of being a director. Truly, in recent times an abbot [*shukuhanjū*] such as Yangqi is difficult to find in all the ten directions!

Here is an example of someone who had [the mind of] the Way and served as inō.

Great Teacher Baoji of Huayan Temple in Jingzhao, whose personal name was Xiujing, was a successor to Dongshan [Liangjie]. Jingzhao became inō at Yaopu. [One day] he hit the tsui chin to announce community work and said, "Those in the north half will carry firewood, and those in the south half will plow the ground."[26] Then the head monk asked, "What about Manjushri [on the central altar]?" [Baoji] Jingzhao answered, "In the hall, [he] does not sit straight; how can he go to work on both sides?"[27]

The inō of Yaopo became a Dharma successor to Dongshan. This esteemed elder was not insignificant, and left praiseworthy remains of the Way. If we want to compare [Baoji] Jingzhao when he was inō with those who are now worthy seniors [i.e., abbots], today's abbots do not even match Jingzhao when he was inō.

Here is an example of an inō's great awakening.

Zen Master Zhu'an Shigui of Longxiang in Wen Province was an heir of High Priest Foyan Qingyuan. When Zhu'an first climbed Longmen ["Dragon Gate"; Foyan's mountain], he spoke to Foyan about his everyday understanding. Foyan said, "You already have released your mind with exhaustive study. However, you still lack in exerting strength and opening the eye."

Later, [Shigui] was assigned the job of manager of the hall [inō]. One day when he was standing in attendance, he asked [Foyan], "What is it like when going beyond dichotomies?"[28] Foyan said, "It's just like when you hit the tsui chin in the hall." Shigui did not relinguish the matter. That evening, Foyan went to the inō. Shigui resumed questioning about the previous conversation. Foyan said, "Useless talk." With these words, Shigui was greatly awakened. Foyan said, "Now there is nothing more to say."

Foyan was a leading disciple of High Priest Fayan of Wuzu Mountain.[29] During the time he was inō, Master Shigui received the vigorous blood of the ancestral essence. Truly this encounter was at a good time. Now Shigui is known as Kushan.[30] In verse he praised, and with prose comment he turned the ancient expressions of the buddhas and ancestors. Few are equal in stature to Shigui's honor and reknown.

Here are examples of those who brought forth and clarified the great matter when tenzo.

The great Guishan was tenzo at Baizhang's. One day he was standing by the abbot's room. The abbot asked, "Who is it?"

Guishan said, "Lingyou."[31]

Baizhang said, "Would you dig in the fire pot and see if there is fire or not."

Lingyou stirred it and said, "No fire."

Baizhang got up and dug deeply [in the fire pot], and found a small ember. He held it up and said, "Isn't this fire?" Lingyou was enlightened and prostrated himself in gratitude, then expressed his understanding.

Baizhang said, "This is only a temporary juncture.[32] A sutra says, 'If you want to see buddha nature, watch for the opportunity of causes and conditions.'³³ The opportunity has already arrived, and it is like the deluded suddenly enlightened, like the forgotten suddenly remembered.³⁴ When truly examined, it is something of one's own, not obtained from others. Therefore, the ancestral teacher [Dhrtaka] says, 'Having been completely enlightened is the same as not yet being enlightened. There is no mind and no dharma to get.'³⁵ It is simply that there are no vain illusions; ordinary people and sages equally share the original mind. From the beginning the dharma is fully endowed in one's self. Now you are already like this; you should protect and maintain it well."

[Later] the wandering ascetic Sima came from Hunan [South of the Lake]. Baizhang questioned him, saying, "This old monk wants to move to Mount Gui; what do you think?"³⁶

Sima said, "Mount Gui is precipitous and awesome, such that an assembly of fifteen hundred could gather there. However, it is not the place for the high priest [Baizhang] to live."

Baizhang asked, "How come?"

He replied, "The high priest is a bony person, but this is a fleshy mountain.³⁷ If you reside there, it will not mature to even a thousand students."

Baizhang asked, "Is there anyone in my assembly who could take up residence there?"

He answered, "Wait till I observe them individually."

Baizhang asked the jisha to summon the head monk (who was Hualin).³⁸ Baizhang asked, "How about this person?"

Sima asked him to cough once, then to take several steps. Then Sima said, "This person is not suitable."

Then Baizhang summoned the tenzo (who was Lingyou). Sima said, "This is truly the master of Mount Gui."

That night Baizhang invited Lingyou to his room and entrusted him, saying, "My affinity for teaching is here. Mount

Gui is an excellent place for you to reside, however, and transmit and continue our school by fully training many later students."

When Hualin heard about this, he said, "This person [myself] humbly occupies the position of head monk, so how can the monk Lingyou become an abbot [before me]?"

Baizhang said, "If before the assembly you can utter an expression that goes beyond status, I will make you the abbot."[39]

Then [Baizhang] pointed to a water jug and asked, "You cannot call this a water jug; what do you call it?"

Hualin said, "It cannot be called a wooden stake."

Baizhang did not agree and asked Lingyou, who kicked over the water jug. Baizhang laughed and said, "The head monk is defeated by the mountain boy."

Finally Lingyou was dispatched to Mount Gui. This mountain was high and steep, far beyond the smoke of homes. Lingyou had gibbons and other monkeys for companions, and horse chestnuts and other nuts for food. The people living at the foot of the mountain gradually came to know of him. Together with some monks, Lingyou built a practice hall.[40] Finally Li Jingrang reported to the emperor, and the temple was named Tongqing [Rejoice together]. Prime Minister Pei Xiugong came to inquire about the profound core [of the teaching]. Then Zen students from all over the country converged there.

Zen Master Jianyuan Zhongxing was tenzo in the assembly of Daowu Yuanzhi. One day he accompanied Daowu on a condolence visit to a deceased supporter's house. Zhongxing slapped the coffin with his hand and said, "Alive or dead?"

Daowu said, "I do not say alive; I do not say dead."

Zhongxing said, "Why don't you say?"

Daowu said, "I won't say. I won't say."

After the visit, as they were returning, Zhongxing said, "High Priest, you must tell me. If you still will not say, then I'll beat you up."

Daowu said, "Strike me if you'd like, but I won't say alive, I won't say dead." Zhongxing finally hit Daowu with a number of punches.

Daowu returned to the temple but made Zhongxing leave, saying, "[You had better go] for a little while, because after the director finds out, he will attack you." Zhongxing then bowed and left, and went to visit Shishuang.[41] There he brought up the matter of the previous conversation, which ended up with his hitting Daowu. [Then Zhongxing said,] "Now I ask you to tell me."

Shishuang said, "Don't you see that Daowu said, 'I do not say alive; I do not say dead'!" At that, Zhongxing was greatly awakened, and he offered a memorial meal in repentance.

Venerable Wuzhuo was tenzo on Mount Wutai.[42] Manjushri appeared above the rice pot. Wuzhuo finally hit him and said, "Even if old man Shakyamuni came, I would also hit him."

High Priest [Shexian] Guisheng of She Prefecture was cold and severe, tough and frugal. Patch-robed monks respected and feared him. When they were monks [in training], Zen masters Fushan Fayuan of Shu Province and Yihuai of Tianyi Mountain in Yue Province specially came to visit and study [with Guisheng].[43] They arrived in the middle of a snowy winter. Guisheng harshly reviled them and tried to chase them away, even pouring water on them in the visitors' room so that their clothing got all wet.[44] The other [visiting] monks all got angry and left. But Fayuan and [Tianyi] Yihuai only spread out their zagus, adjusted their robes, and continued to sit in the visitors' room. Guisheng came and scolded them, saying, "If you do not leave right now, I will beat you."

Yihuai went before him and said, "The two of us have come a thousand miles just to study Zen with you, how could we leave from just one scoop of water dumped on us? Even if you beat us to death, we will not go."

Guisheng laughed and said, "You two need to practice Zen, so go hang up your belongings."

Later, Fayuan was asked to serve as tenzo. The assembly suffered from the coarse and poor [quality and quantity of food]. One time, Guisheng went out to the village. Fayuan stole the key [to the storehouse], and took some wheat flour to prepare five-flavored gruel.[45] Guisheng suddenly returned and went to the hall. After eating, he sat in the outer hall and sent for the tenzo, and Fayuan came. Guisheng said, "Is it true that you stole flour to cook the gruel?" [Fayuan] admitted it and implored Guisheng to punish him. Guisheng had him calculate the price [of the flour], and sell his robes and bowls to repay it. Then Guisheng struck Fayuan thirty blows with his staff and expelled him from the temple.

Fayuan stayed in the city and begged some fellow practitioners to seek forgiveness for him, but Guisheng would not allow it. Then [Fayuan] said that even if he was not permitted to move back, he wanted only to follow the monks into the room [to meet with the teacher]. Guisheng again did not allow it.

One day Guisheng went out to the town and saw Fayuan standing alone in front of a lodging house. Guisheng said, "This is an apartment building belonging to the temple. During the time you have been staying here have you paid or not?" Then he told Fayuan to calculate what was owed and repay it. Fayuan was not bothered by this, but carried his bowl through the city and sent the money he received [to the temple].

Another day Guisheng went to the town and saw Fayuan holding his bowl. Guisheng returned to the assembly and said, "Fayuan truly has the determination to study Zen." Finally he was summoned to return.

The great Guishan, after he was appointed tenzo under Baizhang, carried water and firewood without being troubled by the many toils and without counting the passing years. The result was that Baizhang bestowed on him the appointment as master of Mount Gui. When he went to live at Mount Gui, all the myriad circumstances were very plain and simple. He had not yet received food offerings from celestials or humans, so [he lived on] chestnuts in modest poverty. Cloud-and-water monks had not yet assembled to study, so mountain monkeys were his only companions.[46] Although it was the harsh study of an ancient sage, this is like an inspiration for later students. For the job of tenzo, [this example] is worthy of veneration. The pupil of the eye cannot be deceived; the top of the head is the most high.

Jianyuan [Zhongxing] is an excellent example whose ancient remains we should admire. Wuzhuo left marvelous tracks, which followers of the wonder should not neglect. Especially, we cannot fail to study the tenzo Fayuan's faithful heart, which can be met only once in a thousand years. It is difficult to match for both the wise or foolish. However, if tenzos do not experience dedication like Fayuan's, how can their study of the Way penetrate the innermost precincts of the buddhas and ancestors? The aforementioned tenzos all are dragons and elephants of the buddha ocean and remarkable persons of the ancestral territory. Now when we search for people like them, they cannot be found in the whole world.

Here are examples of people of the Way who were tenzos.

Jiashan was tenzo under Guishan.[47] Guishan asked, "What will we eat in the hall today?"

The tenzo [Jiashan] said, "Year after year, the same single spring."[48]

Guishan said, "With such a dharma, practice all affairs."

The tenzo [Jiashan] said, "A dragon lodges in the phoenix nest."[49]

Zen Master [Furong] Daokai of Dayang Mountain was thoroughly enlightened in meeting with Touzi. When Daokai was serving as tenzo, Touzi asked, "Isn't it difficult to carry out the strenuous duties of the kitchen?"

Daokai said, "It's not so bad."

Touzi asked, "What about cooking the gruel and steaming the rice?"

Daokai said, "Workers clean the rice and make the fire; attendants cook the gruel and steam the rice."

Touzi said, "What is it that you do?"

Daokai said, "High Priest [Touzi], kindly let me be."[50]

Touzi deeply agreed.

Touzi and [Daokai] Dayang were outstanding persons of the ancestral gate. [Touzi] appointed [Daokai] Dayang, who served as tenzo under Touzi. These are excellent relics from the ancestral seat. Therefore common people are not appointed to the tenzo's job. Those who fill this position are dragons and elephants. Compared with [Daokai] Dayang, very few of the ancient or present masters can match his stature. Because of this, those who can appreciate his tones are fairly rare; those who understand him are above the crowd. However, if you wish to receive the bones and marrow of the buddhas and ancestors, you must study the body and mind of [Daokai] Dayang.

Jiashan was the only disciple of [the boatman of] Huating [Chuanzi Dechung], who was a disciple of Yaoshan. This is a noble lineage. After he saw Huating, Jiashan also studied with Guishan and was appointed tenzo. Guishan was a disciple of Baizhang already residing at Mount Gui during Baizhang's time. [Jiashan's] eye of the Way was truly clear. In his expression, the advancing and halting of the Way and the ancient truth of the dharma permeates the abyss and permeates the ocean! Therefore, the family style of tenzos is to see and hear [fully] the piling up of the generations. Together these [examples] are the ancestral teachers' clear, bright meaning.[51] This is what wise people venerate and fools disregard.

Here is an example of a person of the Way who served as work leader.

Zen Master Baofu Benquan of Zhang Province was a Dharma heir of Huitang Zuxin.[52] Once when Huitang [just] raised his fist, [Benquan] was struck through and actualized the source. He was eloquent and sharp-witted. When government official Shanku Huang first entered [practice], he asked Huitang, "Which persons here are worthy of having discussions with?" Huitang said, "Benquan of Zhang Province now is supervising workers in constructing rice fields."

Shanku went there together with Huitang, and said to Benquan, "Work Leader, tell me. Do you know that a free-standing pillar gives birth to a child?"

Benquan answered, "Is it a boy or a girl?"[53]

Shanku hesitated. Benquan shook him. Huitang said, "Do not be rude."

Benquan said, "If I do not hit this wooden dummy, when will he ever get it?"

Shanku laughed loudly.

Temple administrators and department heads should not simply give priority to purity.[54] Definitely only those who embody the Way should be selected to fill these jobs.

Here are some examples of minor department heads who expressed the Way.

Zhaozhou was fire manager at Nanquan's monastery.[55] One day he fastened the doors of a building and started a fire inside. When the building was full of smoke he yelled, "Help, Fire! Help, Fire!" When all the monks arrived, Zhaozhou said, "If you can say something, I will open the doors."

The monks all had no response, but through the window Nanquan handed Zhaozhou a lock. Zhaozhou immediately opened the door.

Xuefeng was rice manager at Dongshan [Liangjie's] assembly. When he was cleaning rice, Dongshan asked him, "Do you sift the rice from the sand, or do you sift the sand from the rice?"

Xuefeng said, "I remove the rice and sand at the same time."

Dongshan asked, "What will the assembly eat?"

At that, Xuefeng overturned the bowl.

Dongshan said, "In accord with your causal conditioning you will [later] meet Deshan."[56]

Zen Master Shishuang Qingzhu became rice manager at Guishan's dharma assembly. One day Shishuang was in the rice storehouse sifting rice. Guishan said, "Food from donors should not be scattered around."

Shishuang said, "It's not scattered around."

Guishan picked up one grain from the floor and said, "You say it's not scattered around, but where does this come from?"

Shishuang did not reply. Guishan again said, "Do not disdain even this single grain. A hundred thousand grains can be born from this single grain."

Shishuang said, "A hundred thousand grains can be born from this single grain. But it's not yet clear; where did this single grain come from?"

Guishan laughed loudly, "Ho! Ho!" and returned to the abbot's quarters. Later in the evening he went up to lecture in the hall and said, "Oh, great assembly, there is a worm in the rice."

After he had attainment under Linji, Zen Master Guanzhi Zhixian left Linji and traveled around until arriving at the nun Moshan Laoran's place. When he first arrived he said [to her], "If we accord with each other I will stay here. If not, then I will knock over your Zen seat." Then he entered into the hall, and she sent a jisha to ask him whether he had come for amusement [*yusan*] or for the sake of Buddha Dharma. Zhixian said, "I came for the sake of Buddha Dharma."

Moshan climbed the seat [in the dharma hall to have public interviews with students]. Zhixian came up for a dialogue.

Moshan asked, "Today where have you arrived from?"

Zhixian said, "I only came from the mouth of the road."

Moshan said, "Why didn't you cover it before coming?"[57]

Zhixian could not respond. Only then did he first make a full prostration and then ask, "How is Moshan [Mount Mo]?"[58]

Moshan said, "Not an exposed peak."

Zhixian asked, "How is the master of Moshan?"

Moshan said, "Neither man nor woman."

Zhixian yelled, "Kaaa!" and said, "Then why haven't you transformed [into a man]?"

Moshan said, "Neither a god nor a demon, why should I make transformations?"[59]

With that, Zhixian did a prostration and venerated her. Then he became manager of the gardens [at Moshan] for three years. Later when Zhixian was abbot at a temple, he said to the assembly, "I was at father Linji's where I got half a scoop and at mother Moshan's where I got half a scoop. Together they made one full ladle that I drank completely, so that even until now I am satisfied through and through."

> The job of garden manager [*enju*] is most difficult and extremely troublesome. [Only] people who have the mind of the Way have served in this job. People without the

mind of the Way cannot fill this position. [The garden manager] always must be at the vegetable garden to plant seeds in accord with the season. With the face of buddhas and ancestors, [they must have] horse and donkey legs, like farmworkers and field hands. Without holding back their own life energy, throughout the day they must carry spades and hoes, plow and till by themselves, and haul manure. They can only wait for the vegetables to ripen, and then must not miss their time. When they plow the ground and sow seeds, they do not wear their two-piece robes [*sankun*], one-piece robes [*jikitotsu*], or their okesa. They only wear coarse workclothes. However, when it is time for the whole community together to chant sutras, do *nenju*, go up in the hall [for the abbot's lectures], or enter the room [for interview with the abbot], the garden manager must definitely go along with the assembly.[60] They must not fail to practice. Morning and evening in the vegetable garden they must offer incense, do prostrations, chant, and recite dedications to *Ryūten* and *Dōji*, without ever becoming lazy or negligent.[61] Even at night they sleep at [a hut near] the vegetable garden. Workers provided for the garden are sometimes rotated according to the supervision of the work leader [and must be trained by the garden manager]. Truly people with the mind of the Way and people of great reknown have filled this position. Fellows of little ability and the crowd of mediocrities have never served in this job.

In the community of my late teacher, the old buddha Tiantong [Rujing], an old monk named Pu from Xishu [Sichuan] was first appointed to this job when he was over sixty years old. In [Rujing's] assembly, he never changed his assignment. Throughout three years the monks admired [his practice], and my late teacher deeply appreciated him. If we compare old Pu to elders [abbots] of various temples, those elders cannot match garden manager Pu.

Zen Master Wuzu Fayan of Qi Province, thanks to High Priest Haihui Shouduan of Baiyun Mountain in Shu Province, settled his investigation of the great matter and deeply penetrated the bones and marrow. Shouduan made him manager of the mill at the foot of the mountain. Each year [Wuzu] Fayan got money from grinding rice and wheat. He opened a pawnshop to earn interest, hired workers, and except for making food offerings, put the remaining money in the temple accounts. People [from the temple] constantly spied on [Wuzu] Fayan and criticized his conduct to Shouduan, claiming that [Wuzu] Fayan spent his days at the mill drinking wine, eating meat, and feeding women guests. The whole temple was in an uproar. When [Wuzu] Fayan heard this, he intentionally bought meat and alcohol and hung them out in front of the mill, and also bought cosmetics and makeup for his women friends. Whenever Zen monks came around the mill, [Wuzu] Fayan would touch the women and laughingly banter and tease them, completely without restraint.

One day Shouduan called him to the abbot's quarters and questioned if this was true, to which [Wuzu] Fayan nodded agreement without further words. Shouduan suddenly slapped his face. [Wuzu] Fayan's expression did not change, and he made a prostration as he was leaving. Shouduan scolded him, saying, "Just leave immediately." [Wuzu] Fayan said, "Please wait for me to finish my calculations and list the accounts for the next person."

Some days later [Wuzu] Fayan told Shouduan, "After excluding expenses for buying alcohol and meat, there remains three hundred thousand in cash to put into the temple accounts." Shouduan was greatly amazed at this, and understood that petty people had just been jealous [of Wuzu Fayan].

At that time Zen Master Yuantong Faxiu was the head monk, and was invited to be the abbot at Simian [Four-Face] Mountain.

Yuantong invited Fayan to come together with him and take the first seat.[62]

> The mill house, called *mage*, *ma'in*, or *masu*, is the office for grinding rice and polishing wheat, built from five or six, up to as many as ten or so *cho* away from the temple compound.[63] One person is appointed manager of the mill. This was Ancestor [Wuzu] Fayan's responsibility. In ancient times persons with the mind of the Way fulfilled this job. Mediocre persons have never served in it. Nowadays it is difficult to find anyone with the mind of the Way. So for now we must use people with adequate intelligence, whether or not they have [bodhi mind]. We must be sad at the decadence of this world. When we contemplate old buddha [Wuzu] Fayan's straightforward activity, nobody from ancient to modern times can compare to him. The color of peach and plum blossoms and the faithfulness of pines and cedars are not broken by the north wind; how could they be overcome by frost and snow? We should know the honest diligence of studying the Way, and should become intimate with the noble character of sincere faith. Even if we later students meet such difficulties [as Wuzu Fayan's], we must not retreat from our intention to exert the Way. How can we not see the wisdom of those eminent persons who ascended [and widened their view], without thinking of being the same? As we are able to clarify the depths or superficiality of those ancient virtuous ones who had the mind of the Way, we must admire all the more their increasing loftiness and firmness.

Here is an example of arduous study with frugal care, [which is the practice even] after attaining the Way.

Great Teacher Huizhao of Linji Temple was on Huangbo Mountain planting pine trees when Huangbo asked, "For what purpose do you plant so many pines deep in the remote mountains?"

Linji said, "First, to make some scenery for the mountain gate [i.e., the monastery]; second, to make a guidepost for later generations." As he finished speaking he struck the ground once or twice with the head of his hoe.

Huangbo said, "Although it is like this, you have received my thirty blows."

Linji again struck the head of the hoe on the ground twice and whispered, "Shh" [i.e., be quiet].

Huangbo said, "When you take up our lineage it will greatly flourish in the world."

Guishan brought up this previous situation and asked Yangshan, "At that time did Huangbo entrust only Linji, or was there some other person?"

Yangshan said, "There was. But this person was from a very remote era, so I cannot tell the High Priest [Guishan]."

Guishan said, "Even if this is the case, I still want to know, so just try to tell me."

Yangshan said, "One person will head south and [his teaching] will rule over Wu and Yue [Provinces]; but he will meet with a great wind and then rest."[64]

Linji was at Huangbo's for twenty years, doing nothing but strenuously studying and exerting the Way. Sometimes he planted pines; sometimes he planted cedars. Is this not the intimate discussion and intimate practice of the single mountain's scenery and the ten thousand ancient ones' guidepost? In the world it is said that the wise and noble do not forget virtue, whereas petty people do not repay generosity. How much more must children in the house of the buddha ancestors repay the deep kindness of the milk of the Dharma? What we call repaying this blessing is to plant pines and cedars, and to be satisfied with our gruel and rice.[65] Even for the sake of those from extremely distant ages, we return to plant trees in the remote mountains. The head of the hoe struck the ground. Already you received my blows. When our teaching reaches you it will greatly flourish in the world. If you yearn to be a bridge to the buddha way, you must become familiar with this time of Linji's.

Here is an example of not arbitrarily bestowing even a minor position.

One day Huitang saw that Huanglong seemed to have an uneasy expression. When asked about it, Huanglong said he had not yet found someone to be the accountant.[66] Thereupon Huitang recommended the treasurer [Nanyueh] Cikan. Huanglong said, "Cikan is still rather aggressive, so I am afraid that petty people may try to resist and deceive him."

Huitang said, "Attendant [Shuangling] Hua is fairly honest and prudent."

Huanglong responded, "Although you may call Hua honest and prudent, he's not as magnanimous and devoted as property manager [Guishan] Huaixiu."[67]

Lingyuan [Weiqing] later asked Huitang, "Why did Huanglong deliberate to such extent for one accountant position?"

Huitang said, "For maintaining a country or a family this is fundamental. Not only Huanglong has especially acted thus, but other former sages have admonished us about this."

[Later the three priests Huanglong and Huinan had discussed,] Guishan [Huai] Xiu, Shuanglong Hua, and [Nanyue] Tiemien Kan, all became nationally known teachers. Even people of this stature previously had filled positions such as accountant, property manager, and treasurer. Searching for such people now is like looking to acquire horses like Feitu and Luer [legendary steeds of an ancient emperor]. Fellows who serve even as director today all have crude countenances and rough characters. Nevertheless, at this time we must employ those who are [at least] clever. Just as Huanglong was frugal with the Way and prudent with the Dharma, we should not recklessly bestow [these jobs]. Arbitrarily granting them, faults will immediately appear!

Here is an example showing that temple administrators should not construct luxurious buildings to be made into lofty halls or great towers.

High Priest Wuzu Fayan announced to the assembly, "When my teacher's teacher [Yangqi Fanghui] first lived at Yangqi Mountain, the rafters of the old roof were rotting and barely covered [the monks] from the wind and rain. On a severe winter evening they were confronted with snow and hailstones covering the sitting platforms, so there was no space for them to be at ease. The patch-robed monks sincerely requested that [the temple] be repaired. My teacher's teacher [Yangqi] refused, saying, 'Our Buddha has said that in this age of decreasing [life expectancy], even tall cliffs and deep valleys are impermanent and always shifting.[68] How is it possible to seek satisfaction of your own desires and claim this is sufficient? You all have left home to study the Way, but your everyday activities are still not peaceful.[69] You are already in your forties or fifties. How could you have the leisure to concern yourselves with making a luxurious building?' Finally he did not comply [with their request].

"The next day [Yangqi] came to the hall to lecture and said: 'When first living at Yangqi, the roof and walls are broken down,/ platforms all sprinkled with snow like precious jewels./ Instead of hunching your shoulders, grieving, and sighing in the gloom,/ look back and recall the ancients who lived under trees.'"

Now, those in the world as well as monastics have been cautioned about constructing lofty halls and [ornate] pavilions with scenic ponds. The *Shitsu* says, "Wishing to contemplate the conduct of the Yellow Emperor, observe the 'Meeting Palace.' Wishing to contemplate the conduct of Yao and Shun, observe 'Total Clarity.'[70] The Yellow Emperor's bright hall [national palace] had a thatch roof and was called 'Meeting Palace.' Yao and Shun's bright hall [national palace] had a thatch roof and was called 'Total Clarity.'" You should understand from this that ancient wise lords did not raise up their palace walls or ceilings, and did not clip the reeds and briars from their thatched roofs. So all the more, which of the descendants of buddha ancestors would work to construct elegant buildings with vermilion towers and jeweled roofs? There is not much time in this single life; do not pass it vainly. For the past twenty years I have observed the two nations [of Japan and China], and there were elders and those in their prime who did not value their moments, but many lost their bearings in busy haste while taking meaningless trouble to engage in construction projects.[71] How pitiful; how bitter! It is as if they threw away good dharma and have not yet abandoned bad karma.[72] If you awaken to the briefness of the remainder of your life, how could you indulge in erecting great lofty merit? Simply this is Ancestor [Wuzu] Fayan's intention.

Director [Kan'in]

The single job of director governs all the general affairs of the temple,[73] such as: responding to government officials; overseeing the assembly's meetings with the abbot; taking charge of documents [that designate appointees]; arranging to send messages of gratitude or congratulations [to other temples]; gathering the assembly for ceremonies; meeting together with donors; extending congratulations and condolences as appropriate in fortune or misfortune; keeping accounts of lending and borrowing; [deciding] the temple's annual budget; [watching over] the supply of money and grain; supervising expenses and incomes; and making arrangements for receiving food and other materials for annual celebrations. When to buy rice or barley and make miso or vinegar should depend on the season. Extracting oil and milling grains also should be kept in mind. [The director must have] an excellent heart for always arranging meals for the assembled monks, welcoming those who come from all the four directions without disregarding any of them.

At the winter [solstice] celebration; New Year's celebration; celebrations for opening and closing the summer practice period; the Eggplant Roasting Ceremony; Boys' Festival [the fifth day of the fifth month]; Festival of the Weaver [the seventh day of the seventh month]; double nine festival [the ninth day of the ninth month]; the opening and closing of the monks' hall furnace; *Rōhatsu* [the December eighth commemoration of Shakyamuni's enlightenment]; and the mid-February commemoration [of his passing into parinirvana]; and other such great celebrations, if the director has the energy he should personally manage them [including ceremonies and feasts].[74] If [the director's] strength is not sufficient, he should request someone to undertake them.

Minor affairs of the temple—for example, everyday matters—can be handled on one's own. For substantial matters or unprecedented situations effecting the temple's dignity, then the temple administrators and department heads together should deliberate and then get the abbot's approval. If anyone, from the abbot down through all the assembly members, has not been in accord with the regulations or has gone against people's feelings in either large or small matters, in each case [the director] should gently but fully express it. Do not fail to speak out of reticence, but also do not speak crudely or harshly.

The manner for instructing novice monks is first to attempt it by effectively employing skillful means.[75] Do not recklessly beat them. If you have to carry out disciplinary punishment, it should be performed in front of [some] other monks in the administrators' office building.[76] Do not exceed ten or so blows before ceasing. [To prevent] unexpected problems, you must not strike immoderately.

If you expel an attendant monk from the temple, the monk must have incurred sufficient blame and confessed the circumstances, and you must get the abbot's approval.[77] Of course, you should not settle on and carry out such an action in a manner that can incur criticism from the government authorities.[78] When inviting [someone] to take such positions as fund-raiser, property manager, charcoal manager, miso manager, gruel manager, *Prajnaparamita Sutra* lecturer, *Kegon [Avatamsaka] Sutra* lecturer, bath attendant, water manager, garden manager, mill manager, or lamp manager, consult the department heads to [find people who will] help and benefit the community.[79] When you have done so you must get the approval of the abbot. Do not carelessly procrastinate [in these appointments].

When donors enter the temple, arrange the guest places, and greet and attend to them [appropriately] according to dharma. Before conducting a great celebration, [the director] should deliberate with the temple administrators [*chiji*] and department heads [*chōshū*] to avoid overlooking anything during the event. The essence of the director position is to respect the wise and openly accept [everyone in] the assembly, [so that] seniors and juniors peacefully stay in harmony and friendship, and function cooperatively in the great assembly in order for everyone to have a happy heart.[80] [The director] must not overexert and rely on their power, thoughtlessly staying aloof from the great assembly. Also, do not carry out responsibilities at your own discretion, disturbing the peace of the assembly.

Unless sick or meeting with official guests, [the director] should always proceed to the hall [for practice with the assembly] at the appropriate times. This is important so that the serving monks for both meals are not disrupted.[81] If the storehouse's available funds are meager [and supplies are needed], the director should endeavor with all due strength to devise some plan. Do not disturb the abbot about it or raise concern in the assembly.

Among the people working with the director, those who are talented and virtuous should be encouraged and praised. If the work of some does not progress and the sincerity of their practice is questionable, admonish them in a discreet place and indignantly reprimand them, so they may renew themselves and abide in dharma for a long time.[82] If some large mistake has been done intentionally and harms the temple, also let the abbot know in private. For the many other affairs that may appear before us, just sit and watch [how] they succeed.[83]

The director's job is fulfilled for the sake of the public [i.e., everyone, both in the community and all beings]. To say for the sake of the public means without [acting on] private inclinations. [Acting] without private inclinations is contemplating the ancients and yearning for the Way.[84] To yearn for the Way is to follow the Way. First read the *Shingi* and understand as a whole, then act with your determination in accord with the Way.[85] When dealing with affairs, definitely consult with the temple administrators before carrying them out. Without taking things as large or small, consult with people before taking care of business. That is exactly acting for the sake of the public. Although you conduct deliberations, if others' words are not considered it is as if you did not consult them.

The director's duty is to accept [all] the monks and work for the peace of the assembly. But do not take it as important for there to be many monks; do not take the monks lightly when they are few. For example, Devadatta enticed five hundred monks to follow him but the result was wickedness.[86] Leading a large assembly of monks but being outside the Way is completely wrong. Yaoshan was an ancient buddha, but there were not as many as ten monks in his assembly. Zhaozhou also was an ancient buddha, but there were not as many as twenty monks in his assembly. Fenyang's assembly was as small as seven or eight monks. Just see that buddha ancestors together with great [awakened] dragons are not limited by [the size of] their assemblies. They only value having the Way, not whether there is a crowded assembly. Now and hereafter, [many] having the Way and having virtue are under [the lineage of] Yaoshan and descendants of Fenyang. We must value Yaoshan's family style and must venerate the excellent example of Fenyang.[87] You should know that even if there are one hundred, one thousand, or ten thousand monks, without the mind of the Way and without practice of contemplating the ancients, [the assembly] is inferior to toads and lower than earthworms. Even an assembly of seven, eight, or nine monks who have the mind of the Way and contemplate the ancients is superior to dragons and elephants and excels the wisdom of the sages.

What is called the mind of the Way is not to abandon or scatter about the great Way of the buddha ancestors, but deeply to protect and esteem their great Way. Therefore having abandoned fame and gain and departed your homeland, consider gold as excrement and honor as spittle, and without obscuring the truth or obeying falsehoods, maintain the regulations of right and wrong and entrust everything to the guidelines for conduct. After all, not to sell cheaply or debase the worth of the ordinary tea and rice of the buddha ancestors' house is exactly the mind of the Way.

Furthermore, reflecting that inhalation does not wait for exhalation also is the mind of the Way and is diligence.[88] Contemplating the ancients enables the eye of the ancestors' essence to observe intently, and enables the ear of [both] past and present to listen vigilantly, so that we accept our bodies as hollowed out caverns of the whole empty sky, and just sit, piercing through all the skulls under heaven, opening wide our fists and staying with our own nostrils. This is carrying the clear, transparent sky to dye the white clouds and conveying the waters of autumn to wash the bright moon, and is the fulfillment of the practice of contemplating the ancients. If such an assembly has seven or eight monks it can be a great monastery. This is like being able to see all the buddhas in the ten directions when you see the single Buddha Shakyamuni. If the assembly is not like this, even with a million monks it is not a genuine monastery, and is not an assembly of the buddha way.

Upon seeing honorable persons with the mind of the Way or who practice contemplating the ancients, the director should deeply arouse consideration for them with appreciation and compassionate care. However, encountering people without faith or loyalty to the triple jewels even when they have actually met with teachers or [read] sutras, or those who are not mindful of the Way and do not practice contemplating the ancients, then [the director] must be aware that they are of demonic inclination or lack the requisite faith for entering practice.[89] Knowing this, do not accept them into the assembly. Buddha said, "People without faith are like broken jars."[90] Therefore living beings without faith in Buddha Dharma of course cannot become vessels of Buddha Dharma. Buddha said, "The great ocean of Buddha Dharma can be entered due to faith."[91] Clearly understand that we should not live together with beings who have no faith.

Zen Master Huanglong Huinan said, "This is the end of the Semblance Dharma Age [zōhō], so many people are intoxicated with arrogance and love many vanities while detesting even a little of the truth. Comprehend that loving many vanities leads to falsehood."

Venerable Sanghanandi, knowing the assembly was becoming proud, said, "It is more than eight hundred years since the passing into parinirvana [of Shakyamuni] under the twin sala trees; people lack persevering faith and right mindfulness has become feeble.[92] [They] do not respect suchness but only love supernatural powers."[93] How deplorable that after [only] eight hundred years, still within two thousand years [of Shakyamuni, i.e., before the degenerate Final Dharma Age], already they did not have sincere faith, and right mindfulness was weak. How much more can today's vices not be compared to that time? What can we do with the four upside-down views? The three poisons are difficult to let go.[94] Even if able people can be located in the mountains and fields, can they easily be found in the monasteries?[95] To prepare them to select the genuine from the false, the road of wisdom must not be shut off.

Seeing someone [dedicated to the Way, the director] should definitely promote that person [to responsible positions in the community]. If the person is promoted but does not accept, do not regret it. In general, not to be shortsighted but to take the long view is the only helpful mental attitude.[96] When seeing some advantage, the director should not be pleased, and when seeing some disadvantage the director should not worry. Cultivating fame, praise, and advantage seriously obstruct the Way. Therefore, in ancient times laypeople and home-leavers who yearned for the Way all relinquished [such gaining thoughts]. How much less could the descendants of buddha ancestors who completely foster monastic practice ever indulge in fame, gain, or wealth?[97]

PURE STANDARDS FOR THE TEMPLE ADMINISTRATORS   159

Formerly Zen Master [Dongkeng] Yanjun of Kannon Temple in Dongkeng was a student of Zen Master [Touzi] Datong of Touzi Mountain. When he studied widely at ancestral seats he traveled around to Heng, Lu, and Min Mountains, and Xishu [Sichuan].[98] Once as he passed through a deep valley in Fengling [Phoenix Forest] he suddenly came upon a valuable jewel. His traveling companions also noticed it and were just about to take it. Yanjun said, "An ancient struck some gold pieces while plowing a field, but [ignored them] as if they were tiles and pebbles.[99] Wait till I have managed to cover a peak [by establishing a temple]; then I shall use this jewel to serve monks coming from the four directions." After he said this they discarded the jewel and went on their way.

You should know that to see gold pieces while plowing a field and yet [ignore them] like tiles and pebbles is the path of wisdom [even] of a worldly person. To see a valuable jewel in a deep valley and discard it and leave is the footprint left by a buddha ancestor. To succeed to the life pulse of the buddha ancestors, do not seek after worldly profits. What is called worldly profit is the offerings of humans and heavenly beings and the patronage of kings and ministers.[100] Do not receive without being in accord with dharma. Humbly wish to be a teacher of home-leaver monks, and not a teacher of kings and ministers. So put home-leavers first and householders after, esteeming monks while taking worldly people [more] lightly.[101]

Furthermore, Zen Master Mingzhao said, "Zen Master Daixue Huailian resided at Guanri [Vast Benefit] Zen Temple on Ayuwang Mountain.[102] It happened that two monks would not cease quarreling over who should benefit from a donation. The temple administrators were not able to arrive at a judgment. Zen Master Daixue called the two monks and admonished them thus, 'Once official Bao was a judge at Kaifeng and a citizen stated that someone who had lent him a hundred coins of silver had died.[103] Now he wanted to return it to the family, but the son would not accept it. He requested the judge to summon the son so that the money could be returned. The judge was moved at such an unusual situation, and summoned the son and discussed it. The son refused the money, saying that his late father did not have personal [supplies of] silver to lend to other people. For a long time each of the two men unyieldingly insisted that the money was the other's. The judge could do nothing, and decreed that they donate the money to Buddhist and Taoist temples in the city for ceremonies dedicated to the dead man's blessing in the unknown realms after death.[104] I [Daixue] witnessed this affair myself. Therefore, even people like this who labor in the dusty world are still able to shun wealth and yearn for justice. You who have become Buddha's disciples do not know integrity like this.' Finally [Daixue] expelled both [the quarreling monks] according to the monastery code." (This is from the *West Lake Extensive Record*; now also described in the *Zen Gate Jeweled Instructions*.)[105]

Now, as I reflect on this son not accepting [the money], how could he have simply spurned wealth and adored justice like this? Certainly this was all from maintaining his family and respect for his father. Do not call this [only] the faithful heart of a person working in the world. This is just like the jewel in the topknot of one who has left home to study the Way.[106] Shukan of the Han dynasty said, "With much wealth the wise will lose their aspiration. With much wealth the foolish will increase their faults." If worldly people are like this, how can monks covet profit? The wise and foolish alike are cautioned about great wealth. Should a thousand gold pieces be loved more than the words of this ancient wise person?

The *Luzhi Chunqiu* says, "Emperor Yao called Xuyu from among the multitude of commoners to be the teacher of all those under heaven [i.e., in the kingdom]. Xuyu declined and hid at Jiashan Mountain."[107] You should know that even a layperson dismissed [rule over] the country and valued the Way. How much less could Buddha's children ever indulge in large or small gain, and not pay attention to [wealth's] damage to oneself and damage to others? When cultivating the buddha way, to see profit as like a snake, like poison, like spit, or like excrement is purity and honesty. The *Shingi* says [to consider], "whether one is expounding the dharma for the sake of profit or not."[108]

If the director meets any human or heavenly being who wants to make offerings to the assembly or [make donations for] erecting buildings, [the director] must first examine in detail whether the donor has true faith or lack of faith and purity or lack of purity, and then consult and consider it together with the abbot. If their pure faith and right view is confirmed, then approve [the offering]; otherwise do not permit it.[109] It is called true faith if it is like Sudatta's faithful heart or Prince Jeta's benevolent justice. Sudatta was [admired as] Sudatta not because he had great wealth. Jeta was Jeta because he truly had noble poverty. Because of their true faith they were received with the Tathagata's approval. Even if those who previously did not have true faith in the three jewels, when facing the end of their life, cultivate some small merit and virtue [by making an offering, their offering] should quickly be approved.

In the third section of the "Increasing by One" Agama, it says, "When he was in the Jetavana vihara, Buddha informed the monks that they should revere donors and patrons as if with the filial piety of supporting and serving fathers and mothers.[110] Donors enable [monks] to carry out precepts, concentration, and wisdom with their many abundant benefits, without any obstacles in the three jewels. [Donors] are able to give the four necessities [food, clothing, bedding, and medicine], so monks should have a compassionate heart toward donors. If even a small kindness should not be forgotten, how much more a great one? Therefore you must be diligent in the three actions [of body, speech, and mind] so as not to discard vainly those donors' blessing, but consequently obtain the great result [of buddhahood] and circulate their fame [for their generosity]. Moreover, [honor patrons] just as you would point out the road to the lost, or end the distress of the frightened, or give shelter to the homeless, or feed the poor, or give sight to the blind." Therefore, [we can see that] to venerate and extend compassionate heart to donors and patrons was the teaching and decree of the World-Honored Tathagata [Shakyamuni].

Although experiencing the great result [of buddhahood] is possible from small causes, this is only within the blessing field of the three jewels.[111] The ancestral teacher Nagarjuna said, "Small good deeds are able to produce the great result, for example seeking the result of buddhahood by praising [buddha] with a single verse or a single "namu butsu" [name of buddha] invocation, by lighting a single stick of incense, or by making an offering of a single flower. Slight actions like this definitely can produce buddhahood."

In general, monks' subsistence must be separate from the four wrong [livelihoods] or the five wrongs.[112] The food of monks in monasteries also must be received like this. The director and abbot must clearly heed this warning. What are called the four wrong livelihoods are:

First, the so-called directive wrong of conveying orders for the national [government].[113]
Second, the so-called binding wrong of medicine or fortune-telling and geomancy.
Third, the so-called upward gazing wrong of divination techniques from gazing up to observe the sun, moon, and constellations.[114]
Fourth, the so-called underground wrong of sowing seeds or planting roots of the five grains.[115]

The above four wrong livelihoods are also called the four mouth livelihoods, and also called the four impure foods. They should not be eaten.

The five wrongs are:

First, for the sake of receiving offerings, presenting an unusual, majestic appearance.
Second, for the sake of receiving offerings, expounding on one's own merits.
Third, foretelling good and bad fortune while expounding the Dharma for people.
Fourth, using a strong voice to appear dignified and elicit people's awe.
Fifth, moving people's hearts by expounding on what can be gained by making offerings.

Food obtained through the five wrong causal conditions should not be eaten. For buddha's disciples who are good spiritual friends, quickly departing from these five wrongs is right livelihood.[116] The [Zen'en] Shingi says, "Consider whether or not the temple property has been damaged." What is called not damaging the temple property is not to accept anything coming from those four wrongs or five wrongs. This is because those who eat from the four wrong or five wrong [livelihoods] have difficulty realizing right view.

The director should always avoid companionship with persons without the mind of the Way or associating with those who do not practice reflecting on the ancients. Intimacy with such people will impede the Way, and backsliding on the Way will promptly appear. One who has heart for the Way is a noble person of the buddha way. A person without the heart of the Way is a small person in the buddha way.

Zhuangzi said, "Everyone under heaven has some ardent desire. If their yearning is for benevolence and justice, worldly people call them noble persons. If their yearning is for material wealth, worldly people call them small persons."[117] Chen Xiuwen said, "Noble and small persons are titles for classifying people. Treading on the Way one becomes noble. Otherwise one becomes small." The buddha way is also like this. Whether with suffering or success, we must be persistently responsive to the mind of the Way. Therefore, hearing of former words and previous actions of the mind of the Way, make them today's innermost heart and eye pupil.

The director cultivates dharma decorum so that the dignified manners that have deteriorated will begin to flourish. The [Zen'en] Shingi says, "Outwardly obey the government laws; inwardly abide by the [monastery] regulations." The buddha ancestors' exalted assembly, the spiritual friends' monastery, is where the dharma law is solemnly observed and the respectful manner is maintained.[118] If decorum is not [actually] displayed, the Way becomes nonsensical. When decorum is not displayed, what is not decorum is called decorum; when the Way is nonsensical, what is not the Way is called the Way.

Chengjin of the Later Han dynasty was governor of Nanyang, but he only sat and chattered as if ignoring his duties. In three years much was accomplished. Although this was influence within the dusty [lay] society, it was a marvel for the world. We should realize that great accomplishments are not related to speaking or not speaking, or to exertion or lack of exertion. Such exertion is the most excellent. What is called most excellent is not acting except in accord with truth.

In the Han Chronicles the Emperor Cheng said, "Heaven created the masses of people but they were not able to regulate themselves, so a lord was elevated to govern with justice."[119] Buddhist temples are the same. Cloud-and-water monks were not able to regulate each other, so an abbot [shukuhanjū] was elevated to govern with justice.

Mozi said, "The ancients' righteousness was the same as heaven's. Because of this they chose a wise person when they established the [emperor as] Son of Heaven. As the Son of Heaven's wisdom and strength was not sufficient to govern all under heaven by himself, therefore three ministers were established beneath him." Now it seems that corresponding with these words, the buddhas imparted to each other and the ancestors correctly transmitted the establishment of guest and host, and respect for [the relationship of] teachers and disciples [as their assistants]. The [Zen'en] Shingi says, "Today temporarily we are guest and host, but till the end of our lives we shall be teachers and disciples."[120] This is the same meaning.

Whenever seeing the countenance of any monk from the ten directions, the director thereupon inwardly dances with joy and is delighted. The [Zen'en] Shingi says, "If their capacity for accepting monks is not generous and their heart of affection for monks is not warm, the director cannot protect the assembly." The Buddha told Ananda, "When bodhisattva-mahasattvas [great beings] dwell together, it is like seeing the World-Honored One. This is because they are my true companions. Like riding in a single boat, they study what I study." Therefore, the temple abbot, administrators, department heads, and all the monks should circulate the Buddha's instructions to live together and see each other as the World-Honored One. In the essential path of emancipation, nothing is more important than this.

The director instructs newly arrived monks. *The Sutra of the Three Thousand Deportments* says, "There are ten things to provide for newly arrived monks. First is to give them a room to rest in.[121] Second is to supply necessities. Third is to call on and greet them morning and evening. Fourth is to tell them about the customs and conventions of the region. Fifth is to teach them to avoid personal names [of the deceased, instead of their posthumous names].[122] Sixth is to tell them the routes for begging rounds.

Seventh is to tell them about what is required of monks [at that temple]. Eighth is to tell them what they should eat. Ninth is to tell them about prohibitions in the district laws. Tenth is to tell them where it is safe from muggers and thieves."

Also [*The Sutra of the Three Thousand Deportments*] says, "If donors come and say they want to make an offering, without having seen what it is, [the director] should not tell others about it." [*The Sutra of the Three Thousand Deportments*] also says, "There are five instructions to give the person who shops in the town. First, instruct them not to quarrel with people. Second, instruct them to buy pure goods. Third is not to disturb or intrude on anyone. Fourth is not to expect people to run around and serve them. Fifth is to be considerate of people's thinking." When having server monks or workers go to shop in town, first the director should explain in detail before sending them out.

Although the [*Zen'en*] *Shingi* talks about such ceremonies as Boys' Festival and the Festival of the Weaver, yet for the family style of the buddha ancestors I'm apprehensive about these worldly customs.[123] In remote mountains and hazy valleys, in reed-covered halls with brushwood doors, who could endure such elaborate preparations? Just simply to make offerings to the assembly and bring peace to the assembly, and not to look for faults and shortcomings of monks is the director's helpful mental attitude.

Now we are in the country of Japan, a distant, remote island, more than 110 thousand li [about 270,000 miles] away from the country of Buddha's birth. Since Buddha's passing into parinirvana it is about twenty-two hundred years.[124] Although we must truly grieve at being so remote in time from the sage, we can still rejoice to see monks and hear the Dharma. Engaging joyfully in our own diligent practice and requiting the benevolent virtue of the ancestors' essence, we expound the lofty deeds of [Wuzu] Fayan and consider the helpful attitude of [Fushan] Fayuan.

Inō [Supervisor of Monks]

The inō [a term derived] from the Sanskrit, here [in China] is called *yuezhong* [giver of joy to the assembly].[125] Generally, [the inō] supervises all the affairs of monks. Those newly arrived to hang up their belongings as residents in the assembly should be cared for with courtesy and esteem. Those who have worked elsewhere as temple administrators [*chiji*] and any noted virtuous monks should especially be assigned to a superior dormitory.[126] Former abbots retired from their temples should be assigned seat positions for meals in the monks' hall at the three head seats [*seidō, godō,* and *tantō*], according to the seniority of the histories in their record book as abbot or their documents of opening the hall.[127] Similarly, other reknowned, virtuous monks should be placed next to the three head seats according to their ordination age.

In the monks' hall in winter and summer, [the inō has the responsibility] to add or remove the woolen matting from the platforms, exchange the warm cloth curtains and the cool bamboo curtains at the entrances, and open up or shut the charcoal pit [behind the altar, for warming the hall]. A signboard with everyone listed in order of ordination age should be prepared before the summer practice period.

[The inō] should always have Manjushri's jisha prepare the incense and lamps at the altars and clean the offering trays in front of the hall before the assembly comes. The inō and the dōan assistants take care of the doorways and windows in the various monks' dormitories, and check the curtains [before the bedding cabinets] at each place on the sitting platforms. They also make sure that the various implements and supplies are in working order, and must always notice if they are kept neatly. If there is something broken or lacking, ask the director or the work leader [*shissui*] to replace it.

Together with the infirmary hall manager, [the inō] should have attendants take care of food, bedding, and other needs of sick monks, never allowing sick people to be neglected.[128] In the temple such positions as the department managers, the abbot's jishas, the infirmary hall manager, the charcoal pit manager, the study hall manager, the head monk, and the librarian are all recommended by the inō. When generous amounts of offering money are left at the buddha hall or other altar halls, the abbot appoints someone [to collect it].

If there is a violation of the rules, for serious matters, after getting the abbot's approval, expel the person from the assembly. For a minor matter only have the person change *ryō*, [i.e., work position and/or resting space]. If there is some troublesome dispute, it should be settled by having [the parties] courteously reconciled. If the two people quarreling do not bow [to the inō's mediation], then it should be judged according to the rules. If something is missing in the assembly and the person who lost it firmly demands a thorough inspection, then [the inō should] tell the monks and search the particular study room. If it is not found in the search, then that monk should leave the assembly or transfer rooms. If a lost item is not important, then [the inō] should try to persuade the person making the request to desist, and avoid troubling the assembly and retarding the spirit of the monastery.

When money is offered to the sacred image [of Manjushri in the monks' hall], it should only be for buying incense, lamps, and offering vessels, not used for other purposes.[129] When the offering box is opened, the money should be placed in the inō's keeping, and then together with Manjushri's jisha, [the inō] enters it in the accounts and uses it for expenses.

If there is something that concerns the government registry of ordination, [the inō] must wait for the authorities to announce their instructions and then put up a signboard declaring it.[130] Upon receiving a monk's personal history, [the inō] should check it with the government bureau. According to the current procedures and custom [of each temple and Chinese district], the temple pays money to register the monks.[131] Although submitting documents for certification is solely the director's duty to dispatch, if they come by way of the inō's office, of course consider them sincerely and in detail. The government bureau's documents of certification of the monks in residence all must be examined [by the inō] as to whether or not they are authentic. This should not be done carelessly or abruptly.

If a monk is sick the authorities should be informed. After the funeral for a dead monk, [the inō] quotes a price for the robes and belongings, and delivers back to the authorities the dead monk's ordination certificate or their document awarding a national teacher name and purple robe. The inō alone attends to all of this, and informs the director, who declares it to the authorities. Delivering to the authorities the public documents and the ordination certificate of the dead monk should be done within the official time limit.

[The inō] should hit the tsui chin and recite the dedication, identifying clearly and in detail [a donation of a meal] to support the donor's arousal of goodness.

Especially when serving tea to newly arrived [monks], no courtesy should be lacking. As soon as they arrive, their ordination date must be reported to the [abbot's] jisha, the temple administrators, the department heads, and the department where they are assigned. It is important to make known the level of seniority of their ordination age. (Some newly arrived monks sit in senior seats. The more recently ordained are in lower seats.)[132] [The inō] should have the study hall make for each new monk one nameplate for entering the hall and one nameplate of ordination age, to be posted or removed at the appropriate occasions. What is most important is not to make mistakes with either the seating positions for serving tea or the rotation for being study hall manager, which might upset and disturb the assembly.

For community work [*fushin*], all monks must participate equally except the study hall manager and the jikidō.[133] [Even] the abbot is not excused unless sick or meeting with official guests, and [if the abbot] does not proceed to work at once, their jisha must leave the temple.[134]

The inō job is called the delight of the assembly in China. Although [the position of inō] is the remains of Venerable Maudgalyayana, it is just like the majestic dignity of all the buddha tathagatas. So this is called [the inō's] regarding with love all who arrive and compassionately nourishing monks, so that the assembly's heart becomes the [inō's] own heart and the mindfulness of the Way becomes the [inō's] own mindfulness. Therefore [this attitude] can make parents into [nurturing] parents and can make children into [loving] children. In that case, [the inō] is just like the rudder of a boat crossing the great river or a long rainy spell after a great drought.

The Sutra of the Three Thousand Deportments says, "There are seven matters to welcome newly arrived monks with: first, as soon as they arrive, to inquire about their well-being [after their travels]; second, to give them a seat according to seniority; third, to provide them with a vacant room;[135] fourth, to provide bedding, a quilt, and a pillow; fifth, to provide lamps; sixth, to tell them the instructions for monks [at that temple]; seventh, to tell them the regional customs and conventions." Therefore, if you see a newly arrived monk, first ask whether or not they have practice equipment.[136] Then ask how far it is to their native place. Ask if their original [ordination] teacher is alive or not, then what temple they have just arrived from. After that, according to dharma [appropriately] get them settled.

Tenzo [Chief Cook]

The tenzo's job is to manage the great assembly's meals.[137] The tenzo must activate the mind of the Way, altering [the food] in accord with the time, to bring the assembly satisfaction, peace, and joy. Also the tenzo must not carelessly waste the temple's food ingredients. The whole kitchen must be checked in detail to prevent disorder and things being scattered about. Competent monks should be chosen for the kitchen crew. The tenzo's bearing should not be too severe, as that may disturb the monks. But also [the tone] should not be too relaxed, as laxity will bring mistakes in the work.

When food is prepared [the tenzo] must energetically manage it personally, [so that everything is] naturally clean and orderly. For putting ingredients together for lunch and breakfast, the combination of flavors must be considered and arranged after first deliberating with the director and temple administrators. Such foods as miso, vinegar, pickles, and dried vegetables must be prepared solely with the tenzo's direction, without any mistakes in their timing. Always [the tenzo] takes charge of lighting all the [kitchen] lamps and fires at the proper time.

Food donations must be shared as equally as possible. Anything concerning the director or work leader should be carried out only after deliberating with each of them, and [the tenzo's] arrangements must not intrude on their authority and disturb their work. If the stove, pots, or other utensils in the kitchen are old and damaged, [the tenzo] must replace them as needed.

Instruct the [kitchen] attendant monks [anjas] so they can work according to regulations. For serving in the monks' hall or offering [food] at the various dormitories, [the tenzo] must arrange to teach [the serving monks] in detail, so they will thoroughly know the prescribed procedures. When seeing senior teachers, the monks should bow and stand to the side. Select attendant monks who are bright and sharp to prepare and offer meals at the rooms of the abbot, temple administrators, and department managers [when they are not eating in the monks' hall]. Always observe the attendant monks from the various offices and consider whether or not they are too inflexible and dull to distribute the food. If the temple administrators or department managers want to be served again by a particular attendant monk, then respecting their authority, follow their wishes without stubbornly desiring to keep the usual [serving] rotation.

The tenzo's own meal is taken in the kitchen, but the food should not be different from that of the assembly. After preparing both meals, first offer incense and do prostrations toward the monks' hall before sending out the food.[138]

The *Zen'en Shingi* says, "For offering food to the assembly there is the tenzo." Since ancient times respected teachers with the mind of the Way have filled this position, and those not resembling this company [of accomplished masters] never were found in this position. In olden days teachers of the essence such as Guishan, Jiashan, Wuzhuo, and Jianyuan have served [as tenzo]. As for serving food to the assembly of monks, the *Zen'en Shingi* says, "Without being common or sacred, monks come together from the ten directions." Therefore at the monastery, cloud-and-water monks from all directions, whether mediocre or sage, are all served food prepared with excellence and abundance.

The tenzo obtains the ingredients for lunch and breakfast, each grain of rice and each stalk of vegetable being obtained through [all] the experience of the tenzo's own hands. This is the merit and virtue of the tenzo's fists.[139] Prepare [food] to feed the buddha ancestors; prepare it to offer the monks. Do not see how it is produced with the fleshy [common] eye. Do not measure where it belongs with mundane considerations. The virtue and blessing of the heavenly lord of creation and of a wheel-turning king do not surpass the virtue and blessing of a tenzo.[140] The rice and vegetables obtained by the tenzo, although not created in the past, present, or future, also are not like what comes simply from [either] the heaven, earth, or human realms.[141] They are obtained through raising the arms, and become intimate through picking them up. Therefore the tenzo has the job of offering the Way to the Way. It is the time of offering mind to the mind. Thus the tenzo always serves the community. Therefore the *Zen'en Shingi* says, "Receiving this food for the sake of attaining the Way you will repay the tenzo." So it is said that the giver and receiver equally attain the Way. For this purpose accept the food.

To enable the receiver to depart from wrongs, nothing is as good as food made by the tenzo. Therefore the Tathagata allowed Mahakashyapa to receive food with the monks [after he became aged.] Begging for food was like a case of obstructing the Way on this occasion.[142] Deeply understand that meals in the assembly of temples of the buddha ancestors are the supreme food. Therefore they have the same virtue as begging for meals.

When you get the ingredients for cooking the next day's breakfast and lunch, protect them as if they were as precious as your own eyes. Zen Master [Baoming] Renyong of Baoming Temple said, "Always guard temple property as your own eyes." Now I consider that we must guard temple property even more closely than our eyes. [It is said that Sharipuṭra] formerly gave his eyes to a Brahman and was greatly retarded [in his progress on the path].[143] The temple property should not be given to those outside the Way, so that we do not retreat on the Way. It must be revered just like food offered to the emperor.

While cooking, not to taste or sample salt, vinegar, oil, miso, and so on is the teaching about the food offered to the three treasures. When speaking of rice or vegetables, we speak with words of reverence. Do not [treat them] unceremoniously and harshly. Do not abuse rice, vegetables, or soup with crude, unsavory, or indecent language [while preparing them].

The *Zen'en Shingi* says, "When putting together ingredients and calculating flavors, before you settle on a combination discuss it with the director and other temple administrators." The tenzo should not proceed according to their own tastes, but must first entrust it to consultation with the administrators. Their agreement must be sought again and again, not done hastily. The temple administrators also must not make decisions based on their own personal inclinations. Just consult together using public mind [dedicated to everyone] and the mind of the Way.

As soon as agreement is reached, post the written menu on the special signboards at the various halls such as the abbot's hall, the monks' study hall, the hall for aged monks, and the residences for retired temple administrators and department managers. Have this written by a novice so that the various items for lunch and breakfast will be announced in detail.

After that, prepare the next morning's breakfast. When cleaning the rice and selecting the vegetables, do it with your own hands and personal inspection, with diligence and sincerity. Do not have a single negligent or careless thought, so that you oversee one matter and fail to oversee another. What this means is that [the tenzo] must add even a single speck of dust on top of the mountain of good actions, and must not give away even a single drop from the ocean of virtues.

The Sutra of the Three Thousand Deportments says, "There are five things to know about sorting or cleaning rice. First, by yourself examine the quantity. Second, do not have any grass or weeds mixed in. Third, remove any mouse droppings. Fourth, do not allow any rice bran. Fifth, carry this out in a clean place."

The *Zen'en Shingi* says, "The tenzo should not offer food to the community without the excellence of the six flavors and without the endowment of the three virtues." The six flavors are bitter, sour, sweet, spicy, salty, and simple. The three virtues [for food] according to the *Maha [Paranirvana] Sutra* are: first, being plain and soft; second, clean and pure; and third, [prepared] in accord with dharma.

Next sort out the rice and sand, watching for sand and rice minutely according to dharma. Xuefeng was tenzo when he was at Dongshan [Liangjie]'s temple.[144] One day when [Xuefeng] was cleaning rice, Dongshan asked, "Do you sift out the rice from the sand or sift out the sand from the rice?"

Xuefeng said, "I sift out the sand and rice at the same time."
Dongshan asked, "Then what will the great assembly eat?"
Xuefeng thereupon overturned the bowl.
Dongshan said, "After you leave you will meet and settle with someone else."

Ancient buddhas of the Way worked all the more diligently at this position with their own hands. How can the common flow of their successors and late arriving practitioners be aimlessly lax and negligent? If they are diligent in accord with the dharma, then even those today will be in the Way.

After washing the kettle add the ingredients for the meal, examining them clearly to be sure of their cleanliness. *The Sutra of the Three Thousand Deportments* says, "There are five things to teach people about cleaning rice. First, use a sturdy container. Second, use clean water. Third, rinse [the rice] by changing the water five times. Fourth, put it in a screened off [safe] place. Fifth, cover the top to keep it secure."

The *Zen'en Shingi* says, "When cooking food, you must intimately and personally look after it so that it will be natural and pure." After putting rice or vegetables in a pot on the stove, make certain that they remain well protected. Do not allow old mice to get in [the food], and make sure that people passing by do not examine or touch it. Even if using attendant monks or workers to keep an eye on it, the tenzo still must personally protect the food.

The Sutra of the Three Thousand Deportments says, "There are five points about washing pots. First is not to poke ladle handles sharply against the pot bottom. Second is to pour out the old, dirty water into a container that can be covered, before discarding it. Third is to fill [the pot] with water to the brim [for thorough washing]. Fourth is when it is clean, to cover it with a washed wooden lid. Fifth is to keep it covered tightly night and day." Utensils used in today's lunch must be put away properly. This is to say that rice buckets, soup pots, platters, and the various containers and utensils should be washed clean and wiped, and what belongs in high places should be placed up high, and those that belong in low places should be placed down low. High places are high level; low places are low level.[145] Wooden and iron ladles and bamboo chopsticks should all be placed neatly with sincerity and kept carefully, picked up and put down with a gentle touch.

Thereafter, for preparing tomorrow's lunch ingredients first sort the rice, removing insects, inedible beans, sediments or rice husks, grasses, and pebbles until it is cleaned and pure. Then store it in a clean place. Next select the next day's lunch soup and vegetables. *The Sutra of the Three Thousand Deportments* says, "There are five aspects to preparing vegetables. First, remove all the roots. Second, arrange them all [in order by size]. Third, never put green and yellow [i.e., withered, vegetables] together. Fourth, wash them clean. Fifth, put them all toward the fire [so as to cook evenly]." Knowing this you can arrange them to be cooked.

When the tenzo has prepared the rice and vegetables, the attendant monk chants sutras dedicated to the oven guardian deity.[146] The sutras chanted are: the chapter "Peaceful and Blissful Conduct" [from the *Lotus Sutra*]; the *Vajra Prajna* [*Paramita*; i.e., *Diamond*] *Sutra*; the "Universal Gate" chapter [from the *Lotus Sutra*]; the "Surangama Dharani"; the "Great Compassionate Heart Dharani"; the chapter on emptiness from the *Golden Radiance Sutra*; Yongjia's "Song of Enlightenment of the Way"; the *Admonitions of Guishan*; or the Third Ancestor's "Inscription on Faith in Mind."[147] Any of these sutras may be chanted according to the occasion [and available time, the merit of the chanting transferred and] dedicated to the guardian deity of the oven. The dedication goes, "We have chanted the [such-named] sutra." Further, "The merit and virtue of having chanted this sutra we dedicate to the true guardianship of the oven deity of this temple, to protect the dharma and bring peace to beings. [Thus we call on] all buddhas in the ten directions and three times, venerable bodhisattva-mahasattvas, mahaprajnaparamita." Ask a capable attendant monk to lead this chanting [and recite the dedication].

When the attendant monks prepare rice or vegetables, the tenzo must personally watch and carefully examine [the food]. Concerning the ingredients received from the director, the tenzo should not comment on their quantity or make judgments about their quality, but only prepare them with sincerity. Definitely avoid emotional contention about the quantity of the ingredients. To the end of the day and through the night diligently exert the Way. While boiling the gruel, steaming the rice, making the soup, or preparing the vegetables, the tenzo should not leave the kitchen. With clear eyes personally watch not to waste one grain and not to break one stalk.

The Sutra of the Three Thousand Deportments says, "For making soup there are five aspects. First is to add ingredients to the soup in proper sequence. Second is to make sure it is fully cooked. Third is to give it an agreeable flavor. Fourth is to watch it personally and make sure it is pure. Fifth, as soon as it is ready, remove the fire [i.e., the burning wood in the stove under the soup] and cover [the pot]."

If using an attendant or worker to steam the rice or make the soup, have that person light the fire. *The Sutra of the Three Thousand Deportments* says, "For making a fire there are five points. First, when building the fire do not insert the firewood crosswise, i.e., horizontally [but rather lengthwise in the stove front to back]. Second, do not use green firewood. Third, when heating the pot, do not let it fall down into the firewood. Fourth, do not blow on the fire with your mouth to fan it.[148] Fifth, do not keep the water boiling so that it boils over and extinguishes the fire."

When the rice is steamed and the soup is finished, then put the rice in a bamboo basket and the soup in a bucket and place them on the table. If you venerate the food according to dharma, then you will see the buddha ancestors and finally penetrate to Guishan and bump against Shishuang. Then the tenzo can pluck a single blade of grass and erect a sanctuary for the jewel king, and twirl a single atom and turn the great dharma wheel.[149] Therefore, providing water in the bucket and rice in the bowls is just like turning this food wheel or turning the dharma wheel.[150]

After putting the food on the table with reverence, when [the monks' hall] is ready, offer incense. Then facing toward the rice and soup table and the monks' hall, unfold the zagu and do nine prostrations; then pick up the zagu and bow, and then stand in shashu as the wooden fish [at the monks' hall; *hou*] is being struck. As the food is taken out, bow to the rice and soup. The tenzo follows after the food and proceeds to the hall if the lunch gathering is unusually large, in which case the tenzo, together with the kitchen monks, helps serve the meal. When serving do not put on the okesa, but tie up your robe [sleeves] and go to the monks' hall. For usual meals this is not necessary.

When tenzos are engaged in cooking, although they encounter coarse [ingredients] they should not arouse negligence; although they encounter delicacies they should be all the more diligent. Therefore, to fulfill these duties for one day and night is to delight in participating in practice.[151] Without the Great Teacher Shakyamuni's compassion and approval, how could one receive on one's own the merit and virtue of one day and night in this degenerate [age] and remote place, while toiling to prepare food for monks for an entire day? How much more [must we be grateful for one day of this job], having heard and been transmitted the skill of the Way in accord with dharma? If we had not flowed into the ocean of virtue of the three treasures, how could we perform such an activity?[152] How much more [is this so] for one year of this job? When doing this we are accordingly delighted in our self's merit and virtue. Appropriately enjoying our self's merit and virtue is exactly appropriate enjoyment of the merit and virtue belonging to buddhas.[153] Thereby we delightfully participate in the buddhas' radiance shining toward the tenzo. We must always set in our minds the former saying, to make [doing so with] respect and esteem the essence of the dharma for feeding monks.[154] Study minutely the significance of the tenzo entering the kitchen.[155]

Work Leader [Shissui]

The job of work leader is generally to take charge of arranging all the work in the temple.[156] They must conduct all repairs in the temple including dormitories, gates and windows, fences and walls, and all the daily work tools and equipment, and as the time requires, take care of repairs and replacements of decorations and ornaments. [The work leader] must take care of the grain mill, the fields and gardens, the workrooms and shops, the oil refining shop, the latrine tanks, the horse stables, boats and carts, general cleaning, and the sowing of seeds.[157] Circulating throughout the temple, [the work leader] must protect it by keeping out burglars, and must assign and supervise the various workers. All this must be managed with an attitude of serving everyone with strong effort, understanding when and knowing how [each task must be carried out]. If there are major repairs or significant projects, they should be conducted after consultation and getting the approval of the abbot, then conferring with the other temple administrators about the [work leader's] plan. They should not be done only according to [the work leader's] own viewpoint.

The work leader stays in the *kuin* [the kitchen and administrators' offices building], the same as the other temple administrators.[158] However, [the work leader] must always be attending to the work leader's shop and thoroughly review whether or not the workers have accomplished their tasks. Although the work leader's shop is inside the temple, it stands outside the eastern corridor [to the east past the kuin, which is along the eastern corridor], situated so that the sound of axes [chopping wood] does not reach the monks' hall, the dharma hall, the abbot's room, or the kuin.[159]

The Sutra of the Three Thousand Deportments says, "There are five things to teach people about chopping firewood. First is not to do it in pathways. Second is to start by making sure that the axe handle is secure and safely anchored. Third is not to chop green wood for firewood. Fourth is not to chop lumber disrespectfully from monuments.[160] Fifth is to pile up the wood in a place where it can dry."

A temple's water clock is placed in the work leader's shop, where two workers are in charge of it.[161] The work leader cares for and maintains the whole temple with increasing prudence and humility, without neglecting anything. They repair and replace temple property and equipment to keep it neat and shiny. Towards the common laborers and oven attendant workers, [the work leader] has an attitude of helping everyone, without any personal interests.[162]

The [*Zen'en*] *Shingi* says, "For work for the sake of the community of monks, there is the work leader." Therefore even before being informed by monks in the assembly, if there are things that are old and broken, the work leader should repair or replace them. The *Shingi* says, "For monks to be [practicing] peacefully in their quarters and value and protect the temple property is the reward of the work leader." The *Shingi* also says, "For a resident [monk] to receive and use something without thinking of [its use by] later people, is what is not rewarding for the work leader." Therefore, the work leader's efforts are the assembly of monks' efforts. The assembly of monks' rewards are the work leader's rewards. How could this [work leader's job] be only the spreading of conventional truth? How could this be only [something] received and used as a means [to get somewhere] along the road?

The previously enumerated items [throughout the "Pure Standards for Temple Administrators"] all grasp the noses of the ancient buddhas and are the eyes of former sages.[163] They cannot fail to be useful throughout past and present. They cannot fail to match the study and enlightenment of the Way. If the thighs and elbows [i.e., practical activities of daily life] are abandoned, then certainly the crown of the head will also be overthrown. Then how will there be a face to meet the buddha ancestors?

In the summer of the fire-horse year [i.e., 1246] of the Kangen Period [1243–1247], the fifteenth day of the sixth [lunar] month, this was composed by the monk Dōgen, founder of Eiheiji temple in Echizen [modern Fukui].

Notes

1. Nanda was a half-brother of Shakyamuni, both sons of King Suddhodana. After Shakyamuni left home, Nanda became the heir to the throne. "Actualized" here is *shō*, one of the characters used for enlightenment, implying certified or authenticated awakening.

In early and Theravada Buddhism, arhats are people who have attained the highest stage of enlightenment. They are also highly venerated in Zen as exemplars of awakening in the world. There are many groupings of different numbers of arhats, often depicted with eccentric or colorful qualities. Their independent spirit was seen as resonating in the character of Zen masters.

2. The *Womb Treasury Sutra* is *Taizōkyō*, the fifty-sixth of the 120 sutras in the *Maharatnakuta* [Great jewel heap] group of sutras, translated

into Chinese by Bodhirucci (572?–727). For a sampling of some of the others, see Garma C. C. Chang, ed., *A Treasury of Mahayana Sutras: Selections from the Maharatnakuta Sutra* (University Park: Pennsylvania State University Press, 1983). Kapilavastu was the city in Northern India where Shakyamuni grew up, and which was the capital of the Shakya clan.

3. "Ordained as a monk" is *jukai* [to receive precepts], a term used in Sōtō Zen for both lay ordination, *zaike jukai*, and home-leaving monk ordination, *tokudo jukai*.

4. Jambudvipa is the name for the Indian subcontinent in the old Indian cosmology.

5. Apparently Buddha met Nanda in the capital Shravasti, near the Jetavana Monastery where they were staying. The Eastern Garden [Purvarama], an adjunct of Jetavana Monastery east of Shravasti, was donated by Vishakha Mrgaramatr, a devoted female lay disciple of Buddha. Gandha Madana [Fragrance rapture] Mountain was north of the Himalayas in Indian cosmology, and was said to be filled with intoxicating scent.

6. In Buddhist cosmology, the Heaven of the Thirty-three [Trayastrimsa], is the abode of thirty-three Indian deities situated on the top of Mt. Sumeru, and is the second highest of the six heavens in the Realm of Desire [Kamadhatu]. The Pleasure Garden is one of the four gardens in the palace of Indra (*Taishaku Ten* in Japanese), which is in the center of this heaven.

7. "Pure conduct" is *bongyo* [*brahmacharya*], used in India for any religious practice, and also implying ascetic renunciation of desires, particularly including celibacy.

8. "Nirvana" here is *jakumetsu*, serene cessation. This is considered the goal of practice in Theravada Buddhism.

9. The "womb form" refers to the *Womb Treasury Sutra*, in which this story appears, and which describes the universe as the womb of buddhahood.

10. All indented sections of "The Pure Standards for Temple Administrators" are Dōgen's summaries and commentaries on the stories he is citing as examples, some of which are quoted verbatim from the sources and some of which are Dōgen's retellings.

11. "Perfuming refinement" refers to the cumulative positive effect of practice or training as its fragrance more deeply penetrates the mind. This teaching is particularly developed in the psychology of the Yogacara branch of Mahayana Buddhism.

12. "Director" here is *inju*, used the same as *kan'in*, which refers to the first three of the six temple administrators, originally one position.

13. "Director" here is *kansu*, which is assistant director when used for one of the six chiji, but here indicates the first three of the six temple administrators, the same as *kan'in* or *inju*.

14. Qingfeng Zhuanchu is also cited as Xuanze's former teacher in the version of this story in the commentary for case 17 of *The Book of Serenity*. See Thomas Cleary, trans., *The Book of Serenity* (Hudson, N.Y.: Lindisfarne Press, 1990), p. 72. However, in *Keitoku Dentōroku* [Jingde transmission of the lamp], a dialogue similar to this had occurred between Xuanze and Baizhao Zhiyuan. See volume 17 of *Keitoku Dentōroku* in *Taishō Shinshū Daizōkyō*, 51: 196–467. (Tokyo: Taishō Issaikyō Kankokai, 1924–1933).

15. "Fire boy" is *heiteidōji*, which also could be read, "fire-spirit's apprentice," referring to fire as one of the five elements in Chinese cosmology. The *heiteidōji* was the novice in the monastery who attended to the lamps.

16. Xuanze had only realized that the fire boy belongs to fire, not the necessity for him to actualize "comes seeking."

17. "Realization" here is *shō*, literally "see, examine, or reflect." It is commonly used in the Rinzai term *shōgo*, which refers to enlightenment opening experiences. Yangqi is the ancestor of all branches of modern Rinzai Zen.

18. "Director" here is *kusu*, yet another term for *kan'in* or *inju*, the first three of the modern six temple administrators.

19. "Old Lady" is the character for old woman or grandmother. Her exact relationship with Ciming is not clear in the story, but they were certainly good friends.

20. "Knowing this kind of affair" refers to the affairs that Yangqi managed as director, and also "the whole affair" of the one great matter of life and death.

21. "Greatly enlightened" is *daigo*, which is often contrasted to *shōgo*. Traditionally *daigo* is final, absolute enlightenment, contrasted to experiences of glimpsing enlightenment, *shōgo*. For Dōgen, *daigo* is being free from ideas about the distinction between enlightenment and delusion.

22. "Over there" refers to Old Lady Ciming's house, but also indicates the "other" side, as in enlightenment or the absolute. "You should just step aside," implies that everyone must follow the Way for themselves.

23. "Playing out in the mountain" is *yusan* [playing or wandering in mountains], a common Chinese and Japanese expression for going out to enjoy oneself. The text of this paragraph could be read literally as saying that Yangqi hit the drum as soon as Ciming departed, forcing him to return against his wishes. We have added interpolations in brackets, following the common Sōtō Zen commentaries on this story, which indicate that he hit the drum upon Ciming's return. This also is more in accord with Ciming's responses to Yangqi on the muddy path, which Yanqi had accepted.

24. Fenyang was Ciming's teacher.

25. *Nenju* [remembrance chanting], is a ceremony still held afternoons in Sōtō monasteries on days ending with a three or eight in the date. In this ceremony the names of buddha are chanted, and then all monks circumambulate the sōdō [in *jundō*] to reenact their entry into the monastery and refresh their intention. Commonly today this is followed by the *hōsan* procedure releasing the monks from the evening meeting. Apparently in Dōgen's time the evening meeting was still held after *nenju*.

26. "Community work" is *fushin* [everyone invited], a word still used in common Japanese for community work projects. During *fushin*, also called *samu*, everyone in the monastery, without exception, is expected to work. This tradition derives from Baizhang (see story after next), who is famous for saying, "A day without work is a day without eating." "North half" is the right side of the hall where the abbot sits, also called the "upper" half. In some temples the directions may be switched depending on the topography.

PURE STANDARDS FOR THE TEMPLE ADMINISTRATORS 185

27. "In the hall, [he] does not sit straight; how can he go to work on both sides?" is difficult. Not sitting [exactly] straight implies Manjushri's leaning slightly to one side or the other. Many Manjushri statues do so, because he sometimes sits on a lion, often with one leg down, or carries a raised sword or *Prajnaparamita* scroll in one hand. "Straight" also is a term for absolute wisdom, whereas leaning refers to the wisdom's relative function in the world. "Go to work" could also be read as "proceed to function energetically," implying the relative activity or function of the absolute, nondiscriminating wisdom, which is symbolized by Manjushri. "Both sides" could be read as "two heads." This rhetorical question implies a denial of one-sided dualism, i.e., how can he choose to work on only one side? In the context of the inō standing near the center of the sōdō, responding to the head monk's question, this utterance also implies an exhortation to all the monks to bring the spirit of Manjushri to all their activity, whichever side of the hall they are on, and whether they are in the hall or out working. The main point is that the absolute truth must actually be enacted freely in all of one's activity. An alternative reading might possibly be, "He does not truly sit in the hall." This might imply that Manjushri is already working everywhere, so he does not need to go anywhere to work.

28. "Going beyond dichotomies" here refers to experiencing the state of the absolute or unconditional nondualism, as contrasted with the relative, conditioned dualities.

29. Wuzu Fayan was also teacher of Yuanwu, compiler of the *Blue Cliff Record* [*Hekiganroku*]. "Leading disciple" is *jinsoku* [divine feet], also used for the supernatural power to go anywhere or transform oneself at will.

30. Kushan [Drum Mountain; *Kusan* in Japanese] is where Shigui taught and is buried. In the generation following Shigui, Kushan was a famous center of Buddhist publishing.

31. This is the story of how Guishan Lingyou later came to be master of Mount Guishan, so we will refer to him as Lingyou in this story. This entire section on Guishan, beginning, "One day he was standing" all the way to "Then Zen students from all over the country converged there" (before the next story) is almost a verbatim quote from *Keitoku*

Dentōroku [Jingde record of transmission of the lamp]. See the version in Chang Chung-yuan, *Original Teachings of Ch'an Buddhism* (New York: Vintage Books, 1971), pp. 200–202.

32. "This is only a temporary juncture" refers to the situation of digging out the fire of buddha nature from the fire pot (and from Lingyou). Baizhang goes on to discuss the locus of buddha nature in temporal, causal conditions, and also the necessity for Lingyou to proceed with his practice.

33. This is a paraphrase from the *Mahaparinirvana Sutra*, chapter 28 "The Bodhisattva Lion Roar."

34. This passage is discussed in detail in Dōgen's "Buddha Nature" chapter of the *Shōbōgenzō*. See Norman Waddell and Masao Abe, "Shōbōgenzō Buddha Nature," in *Eastern Buddhist* 8, no. 2 (1975): 102–5. The usual understanding of this statement is, "*When* the opportunity [or occasion] arrives, it is like the deluded suddenly enlightened . . ." However, Dōgen's reading, explicated in "Shōbōgenzō Buddha Nature," is: "The opportunity *has already* arrived, and it is like the deluded suddenly enlightened."

35. This quote is from the section on Dhrtaka, the fifth Zen ancestor in India, in *Keitoku Dentōroku*.

36. "Wandering ascetic" is *zuda*, from the Sanskrit *dhuta*, referring to ascetic practitioners. Originally the term referred to a set of twelve specific purifying practices—always remaining outdoors, only taking one meal daily before noon, never lying down, etc. Sima Chengzheng was a lay disciple of Mazu Dao-i, and so a Dharma brother of Baizhang, also Mazu's disciple. Sima was noted for geomantic skill that was useful in determining sites for temples. Sima had found Mount Gui and recommended it to Baizhang as an auspicious place for a monastery. A version of this story appears in the *Gateless Gate* [*Mumonkan*], case 40. See Yamada, *Gateless Gate*, or Thomas Cleary, trans., *No Barrier: Unlocking the Zen Koan, A New Translation of Mumonkan* (New York: Bantam Books, 1993).

37. These were originally geomantic terms, but as a result of this story, in modern Japanese Zen a "bony mountain" is a poor temple and a "fleshy mountain" is a large, rich temple.

38. High Priest Hualin Shanjue was an heir of Mazu, and therefore a younger Dharma brother of Baizhang. According to *Keitoku Dentōroku*, volume 8, when he later became abbot at Hualin, he once was asked by Prime Minister Pei Xiugong if he had any attendants. Hualin called out the names "Large Emptiness" and "Small Emptiness" and two tigers appeared. When Pei Xiugong became frightened, Hualin asked the tigers to leave for a while. They roared and departed.

39. "Go beyond status" refers to abandoning concern for self-serving or egoistic ambition. This foreshadows Linji's ideal of the "True person of no rank." It also implies going beyond any name or relative conception derived from cognitive discriminations.

40. "Practice hall" is *bon'u* [pure building], another word for temple in East Asian Buddhism. This passage might perhaps be read to mean that the people living at the foot of the mountain assembled together with Lingyou to build the practice hall.

41. A version of this story can also be found in the *Hekiganroku*, case 55; see Cleary, trans., *Blue Cliff Record*. According to the *Wudeng Huiyuan* [Five lamps merging at the source], Zhongxing visited Shishuang Qingzhu, also a Dharma heir of Daowu, five years after Zhongxing had left Daowu. Daowu had died in the interval.

42. Mount Wutai, one of the ancient holy mountains of China, is said to be the abode of Manjushri, bodhisattva of penetrating wisdom and insight. See Cleary, trans., *Blue Cliff Record*, case 35, for a previous encounter and dialogue between Wuzhuo Wenxi (a Dharma heir of Yangshan) and Manjushri on Mount Wutai.

43. Tianyi Yihuai became a Dharma heir of Xuedou, while Fushan finally became a Dharma heir of Shexian Guisheng. Later, he also saved the Caodong/Sōtō lineage from extinction by transmitting the Sōtō lineage from his deceased friend Dayang Qingxuan to his own student, Touzi Yiqing. See the glossary and the story after next about Touzi. For Fushan and Touzi, see Francis Cook, trans., *The Record of Transmitting the Light: Zen Master Keizan's Denkōroku* (Los Angeles: Center Publications, 1991), pp. 197–203.

44. "Visitors' room" is *tangaryō*, the place where traveling monks stay when visiting or before they are accepted into the sōdō. Tradition-

ally, for about a week before admittance to a monastery, Zen monks must sit still all day inside the tangaryō and also receive various instructions.

45. "Five-flavored gruel" uses various grains and spices, and traditionally was served in monasteries as a special treat only on Buddha's Enlightenment Day. Some modern Japanese monasteries serve breakfast gruel with milk instead of water on that day.

46. "Cloud-and-water monks," literally "cloud monks and water monks" refers to *unsui*, a common word for monks, implying that they wander freely through the mountains like clouds and rain.

47. Jiashan was already the Dharma heir of Chuanzi, the boatman, when he served as tenzo for Guishan. Chuanzi, a student of Yaoshan, lived in the world as a ferryman after the persecution of Buddhism in 842. After transmitting the Dharma to Jiashan, he overturned the boat and disappeared in the water.

48. "Year after year, the same single spring," in this context implies not deviating from the standard menu.

49. "A dragon lodges in the phoenix nest," may refer to the variety of particulars in the context of sameness. In "Instructions for the Tenzo" Dōgen encourages maintaining the same attitude toward different quality ingredients. In Chinese tradition, dragon's liver and phoenix marrow were extolled as great gourmet delicacies, mentioned as such by Dōgen in *Shōbōgenzō Zuimonki*, section 1–16. See Shohaku Okumura, trans., *Shōbōgenzō Zuimonki* (Kyoto: Kyoto Sōtō Zen Center, 1987), p. 53.

Dragons also represent flexible activity and function, as they fly freely. Phoenixes are known for their excellent and stately forms. Therefore Jiashan refers here to the integration of purity with active functioning necessary for a tenzo.

Although it probably is not the primary meaning in this dialogue, Jiashan's statement also might refer to the fact that he was heir to a different lineage than Guishan. Dōgen mentions this in his subsequent commentary. This interpretation is also suggested by a similar though contrasting line in the transmission poem given by the Rinzai lineage master Fushan (see immediately previous story) to Touzi (see the very next story), when the Sōtō lineage was saved from extinction. In that poem, perhaps adapting this earlier saying by Jiashan, Fushan says, "A golden phoenix lodges in a dragon's nest." See Cook, trans., *Record of Transmitting the Light*, p. 198.

50. A longer version of this story appears in Cook, trans., *Record of Transmitting the Light*, pp. 204–9; or Cleary, trans., *Transmission of Light*, pp. 194–199. "High Priest, kindly let me be," might be read grammatically from the Chinese as a statement rather than a request, i.e., "The high priest has kindly let me be (or freed me)." Cleary and Cook both read it this way. However, in Keizan's original, it is clearly a request, not a flat statement of fact, when he repeats the phrase. Although Keizan and traditional Sōtō school readings make this a request, we cannot be sure how Dōgen understood it or which was [Furong] Daokai's original meaning. However, both readings are included in the fundamental meaning of this story. Daokai's response implies that Touzi need not bother him because Daokai is already taking care of his job, and also indicates his gratitude to Touzi's compassion for teaching Daokai how to be free just to do his work. A point about the tenzo's practice in this story concerns the tenzo's responsibility to be constantly aware of all the matters involved in the kitchen.

Furthermore, the version of the dialogue given by Keizan in the context of the longer story includes the pronoun "he" ["kindly let him be"], which is not present in the version Dōgen gives here.

51. "The ancestral teachers' clear, bright meaning" is quoted from a dialogue between the famous adept Layman Pang and his daughter. See Ruth Fuller Sasaki, Yoshitaka Iriya, and Dana Fraser, trans., *A Man of Zen: The Recorded Sayings of Layman P'ang* (New York: Weatherhill, 1971), p. 75.

52. Huitang taught by raising a fist and saying, "If you call this a fist you've said too much. If you say it's not a fist you do not hit the mark."

53. "Free-standing pillar" may represent any inanimate object, i.e., one with no-mind, or beyond the mind of deliberation. "A boy or a girl?" tests if Shanku has truly, personally realized it.

54. "Temple administrators and department heads" are *chiji* and *chōshū*. Dōgen here indicates that pure intentions (as well as views of purity) without energetic function are not sufficient.

55. The "fire manager" was responsible for making and tending fires and maintaining the supply of firewood.

56. In the prior version of this story in "Instructions for the Tenzo," Dōgen said that Xuefeng was the tenzo during this episode, although here he calls him the "rice manager," a subordinate position in the kitchen. Either way, Xuefeng eventually served as tenzo at many monasteries, and finally became Dharma heir of Deshan, who was famous for aggressive teaching methods such as blows and shouts.

57. "Cover it" might indicate "putting a lid on" his own mouth out of courtesy, as well as thoroughly mastering the road of practice.

58. Moshan is Mount Mo, the name of the mountain where this temple was and the name she was also known by.

59. "Kaaa!" is an exclamatory shout known as *katsu*, literally, "to yell," used especially in the Linji tradition to induce or express awakening.

At times in early Buddhism, monks expressed the prejudiced notion that nuns would have to become male before they could be fully enlightened. "Gods and demons" are said to have less possibility than humans to fulfill practice, so her response implies that all humans, regardless of gender, are equally capable of awakening.

60. "Go up in the hall" is *jōdō*, to attend a formal lecture of the abbot, in which no text is used, although possibly starting off from a koan or phrase from a sutra.

61. "Recite dedications" is *ekō*, done after all chanting to dedicate and transfer the resulting merit and benefit to all beings. *Ryūten* [dragon heavenly being] is a nature spirit who helps control weather to avoid natural disasters. *Dōji* [land] is a protector spirit of grounds and buildings. Traditionally, all monks in training keep a scroll dedicated to Ryūten and Dōji as guardians and honor it in their personal services. The scroll is opened, hung, and given offerings the first three days of the new year.

62. "Head monk" here is *zagen*, another word for *shuso*, or someone who has been shuso, also called "first seat."

63. One *cho* is 109 meters.

64. Wu and Yue are ancient names for modern Jiangsu and Zhejiang provinces. "Great wind" is said to be a reference to Fengxue Yen-

zhao, whose name means "wind cave." He was three generations after Linji, a successor of Nanyuan Huiyong. Since Nanyuan means "South Temple" he is indicated by "heading south" in Yangshan's statement. All later Rinzai teachers derive from this lineage. It seems a bit strange if this prediction were the only meaning of Yangshan's statement and this dialogue. It may have been added later to the source story Dōgen refers to, in praise of a particular later branch of the Linji lineage. Yangshan is considered to have had prophetic powers.

65. Generosity, kindness, and blessing are all translations of *on*, a traditional Japanese social concept that implies some benefaction in which one incurs a natural response of obligation. Out of gratitude and consideration for those in both the distant past and future, Linji just planted trees in the remote mountains without knowing if they would ever grow.

66. Accountant is *kanshu*, a lesser position under the director [*kan'in*].

67. "Property manager," *sōshu*, is the manager of the fields and minor temple buildings. The term is no longer used.

68. "Age of decreasing" refers to the Buddhist theory, stated in the *Abhidharma Kosha*, that human lifespan was once eighty thousand years and decreases one year every century. The lifespan will start to increase again when it falls to ten years.

69. "Everyday activities" is *sashu kyaku*, literally, "using your arms and legs." "Peaceful" is *odayaka* [calm, quiet, peaceful] and here refers to nirvana.

70. The *Shitsu* (*Shishi* in Japanese) is a book of philosophy by a writer of the same name from the Warring States Period (fourth century B.C.E.). The Yellow Emperor was a legendary ruler of Chinese antiquity who is said to have invented written characters, the calendar, music, and medicine. Yao and Shun were also legendary emperors of ancient China.

71. "Construction projects," *domoku*, literally, "earth and wood," is a common term for engineering as well as building projects.

72. "Good dharma," *byakuhō*, literally, "white dharma," is commonly used in Chinese Buddhism for "wholesome activity" [Sanskrit: *kusala dharma*]. "Bad karma," *kokugō*, literally, "black conduct," is activity that produces suffering.

73. A long initial part of this section is a direct quote of the entire discussion of the kan'in from *Zen'en Shingi*, as is also the case for the following sections on the inō, the tenzo, and the work leader. "Temple" here is *inmon*, "temple gate," one of the many terms used for a temple.

74. These annual ceremonies had particular foods associated with their feasts, for example adzuki beans for the winter solstice. Some of these festivals are still commonly celebrated in China and Japan. In modern Japan there is a girls' festival (on the third day of the third month) as well as the boys' festival. The Festival of the Weaver is based on a romantic myth about two constellations, a boy shepherd and a girl weaver, which meet once a year on this night. The monks' hall furnace was a fire pit located behind the altar in the sōdō, used for some warmth in the winter. *Rōhatsu* is commemorated in the modern era as the culmination of the year's most intense *sesshin*, seven days (or at some other times three or five days) of concentrated zazen practice. In Dōgen's time there was sufficient daily zazen to make such special sesshin periods unnecessary.

75. "Novice monks" is *zun'an*, children raised in the monastery, possibly preparatory to ordination. "Skillful means" is *hōben*, in Sanskrit *upaya*, the traditional Mahayana methodology of conveying the truth appropriately to all various beings with their diverse needs and conditioning. This is especially elaborated in the *Lotus Sutra*.

76. "Administrators' office building," which includes the kitchen as well as roku chiji offices, here is *kudo*, also called *kuin* or *kuri*.

77. "Attendant monk" is *anja*. This seems to indicate dismissal of a monk for improprieties in their work rather than for general violations of temple regulations.

78. Throughout most of Chinese and Japanese history, monks could only be ordained by permission of the government, and usually positions and promotions within the monastery were supervised, at least indirectly, by government officials. This was necessary because monks and temples were tax exempt, and also received significant material support from the government. Obviously this impaired the ability of Buddhist institutions to criticize significantly the established social order.

79. Most of these terms are no longer in use. The "fund-raiser," *gaibō kesshu*, solicited donations from patrons and provided for supplies. Property manager is *sōshu*. Charcoal manager, miso manager, and gruel manager are, respectively, *tanjū*, *shōju*, and *shukujū*. The *Prajnaparamita Sutra* and *Kegon* [*Avatamsaka*] *Sutra* lecturers went to donors' homes to recite and lecture on these sutras and receive donations. They also possibly may have been custodians of those sutras in the temple library. Bath attendant is *yokusu*. The water manager, *suijū*, was responsible for carrying and supplying water throughout the temple. The garden manager, *enju*, is described in detail by Dōgen after the story about Guanzhi Zhixian and Moshan. For mill manager, *majū*, see the previous story about Wuzu Fayan. The lamp manager, *tōju*, took care of lamps and lamp oil.

80. "Function cooperatively" refers to activity and attitude that accepts everyone as fundamentally the same. It is the last of the four integrative modes of bodhisattva practice, the others being generosity, loving speech, and beneficial action. Dōgen discusses these in *Shōbōgenzō Shishōhō*. See translations in Thomas Cleary, trans. *Shōbōgenzō: Zen Essays by Dōgen* (Honolulu; Univ. of Hawaii Press, 1986), pp. 116–20; and in Kazuaki Tanahashi, trans., *Moon in a Dewdrop: Writings of Zen Master Dōgen* (San Francisco: North Point Press, 1985), pp. 44–48.

81. "This is important . . . are not disrupted" is not clear, but seems to refer to the director's absence as affecting the regular schedule of serving monks who might have to serve extra meals to the director.

82. "Sincerity of their practice" is *bongyō*, or pure conduct.

83. "For the many other affairs . . . watch [how] they succeed" is the end of the section quoted from *Zen'en Shingi*. What follows, beginning with "The director's job is fulfilled for the sake of the public," is Dōgen's commentary on the director position.

84. "Contemplating the ancients" is *keiko*, an important term for Dōgen. It refers to practice modeled on study of and reflection on the ancient sages and their standards. In modern Japanese it is a common term for practice of arts and sports, as in practicing tea ceremony, practicing the piano, or practicing karate.

85. "Determination" is *nen*, which also means mindfulness or remembrance, as in *nembutsu* or *nenju*.

86. Devadatta was Shakyamuni Buddha's cousin, who after joining his order tried to become his rival and even tried to have the Buddha killed. Wickedness refers to the five heinous crimes: killing one's mother, father, or an arhat, shedding a buddha's blood, or encouraging contention in the community.

87. In Dōgen's time and also today, all Zen practitioners are descendants either of Yaoshan or of Fenyang, who was early in the Linji/Rinzai lineage. Yaoshan was the teacher of Yunyan, who was the teacher of Dongshan Liangjie, the founder of the Caodong/Sōtō lineage that Dōgen inherited in China.

88. "Reflecting that inhalation does not wait for exhalation" implies impermanence, i.e., that each breath may be our last, and also implies the experiential immediacy and suchness of each event.

89. "Loyalty" is literally "filial piety." "Demonic inclination" is *mato*, literally, "the demons' faction," i.e., those who are possessed by the demons of ego and so are blind to reality. "Lacking the requisite faith for entering practice" is *sendai*, short for *issendai*, which is the standard Japanese transliteration of the Sanskrit word *icchantika*. This is a traditional Indian Buddhist term for beings understood as completely devoid of buddha nature and therefore incapable of enlightenment. It was later interpreted to mean those who were completely lacking in faith but who might possibly later develop some capacity for practice.

90. The quote, "People without faith . . ." is from the early *Ekottara Agama* [Anguttara Nikaya; *Zōitsu Agonkyō* in Japanese].

91. The quote, "The great ocean . . ." is from the *Avatamsaka Sutra* ["Flower ornament"; *Kegon Kyō* in Japanese], in chapter 12 on the bodhisattva Kenju, "Chief in Goodness." See Cleary, *Flower Ornament Sutra* 1: 330–67.

92. Sanghanandi is recognized as the seventeenth Indian ancestor in the Zen lineage. See Cook, *The Record of Transmitting the Light*, pp. 93–97; or Cleary, *Transmission of Light*, pp. 75–80. "Persevering faith" is *shishin*, sincere or complete faith that reaches the ultimate. "Right mindfulness" is *shōnen*, one of the practices of the eightfold noble path taught by Shakyamuni.

93. "Suchness," or ultimate reality, is *shinnyo*, tathata in Sanskrit.

"Supernatural powers" is *jinriki*, unusual psychic capacities resulting as a by-product of practice. Sanghanandi's quote is from the *Keitoku Dentōroku*.

94. "The four upside-down views" are false views involving the denial of the realities of impermanence, suffering, lack of inherent self, and impurity. The three poisons are greed, hate, and delusion.

95. "Mountains and fields" refers to sincere people doing hidden practice as hermits, or possibly working secretly in the world.

96. "Helpful mental attitude" is *shinjutsu*, literally, "mind art, technique, or skillfulness."

97. "Monastic practice" is *soseki*, literally, "monastic seats or places."

98. "Studied widely" or "all-inclusive study" is *henzan*, a term for the traditional practice of a monk's traveling to visit different teachers to test the monk's own (and the teachers') awareness. "Henzan" is the name of one of the chapters in Dōgen's *Shōbōgenzō*, in which he indicates that to study widely [*henzan*] is to study oneself widely. See Tanahashi, *Moon in a Dewdrop*, pp. 197–202.

99. The ancient striking gold is a story from volume 3 of the Sixth Dynasty collection *New Stories of Worldly Opinions* [*Sesetsu Shingo* in Japanese] by Liu Yiqing (403–44; Ryū Gikei in Japanese).

100. "Patronage" is *kie*, literally, "to take refuge," as in taking refuge in buddha, but here referring to the conversion and sincere patronage of socially powerful followers. Historically in China and Japan many Buddhist priests had royal disciples, which Dōgen here warns against as a form of worldly benefit or advantage.

101. "Worldly people" is *zoku*, also called *sezoku*, which also refers to laypeople as opposed to monks. Historically in China and Japan laypeople were often sincere and devoted believers and patrons, but were not always active as practitioners of meditative disciplines, as are many contemporary Western laypeople.

102. Vast Benefit Zen Temple on Ayuwang Mountain is the same temple where later resided the tenzo Dōgen praises in "Instructions for the Tenzo."

103. Official Bao lived 999–1062.

104. "Blessing in the unknown realms after death" is *meifuku*, a

common term still used in association with priests' memorial ceremonies. This *mei* means dark, unknown, or unseen.

105. *The West Lake Extensive Record* is *Xihu Kuangji* in Chinese, *Saiko Kōki* in Japanese. *Zen Gate Jeweled Instructions* [*Chanmen Baoxun* in Chinese, *Zenmon Hōkun* in Japanese] is a collection of stories compiled by the famous Linji lineage teacher Dahui and by Zhu'an Shigui.

106. "The jewel in the topknot" refers to a story in the *Lotus Sutra* in which this jewel represents the most precious teaching, given only to the most worthy. See Hurvitz, trans., *Scripture of the Lotus Blossom of the Fine Dharma*, pp. 218–19.

107. The *Luzhi Chunqiu* (Spring and fall annals of the Lu clan, *Ryoshi Shunju* in Japanese), compiled by Fouwei (d. 235 B.C.E.; Ryohui in Japanese), is a collection of stories of ancient sages. Emperor Yao was a legendary emperor of ancient China. Xuyu is Kyoyu in Japanese.

108. This quotation is from chapter 8 of the *Zen'en Shingi*, "One Hundred Twenty Questions," which describes problems to check for in one's practice.

109. "Right view" is *shōken*, one of the practices of Shakyamuni's noble eightfold path.

110. The Ekottara [Increasing by one] Agama corresponds roughly to the Anguttara Nikaya [Gradual sayings] of the Pali canon.

111. "The blessing field" is an image of the activity of cause and effect, fruits growing from small seeds. Dōgen elsewhere emphasizes the distinctive importance of the belief in cause and effect taught in Buddhism.

112. "Subsistence" here is *shoku*, also commonly meaning to eat, food, or livelihood, and variously translated as such according to context in the following passage. The four wrong livelihoods and the five wrong livelihoods are both from the third chapter of the *Mahaprajnaparamita Commentary* [*Daichido Ron* in Japanese] attributed to Nagarjuna.

113. Directive in "directive wrong" is *kata*, whose meanings include direction, side, method, or person, here implying transmitting messages in many directions.

114. "Fortune-telling and geomancy" in the second wrong is *bokusō*, referring to divination using palm or face reading or geomantic

techniques based on landscape and spatial configuration. "Divination techniques" in the third wrong is *jussu*, referring to divination using astrology or the Chinese five-element or *I Ching* systems. These are both old terms, not in modern use.

115. This fourth wrong livelihood concerning agriculture is obviously anachronistic, as the proscription against agriculture in Indian Buddhism, quoted here, was changed in China and Japan, particularly amongst the Zen communities, which survived by becoming relatively self-sufficient. Dōgen praises the practice of the garden manager earlier in the "Pure Standards for Temple Administrators." Such anachronisms apparently do not interfere with Dōgen's respectful citing of earlier Indian sources.

116. "Spiritual friends" is *chishiki*, a word that may mean teacher, and which has sometimes been translated as such heretofore in this work, but also has the meaning, as in this case, of spiritual friend or guide. It is used as a translation of the Sanskrit term *kalyana mitra*. "Right livelihood" is *shōmyo*, one of the practices in the noble eightfold path of Shakyamuni.

117. Zhuangzi is the name of a book and its writer, highly eminent in early Taoist philosophy and in Chinese literature. See Burton Watson, trans. *The Complete Works of Chuang Tzu* (New York: Columbia University Press, 1968). "Ardent desire" is *jun*. It also implies great sacrifice, such as that by retainers who loyally follow their lords into death via suicide. "Noble person" is *kunshi*, implying a wise, respected person of honor.

118. "Dharma law," *hattō*, is a common term for social legal codes. The second character of this compound here means degree or measure, although in other contexts it can mean time, extent, or to save or "bring across," a term used for salvation in Buddhism.

119. The *Han Chronicles* are *Hanshu* (*Kanjo* in Japanese), a 120-volume history of the Early Han compiled in the Later Han dynasty. The Emperor Cheng reigned 32–9 B.C.E. as the eleventh emperor of the Early Han dynasty.

120. For this quote from *Zen'en Shingi*, see also "Regulations for the Study Hall," note 6, where Dōgen paraphrases this as "we will be buddhas and ancestors."

121. The three thousand in the name of *The Sutra of the Three Thousand Deportments* derives from a bhikshu's approximately two hundred fifty regulations multiplied by four for the positions of walking, sitting, standing, and lying to make one thousand; and then multiplied by three for past, present, and future to make three thousand. This sutra was translated into Chinese by An Shigao, who came to China from Central Asia in 148 C.E.

"A room to rest in" is literally a room to remain secluded in, or a private room. This reflects the practice in India, where the sutras originated, of monks practicing in individual rooms. Such practice is still followed in South Asia, but in China and Japan, in Dōgen's day and today, obviously sōdō style practice does not involve such private space. A newly arrived monk might instead be shown a space for resting in the shuryō, or study hall. Other items in this list of ten, particularly the third, may also anachronistically refer to Indian-style practice rather than that which Dōgen specifies in *Eihei Shingi*, although some items seem more particular to China and Japan.

122. "Avoiding personal names" seems to refer to the former common practice, at least in China and Japan, of only using the posthumous, sacred names given at funeral services when referring to deceased persons. The Chan literature also speaks of taboos against using the emperor's name.

123. For "such ceremonies as Boys' Festival and the Festival of the Weaver," see p. 153, which is from the long opening quotation from the *Zen'en Shingi*. This is a rare occasion of Dōgen clearly criticizing one of the source texts he quotes for monastic procedures, which reflects his vantage point in the "remote mountains and hazy valleys" around Eiheiji, distant from worldly customs and ceremonies.

124. "Parinirvana" is *metsudo*, literally, "extinction and crossing over," referring to a buddha's passing into the ultimate state of nirvana upon death. Our current understanding of history contrasts sharply with the view in Dōgen's time, as does our understanding of geography and the distance between Japan and India. Today we believe that this writing of Dōgen's was written only about 1730 years after Shakyamuni's death in the 480s B.C.E., five centuries later than Dōgen's con-

temporaries had calculated (although some modern scholars believe Shakyamuni's death was even another century later).

125. The opening section of this discussion is a quote of the entire description of the inō position from the *Zen'en Shingi*. The word *inō* derives from the Sanskrit *karmadana*, literally "bestower of conduct" [*karma*], i.e., the one who assigns activities to monks. The *i* of inō comes from the Chinese, meaning "oversee"; while the *nō* of inō is used to transliterate the *na* of karmadana. *Yuezhong* [*esshu* in Japanese] was used as a Chinese translation for the inō position, and means, literally, "joy or delight to the assembly."

126. "Dormitory" is *ryō*, as in the shuryō, or monks' study hall. These ryō refer to spaces in which monks who sleep in the sōdō may study or take breaks; to work spaces or offices for various positions and their staffs (e.g., the tenzo ryō or inō ryō); or sometimes, as in this case, to dormitory spaces where senior monks sleep as well as study. Sometimes ryō also refers to the staff itself of a certain position rather than to a work space, e.g., sometimes "tenzo ryō" refers to the kitchen workers.

127. "The seniority of the histories" refers to records of Dharma age by ordination date, date of being head monk, and dates of being abbot. "Record book as abbot," *jūjichō*, and "documents of opening the hall," *kaidōshō*, are both formal, official documents used as resumés by former abbots. The kaidōshō is recited at an abbot's installation ceremony.

128. "The infirmary hall" is *enjudō*, literally, "the hall for prolonging longevity." While in the enjudō, monks do not participate in any other temple activity.

129. "Money offered to the sacred image" probably refers to donations left by laypeople at the monks' hall; but it might also refer to a practice in which the monks themselves donate money for lamp oil after making some mistake, either in performing ceremonies or in caring for temple property. We are not sure if this practice, still continued in some traditional Japanese monasteries, dates back to Song China and the *Zen'en Shingi*.

130. "The government registry of ordination" is *daisōchō* [great priest registry], which was the Chinese government official record of monk

ordination. All ordinations were approved by the government. Some Sōtō commentators understand this as especially referring to abbots or other high priests. If so, this sentence indicates waiting for government authorities' judgment in the event of questionable conduct by an abbot.

131. Monks' registration with the Chinese government had to be renewed, usually every three years. In the Song dynasty, beginning in 1145, tax money had to be paid for each monk in lieu of military service.

132. "Some newly arrived . . . in lower seats" is a bracketed section in *Zen'en Shingi*, probably indicating that it was added to the original text for clarification, possibly in the early Shohon version, as in previous passages with parentheses. (See "The Textual History of *Eihei Shingi*" section of the introduction.)

133. "Community work" is *fushin* here. The *jikidō* was the person assigned, in turns, to cleaning and taking care of the monks' hall, and who remained in attendance in the hall when all the other monks were elsewhere. In modern times they also carry the *kyōsaku* stick and ring the wake-up bell each morning in between practice periods (during which the head monk does so).

134. The clause "jisha must leave the temple" is the end of the *Zen'en Shingi* discussion of the inō. What follows is Dōgen's brief commentary. The jisha is responsible for keeping the abbot's schedule.

135. This list of ways for the inō to welcome new monks from *The Sutra of the Three Thousand Deportments* parallels the similar list given above for the director. As indicated in note 121, the "vacant room" reflects the practice in India.

136. "Practice equipment" may refer to all or some of the traditional eighteen practice utensils monks are supposed to carry when traveling. These are a toothbrush; soap; three sets of robes (including okesa); a drinking flask; eating bowls; a zagu (bowing mat); a staff with a metal ring top; an incense burner; a water filter; a hand towel; a knife; matches; tweezers; bedding; sutras; a Vinaya regulations text; and buddha and bodhisattva images. See Buddhist Text Translation Society, *The Buddha Speaks the Brahma Net Sutra*, p. 44.

137. The first part of the tenzo section is the entry about the tenzo from the *Zen'en Shingi*.

138. The phrase "before sending out the food" is the end of the *Zen'en Shingi* instructions for the tenzo. Some parts, though not all, of Dōgen's ensuing comments are quotations or paraphrases from the "Instructions for the Tenzo."

139. "All the experience . . . [and] the tenzo's fist" implies that the work of the tenzo is accomplished as a result of the tenzo's whole karmic experience.

140. "The heavenly lord of creation" is the Indian creator god Indra (*Taishaku Ten* in Japanese). "A wheel-turning king" (*chakravartin* in Sanskrit) is a virtuous world ruler. It was predicted of Shakyamuni that he would become one if he did not enter the spiritual path.

141. "Heaven, earth, and human realms" refers to a standard expression in Chinese cosmology for the spiritual, natural, and human societal aspects of the universe.

142. Mahakashyapa had been practicing austerities alone in the forest, living on what he obtained in begging rounds. When this became difficult due to age, Shakyamuni allowed him to share the offerings of the other monks, without begging himself.

143. This story about a former life of Shariputra, one of the ten great disciples of Shakyamuni who was especially noted for wisdom, is from the *Mahaprajnaparamita Commentary* (*Daichido Ron* in Japanese), attributed to Nagarjuna.

144. For this story see "Instructions for the Tenzo" page 35, and "Pure Standards for Temple Administrators," page 144 above. The Chinese ideograms here are exactly the same as in the "Instructions for the Tenzo" version, although we are giving a slightly different possible English reading.

145. For the saying, "High places are high level; low places are low level," see the story about Yangshan and Guishan in "Instructions for the Tenzo," note 8, page 51.

146. For the oven guardian deity, Zaogong (Sōkō in Japanese), see "Instructions for the Tenzo," note 9, page 51.

147. Most of these texts are still regularly chanted in Japanese Zen monasteries. "Peaceful and Blissful Conduct," chapter 14 of the *Lotus Sutra* ("Comfortable Conduct" in Hurvitz, *Scripture of the Lotus Blossom*

of the Fine Dharma) is now only chanted occasionally. The *Diamond Sutra*, which inspired the Sixth Ancestor Dajian Huineng's awakening, remains highly popular. The "Universal Gate of Avalokiteshvara (Kanzeon) Bodhisattva" ("Fumonbon" in Japanese), chapter 25 of the *Lotus Sutra*, is very popular. It is considered a separate sutra and still chanted daily. The "Surangama Dharani" ("Ryōgonshu" in Japanese), is a long section of the *Surangama Sutra*. The "Great Compassionate Heart Dharani" ("Daihi Shin Dharani" in Japanese), is also chanted daily. The chapter on emptiness is chapter 25 from the *Golden Radiance* [*Suvarnaprabhasa*] *Sutra* (*Konkōmyō Kyō* in Japanese), no longer commonly chanted. Yongjia Xuanjie is famous for becoming a successor to the Sixth Ancestor after spending only one night at his temple. Yongjia's "Song of Enlightenment [or Verification] of the Way" ("Shōdōka" in Japanese), remains a popular Zen text. See for example, Master Sheng-Yen, *The Sword of Wisdom; Lectures on "The Song of Enlightenment"* (Elmhurst, N.Y.: Dharma Drum Publications, 1990). Guishan [Lingyou]'s "Admonitions" are still commonly studied but not usually chanted. The popular "Inscription on Faith in Mind" ("Shinjinmei" in Japanese), is attributed to the Third Ancestor Jianzhi Sengcan. See for example Sheng-Yen, *The Poetry of Enlightenment: Poems by Ancient Ch'an Masters* (Elmhurst, N.Y.: Dharma Drum Publications, 1982).

148. "Heating the pot, do not let it fall down into the firewood," is our interpretation of an unclear phrase that literally seems to say, "Heating the pot, do not turn the firewood upside down." Instead of blowing on the fire with your mouth, and maybe getting burnt, usually a bamboo tube is used for blowing, which is also more efficient.

149. The story about venerating rice, involving Guishan and Shishuang Qingzhu not wasting a single grain, is given above in the "Pure Standards for Temple Administrators," see page 144. "Pluck a single blade of grass and erect a sanctuary for the jewel king," previously mentioned in "Instructions for the Tenzo," refers to the story related in case 4 of the *Book of Serenity*. "As the World-Honored One was walking with the congregation, he pointed to the ground with his finger and said, 'This spot is good to build a sanctuary.' Indra, Emperor of the gods, took a blade of grass, stuck it in the ground, and said, 'The sanc-

tuary is built.' The World-Honored One smiled." See Thomas Cleary, trans., *Book of Serenity*, pp. 17-19.

In "pluck a single blade" and "twirl a single atom" the same Chinese character is used to mean "pluck" and "twirl."

150. "Turning the food wheel or turning the dharma wheel" could indicate either the tenzo's activity as turning the wheels, or the wheels just turning on their own. Also this might be understood as the food wheel being the same as the dharma wheel, or also as the food wheel causing the dharma wheel to turn.

151. "Delight in participating in practice" is *zuiki*, a term in Buddhism for the joy of participating in beneficial activity, including ceremonies and other practice activities. It is derived from the *Lotus Sutra*, chapter 18, "The Merit of Appropriate Joy," which describes the zuiki [appropriate joy] of the bodhisattva upon hearing the Dharma or upon seeing others' good deeds or resultant happiness. In the sutra, the bodhisattva Maitreya says in a gatha, "After the World-Honored One's passage into extinction, / If there is one who hears this scripture / And if he can rejoice appropriately [*zuiki*], / How much happiness shall he obtain?" Hurvitz, *Scripture of the Lotus Blossom of the Fine Dharma*, p. 258. In the following passage of the text, according to context we have translated *zuiki* as "accordingly delighted," "appropriately enjoy," "appropriate enjoyment," or "delightfully participate."

152. "Perform such an activity" indicates the meaning of accomplishing this job for one day, but at the same time it also could be read more deeply as "fulfill suchness."

153. "Appropriately enjoying our self's [or our own] merit and virtue" recalls the central teaching in Dōgen's writings on meditation of *jijuyū zammai*, the samadhi [concentration] of self-enjoyment or fulfillment. As exemplified in this paragraph, Dōgen's teachings in *The Pure Standards for the Zen Community* emphasize the satisfaction and fulfillment of jijuyū samadhi right in the midst of everyday activity. See the section entitled "Jijuyū Zammai" in Shohaku Okumura, *Dōgen Zen* (Kyoto: Kyoto Sōtō Zen Center, 1988).

154. "Make respect and esteem ... feeding monks" is from the *Zen'en Shingi*, vol. 10.

155. "The tenzo enters the kitchen" is from the sayings of Luohan Guichen, the teacher of Fayan Wenyi, founder of the Fayan lineage.

156. The first paragraph of this section is the instructions for the work leader in the *Zen'en Shingi*, which is followed by Dōgen's comments.

157. "Latrine tanks" is literally "containers in the back." The latter term may refer to septic tanks, or possibly to livestock feed tanks.

158. "The work leader stays in the *kuin*" is the beginning of Dōgen's own discussion of the work leader after the section from the *Zen'en Shingi*.

159. The major, central buildings of traditional Zen monasteries, including the monks' hall, dharma hall, buddha hall, abbot's room, kuin, founder's hall, toilets, bathhouse, and main gate, are all connected by corridors and are laid out in a prescribed arrangement, in a rectangle usually on a north-south axis (see diagram, p. 59).

160. "Monuments" refers to tall, square pieces of wood used as memorials, as in cemeteries, or as monuments throughout temple grounds for various occasions.

161. The water clock was a vessel with a small hole in the bottom from which water slowly leaked. A marked measuring stick placed perpendicularly in the vessel gave indications of passage of time. The bell signals from the temple were traditional time indications for all the surrounding populace. These signals may have sometimes been based on such a water clock, but also were based on such things as sunrise, sunset, and when the rice was finished cooking.

162. "Attitude of helping everyone" and "personal interests" are literally "public mind" and "private mind," respectively.

163. "Grasp the noses" is a phrase usually used for grasping the nose, or nose ring, of the ox in order to lead it. This indicates catching and controlling the essential point, in this case of the ancient buddhas.

Appendix
AFTERWORD TO THE SHOHON EDITION

by Kōshō Chidō, thirtieth abbot of Eiheiji, 1667[*]

Since Baizhang first resided [as abbot] at Mount Dayu [with clear monastic standards] up to the present, many Zen shingi have appeared. Also we have Dōgen Zenji's writings, which match all the others. From the time he dwelled at Kōshōji in the southern part of the capital [Kyoto], through when he lived at Eiheiji in Echizen, he bestowed model examples in various writings such as the *Tenzokyōkun* and *Chiji Shingi*. [As they were] sealed up in the dust and hidden in the mists, to see a bit of them was rare, to hear of them at all was uncommon. When I had come to stay at this mountain [Eiheiji], I was able to encounter these writings in

---

* This translation is from a version of the afterword "respectfully copied by Ryūrin Genkoku in the Kansei period, year of the sheep [1799], mid-autumn, at Edo [Tokyo]."

their worm-eaten container. It was just like finding a jewel shining in the dark during a long, gloomy night, and I danced with joy.

As I patiently examined them, these words had the natural simplicity of our country's early [literary] style. It had incomplete phrases and expressions, [which were unpolished in form] like the difference between the Chinese characters for "fish" and "foolish" [*gyo* and *ro*, which are very similar]. If we take only flowers but abandon genuine fruits, then how can we follow our predecessor's admonitions and promote the flourishing of his intended bequeathal to us?

Therefore, now I have published these instructions and regulations to inform later generations of how future chiji and tenzos can apprehend and extend [Dōgen's teaching], as I deeply wish to assist these black-robed monks.

This afterword is respectfully written by Kōshō, the present Eiheiji abbot, in the Kambun Period, year of the sheep [1667], first month of summer, on Buddha's birthday in the fourth month [by the lunar calendar].

Glossary of Japanese Terms

These are technical terms from Buddhist or Zen doctrine, the Buddhist monastic tradition, or terms identifying translation ambiguities. The Japanese terms are followed by their Chinese characters and their definitions, and the page number in the text or notes where they first appear or are further clarified in their Japanese form. Some of them may reappear in translated forms, which are not noted.

ajari (阿闍梨) Instructor, used for the Sanskrit *acharya*, any senior monk qualified to have disciples. *126n. 1*

ango (安居) Monastic practice periods, literally, "peaceful abiding." These are ninety-day training periods of concentrated practice without leaving the monastic enclosure (except for monks going out for necessary temple business). They date back to the summer rainy season retreats of Shakyamuni's time. In Japan they have been held twice a year, in summer and winter. *101n. 9*

anja (行者) Usually a junior monk who acts as personal assistant for the abbot or other monks in important positions. *64, 76n. 7 bangaku* (晚學) Mature newcomers, those who first come to practice at a late age. *117n. 9*

bansan (晚參) Evening dharma meeting of the community. See *san*. *52n. 17*

bendō (辨道) "Wholeheartedly engage the Way." This is used in the title of "Bendōhō," the second essay in *Eihei Shingi*, and also in Dōgen's writing "Bendōwa". *54n. 32*

bendōhō (辨道法) Dharma or model for engaging or practicing the Way. *75n. 1*

biku (比立) One of four terms for a monk that Dōgen commonly uses in *Eihei Shingi*, along with *sō, shu,* and *unsui*. Biku, from the Sanskrit *bhikku*, is used for monks who have taken the full Theravada precepts. Dōgen uses it when quoting from Indian sutras or Vinaya (precepts) texts. *53n. 32*

bokusō (卜相) Fortune-telling and geomancy, referring to divination using palm or face reading, or geomantic techniques based on landscape and spatial configuration. *196n. 114*

bongyō (梵行) Pure conduct; in Sanskrit *brahmacharya*, used in India for any religious practice, but also implying ascetic renunciation of desires, particularly including celibacy. *182n. 7*

bon'u (梵宇) Practice hall, literally, "pure building," another word for a temple in East Asian Buddhism. *187n. 40*

byakuhō (白法) Literally, "white dharma," commonly used in Chinese Buddhism for good dharma or wholesome activity [Sanskrit: *kushala dharma*]. *191n. 72*

chiden (知殿) The buddha hall manager. See *chōshū*. *52n. 18*

chiji (知事) Literally, "know, manage, or take care of affairs"; term for the temple administrator positions, which are discussed in detail in the last section of *Eihei Shingi*, "Pure Standards for the Temple Administrators," or *Chiji Shingi*. Today *chiji* often refers to the *roku* [six] *chiji*: the director *tsūsu*, assistant director *kansu*, treasurer *fūsu*, supervisor of the monks' conduct *inō*, chief cook *tenzo*, and work leader *shissui*. At the time of *Chiji Shingi* the first three of the six were consolidated in one director position, *kan'in*. Along with the four primary chiji positions (kan'in, inō, tenzo, and shissui), "Pure Standards for the Temple Administrators" also discusses other positions of responsibility in the monastery, such as the garden manager, the fire manager, and the mill manager. *34, 50n. 4, 102n. 11, 189n. 54*

chinchō (朕兆) Omens or signs, also judgments or predictions. *76n. 4*

chishiki (知識) Spiritual friend; may refer formally to a teacher, but also has the meaning of a spiritual friend or guide, used as a translation of the Sanskrit term *kalyana mitra*. *197n. 116*

chōsan (朝参) Morning dharma meeting of the community. *See san. 52n. 17*

chōshū (頭首) The six heads of the different monastic departments. They are the head monk (*shuso*), the head scribe/secretary (*shoki*), librarian (*zōsu*), guest manager (*shika*), bath attendant (*yokusu*), and buddha hall manager (*chiden*). *52n. 18, 102n. 11, 189n. 54*

dai (大) Literally, "big" or "great"; used for *daishin*, the tenzo's "magnanimous" mind. *56n. 48, 57n. 54*

daigo (大悟) Great realization or enlightenment. Particularly in the Rinzai lineage, but not for Dōgen, daigo is someimes used to indicate a special opening experience resulting from practice. Traditionally, daigo is final, absolute enlightenment, contrasted to experiences of glimpsing enlightenment, *shōgo*. For Dōgen, daigo is being free from ideas about the distinction between enlightenment and delusion. *76n. 4, 184n. 21*

daikaijō (大開静) Same as *kaidaijō*. *80n. 29*

daisan (大参) Dharma meeting of the community in the dharma hall. *See san. 52.n. 17*

dai satori (大悟) Same as *daigo*. *76n. 4*

daisōchō (大僧帳) The government registry of ordination, literally, "great priest registry," which was the Chinese government official record of monk ordination. All ordinations had to be approved by the government. *199n. 130 daiza chato* (大坐茶湯) Tea offered in the sōdō; a ceremony in which tea is offered to the assembly by the abbot or director four times a year: at the winter solstice, New Year's day, and the beginning and end of the summer practice period. *108n. 65*

dajō ippen (打成一片) Literally, "to completely become one piece"; to become integrated. *52n. 14*

danka (檀家) Since the seventeenth century the system of supporters for individual Japanese Buddhist temples. *126n. 7*

danotsu (檀越) Donor, derived from the Sanskrit *danapati*. Dana, generosity, is the first of the six perfections in Mahayana Buddhism. *126n. 7*

datsuraku shinjin (脱落身心) "Body and mind dropped off," a term Dōgen uses for complete awakening, referring to his own enlightenment experience with his teacher Tiantong Rujing in China. *75n. 3*

dōan (堂行) Short for *dōsu kuka anja*. The dōans, literally the inō's anjas or attendants, strike instruments during chanting and make offerings (flowers, incense, etc.) to altars. *80n. 33*

dōchō (堂頭) Literally, "head of the hall," a common term for abbot. *81n. 38*

dōji (土地) Literally, "land," a protector spirit of grounds and buildings. Traditionally, all monks in training keep a scroll dedicated to *Ryūten* (a dragon spirit who helps avoid natural disasters) and Dōji as guardians, and honor it in their personal services. The scroll is opened, hung, and given offerings the first three days of the new year. *146, 190n. 61*

dōjō (道場) A place for practice/realization of the Way; used for the Sanskrit *bodhimandala*, originally the site of Buddha's enlightenment. Now also commonly used for martial arts practice halls. *115, 119n. 21*

domoku (土木) Construction projects; literally, "earth and wood," a common term for engineering as well as building projects. *191n. 71*

dōsu (堂主) The infirmary manager. *102n. 11*

dōsu (堂司) Literally, "hall manager," another name for the inō. *80n. 33*

GLOSSARY OF JAPANESE TERMS   211

dōsu kuka anja (堂司供過行者) Full name for dōans, or possibly a particular dōan job. *80n. 33*

ekō (回向) "Recite dedications," done after all chanting to dedicate and transfer the resulting merit and benefit to all beings. *190n. 61*

ekō henshō (回光返照) Another expression for *taiho henshō*, "Take the backward step of inner illumination," or "learn to withdraw, turning the light inwards, illuminating the Self," which is described in Dōgen's "Fukanzazengi," "The Way of Zazen Recommended to Everyone." *52n. 14*

enju (園頭) Manager of a monastery's gardens and fields. *193n. 79*

enjudō (延壽堂) The infirmary hall, literally, the "hall for prolonging longevity." While sick in the enjudō, monks do not participate in any other temple activity. *199n. 128*

funzō'e (糞掃衣) Literally, "robe from garbage or excrement"; a traditional term for the okesa, which was originally sewn together from patches of old discarded scraps and rags, sometimes taken from charnel grounds. *118n. 17*

fushin (普請) Community work, literally, "everyone invited," a word still used in common Japanese for community work projects. During fushin, also called *samu*, everyone in the monastery, without exception, is expected to work. This tradition derives from Baizhang, who is famous for saying, "A day without work is a day without eating." *184n. 26*

fushiryō (不思量) Not thinking; blank consciousness or absence of thoughts. This is not the goal of Dōgen's zazen. *80n. 36*

fūsu (副寺) The treasurer of a monastery, one of the six temple administrators. See *chiji*. *34, 50n. 4, 102n. 11*

futon (蒲団) Dōgen usually uses this word for the round sitting cushion used in zazen. It is now called a zafu. The *ton* of futon has the meaning "round." In modern Japan a futon is a thick sleeping mattress. The word Dōgen uses for a sleeping mat is *mintan*. *78.n 18, 80n. 35*

gaibō keshu (街坊化主) Fund-raiser or supply provider, literally "town priest teacher," responsible for soliciting donations from patrons and acquiring food provisions. *102n. 11*

gaidō (外堂) [also *gaitan*] The outer hall, which is just outside the curtained entryway to the main or inner hall *naidō*, and where Manjushri's jisha, new or visiting monks, monks who attend to guests, and the temple administrators all have their places. *78n. 14*

gasshō (合掌) Palms joined together in front of one's face, with fingers straight up and fingertips about at nose level, hands one width away from the face. May be used while bowing or erect and connotes gratitude or respect. *76n. 8*

genjōkōan (現成公案) *Genjō* means manifestation, actualization, or the present phenomena. *Kōan*, a term for stories and dialogues of ancient masters, here simply means the essential truth, so together this signifies manifestation of fundamental truth. "Genjōkōan" is also the name of one of Dōgen's major essays in the *Shōbōgenzō*. *76n. 4*

genzen sanbō (現前三寶) One of the three categories of three treasures (buddha, dharma, sangha), i.e., the three treasures of the historically manifested Shakyamuni Buddha. The other two types are *itai sanbō* and *jūji sanbō*. *116n. 4*

godō (後堂) Literally, "back hall," referring to the person who is the head of training in a large monastery, and who sits at the head of the platform by the back entrance of the north side of the hall, opposite the seats of the abbot and head monk. *105n. 34*

gokuka (極果) Ultimate fulfillment or final result; refers to the fruit of practice and is equated with buddhahood. *126n. 8*

han (版) A hanging wooden block that is struck with a wooden mallet, one of the instruments to signal events in the monastery. It is roughly (with some variation) two feet by one-and-a-half feet by four inches. *77n. 12*

hatettsu (鉢㯮) The tiny, slightly concave bowl stand on which the largest eating bowl, *zuhatsu*, sits. *103n. 19*

hatsu-u (鉢盂) Sometimes pronounced *hau*, a set of five eating bowls

GLOSSARY OF JAPANESE TERMS

with wrapping cloth, wiping cloth, lap cloth, utensil bag with utensils, and lacquered paper place mat. It is also called *ōryōki*, the more commonly used word today, although Dōgen does not use *ōryōki* in "The Dharma for Taking Food." In modern times all the bowls are made of black lacquered wood. *103n. 19*

hattan (鉢單) A lacquered paper place mat that the eating bowls are set on to protect the cloth from water. Between meals it is folded up and sits on the bowls inside the wrapping cloth. *103n. 21*

hattō (法度) This is a common term for social legal codes, the second character of the compound meaning degree or measure. When referring to the Dharma of a buddha, the second character means time, extent, or to save or bring across to salvation. *197n. 118*

heiteidōji (丙丁童子) The novice in the monastery who attends to the lamps. Literally, "fire boy" or "fire-spirit's apprentice," referring to fire as one of the five elements in Chinese cosmology. *183n. 15*

henzan (遍參) All-inclusive study, or to study widely, a term for the traditional practice of a monk traveling to visit different teachers to test the monk's own (and the teachers') awareness. "Henzan" is the name of one of the chapters in Dōgen's *Shōbōgenzō*, in which he indicates that to study widely [henzan] is to study oneself widely. *195n. 98*

hi (被) Quilt or thick cloth used to cover oneself when lying down, and folded up in a particular manner when put away. Its use in Zen dates back to the founder, Bodhidharma, often depicted with it covering his head and body while sitting in his cold cave in North China. *78n. 15*

hishiryō (非思量) Beyond-thinking, or, to unthink; used in a dialogue by Yaoshan Weiyan. This is active, open awareness, neither stuck to or pushing away either thinking or not thinking. *80n. 36*

hō (法) Chinese character used for dharma, a Sanskrit word, referring to the teaching of reality (often implying the Buddhist Dharma or teaching); the truth of reality itself; the elements of that realm of reality; and this teaching as means or path to align with that reality. This character also is used for the ordinary meanings of method, procedure, model, custom, or manner. Dōgen often conflates these two realms of meaning, for example to indicate that manners are teachings of reality. *101n. 7*

hōben (方便) Skillful means, in Sanskrit *upaya*, the traditional Mahayana methodology of conveying the truth appropriately to all the various beings with their diverse needs and conditioning. This is especially expounded in the *Lotus Sutra*. *192n. 75*

hōsan (放参) Literally, "release from meeting," indicating no meeting with the teacher that day. In "The Model for Engaging the Way" ("Bendōhō"), the days it occurs is unclear, perhaps occurring only for a period in late afternoon or early evening. In modern Sōtō monasteries, hōsan is announced (in the same manner described in "Bendōhō") on the afternoons of days ending in three or eight, and then the subsequent four or nine days hōsan is observed with some extra break time. *71, 73, 80n. 34, 99*

hōshin (報身) Sambhogakaya, the meditative bliss, reward body of buddha; one of the three bodies of buddha along with the dharmakaya *hosshin*, and the nirmanakaya *keshin*. *104n. 27*

hosshin (法身) Dharmakaya, the universally pervading, reality, or dharma, body of buddha. *104n. 27*

hou (梆) Literally, "wooden fish"; the long, hollow, wooden, fish-shaped drum hanging in the outer hall, and used during the meal ritual. It is struck by a long wooden pole. In Dōgen's time this was called the *mokugyō*. *102n. 12*

inju (院主) Another name for *Kan'in*, the director of a monastery, later divided into the first three of the six chiji positions. *183n. 12*

inmon (院門) "Temple gate," one of the many terms used for a temple. *192n. 73*

inō (維那) The supervisor of the monks' hall, and generally of the monks' conduct, one of the six temple administrators. *See chiji*. The word *inō* derives from the Sanskrit *karmadana*, literally, bestower of conduct [karma], i.e., the one who assigns monks their activities and places in the *sōdō*. The *i* of inō comes from the Chinese,

GLOSSARY OF JAPANESE TERMS 215

meaning oversee; while the *no* of inō is used to transliterate the *na* of karmadana. *Yuezhong* [*esshu* in Japanese] was used as a Chinese translation for the inō position, and means literally, "joy or delight to the assembly." 34, 50n. 4, 135–36, 167–70, 199n. 125

isshu (揖手) Sometimes in "Bendōhō," and in Song Chan, the name for the hand position or mudra called *shashu* in modern Sōtō Zen. 77n. 9

isu (椅子) The abbot's wooden armchair, separate from the monks' platform or *tan*, large enough to sit on cross-legged on a large cushion, but not to sleep on. It is to the right of the front door as one enters, and faces Manjushri, i.e., in front of Manjushri slightly to his left. 76n. 6

itai sanbō (一体三宝) One of the three categories of three treasures (buddha, dharma, sangha), i.e., the universal, omnipresent, unified body as the three treasures. *Genzen sanbō* and *jūji sanbō* are the other two types of three treasures. 116n. 4

jakumetsu (寂滅) Nirvana, literally, "serene cessation," considered the goal of practice in Theravada Buddhism. 182n. 8

ji (事) The phenomenal realm, contrasted philosophically with principle. *See also ri.* Commonly ji also refers to affairs, business, or the situation. 100n. 3

jigō (寺号) Temple name. East Asian Buddhist temples traditionally have both a temple name and a mountain name, *sangō*. 108n. 64

jijuyū zammai (自受用三昧) The samadhi [concentration] of self-enjoyment or fulfillment, a central teaching in Dōgen's writings on meditation, described by him as the criterion for true dharma and zazen. Dōgen's teachings in *The Pure Standards for the Zen Community* emphasize the satisfaction and fulfillment of jijuyū samadhi arising right in the midst of everyday activity. 16–17, 203n. 153

jikidō (直堂) The person assigned, in rotation from the assembly, to cleaning and taking care of the monks' hall and who remains in attendance in the hall when all the other monks are elsewhere. In modern times they also carry the *kyōsaku* stick, and ring the wake-up bell each morning in between the practice periods. 169, 200*n*. 133

jikitotsu (直裰) Literally, "sewn together." A one-piece robe to be worn beneath the okesa, adopted in the twelfth century by Chinese and Japanese monks to replace the two-piece *sankun*. In Dōgen's time monks wore only this one robe under the okesa, but modern Japanese monks wear the okesa over a long robe, *koromo*, with a long underrobe, *kimono*, beneath that. 78*n*. 17

jinriki (神力) Supernatural powers, unusual psychic capacities resulting as a by-product of meditative practice. They are usually disparaged as a goal in Zen, although may be used as skillful means for liberative purpose when appropriate. 195*n*. 93

jinsoku (神足) A leading disciple of a master. Literally meaning "divine feet," this also is used for the supernatural power to go anywhere or transform oneself at will. 185*n*. 29

jisha (侍者) The abbot's attendant, a senior monk who fulfills many functions, including acting as formal attendant during ceremonies and on travels, acting as a secretary, and acting as intermediary with monks or visitors. 64–5, 76*n*. 7, 200*n*. 134

jōdō (成道) To accomplish the Way; used for Shakyamuni Buddha's enlightenment. 106*n*. 41

jōdō (上堂) "Go up in the hall," i.e., to attend a formal lecture of the abbot, in which no text is used, although possibly starting off from a koan or phrase from a sutra. The term is also used for the abbot going to give the lecture. 190*n*. 60

jōen (牀縁) The edge of the monks' sitting platforms toward the center of the room, on which ōryōki are set out during meals. 76*n*. 6

jōken (上肩) Literally, "the left shoulder." This indicates a clockwise turn, "to the right" as we would say in English, i.e. leading *from* the left shoulder, not turning *toward* the left. 101*n*. 10

jōnin (浄人) Literally, "pure people"; name for those who serve meals in the sōdō, usually rotated amongst the monks (except for the six chiji and others whose work precludes it). 106*n*. 37

jōza (上座) A translation for *thera*, the Sanskrit for "elders" in the old Theravada tradition. Jōza originally meant senior monks who had been ordained over twenty years. Gradually it has come to refer to junior monks. In modern Sōtō and sometimes in Dōgen's usage, jōza refers to those who have not yet been shuso in a monastery, although Dōgen uses it interchangeably with *taiko* in "The Dharma when Meeting Senior Instructors." *107n. 56, 126n. 2*

jūji (住持) One of the terms for abbot; literally, "reside in and maintain [the temple]." *76n. 6*

jūjichō (住持帖) "Record book as abbot," a formal, official document used as a resumé by former abbots to demonstrate their seniority according to their dates of being abbots; similar to the *kaidōshō*. *199n. 127*

jūji sanbō (住持三寶) One of the three categories of three treasures (buddha, dharma, sangha), i.e., the three treasures upheld and maintained after Shakyamuni, namely, buddha images, printed sutras, and the community of fellow practitioners. *Jūji* [reside and maintain or uphold] is the same word used for the abbot of a temple. The other two types of three treasures are *itai sanbō* and *genzen sanbō*. *116n. 4*

jukai (受戒) Ordination, literally, "to receive precepts," a term used in Japanese Sōtō Zen for both householder, *zaike*, lay ordination and home-leaving, *tokudo*, monk ordination. *182n. 3*

jun (殉) Ardent desire, also implying great sacrifice, such as that of retainers who loyally follow their lords into death via suicide. *197n. 117*

jundō (巡堂) Circumambulation of the monks' hall. Done by the abbot or officiating priest at the beginning of each day's zazen (in the evening in *Eihei Shingi*, often in the morning in American centers with no sleep-in sōdōs). Jundō is also done by particular monks at ceremonies for entering or leaving the temple, or by all the monks during *nenju* ceremony. When the person(s) doing the jundō pass by, the other monks have hands in gasshō, either while sitting upright at their places for opening zazen, or with standing bows before their places for other jundōs. *77n. 9 junten* (順転) Turning in clockwise direction, the manner in all formal or ritual movements in the monastery. This is considered respectful, and promotes harmony of movement and alignment in the monastic space. *101n. 10*

jussu (術数) Divination techniques using astrology or the Chinese five-element or *I Ching* systems. *197n. 114*

juzu (珠数) A rosary or string of beads used traditionally by Buddhists, originally to count chanting or prostrations. Usually 108 beads for the number of possible delusions, it is sometimes considered an attribute of Avalokiteshvara, the bodhisattva of compassion. *79n. 28*

kahan (火版) Literally, "fire han," this is the first lunch signal. The three strikes on the *unpan*, done when the fire is extinguished under the rice, signals that food will be ready soon. *80n. 32*

kaidaijō (開大静) Literally, "opening the great stillness." The signal of night's end on the unpan and various hans that closes early morning zazen and announces the time to put away bedding, chant the robe verse, and put on the okesa. Also called *daikaijō*. *80n. 29*

kaidōshō (開堂疏) "Documents of opening the hall"; formal, official documents used as resumés by former abbots to indicate their seniority based on the dates of their having become abbots. The kaidōshō is recited at an abbot's installation ceremony. *See also jūjichō. 199n. 127*

kairo (戒臘) Literally, the end of the year precepts [were received]. A monk's ordination age, or years since ordination, is important as the basis for seating and various other arrangements in the monastery. This system of seniority or hierarchy can have an egalitarian aspect, as it counters ambition based on individual qualities. *101n. 8*

kan'in (監院) Director of a monastery. This is the name formerly given to the one person who did the work that was later divided between the director (tsūsu), assistant director (kansu), and treasurer (fūsu), the first three of the six temple administrators. Smaller temples still have just one kan'in position for the three, and some

GLOSSARY OF JAPANESE TERMS 219

larger temples also still have an additional kan'in administrator, whose job includes receiving important guests. *102n. 11, 132–35, 152–66*

kanki (函櫃) The wooden cabinets at the foot of each tan in the sōdō, with two large shelves for monks to store their bedding and some personal items. *77n. 13*

kanshu (監収) Accountant, a position under the director. *191n. 66*

kansu (監寺) The assistant director of a monastery, one of the six temple administrators. *See chiji*. Sometimes also used for the earlier director position; same as *kan'in*. *34, 50n. 4, 102n. 11, 134, 183n. 13*

kasshiki anja (喝食行者) The anja who calls out the names of courses as they are served during meals. Before the serving they also carry to the altar the meal-offering tray, with small portions of that meal's food in miniature monk's bowls. As servers enter, this anja stands just inside the door, bows in shashu, and announces the names of the courses for breakfast and lunch, i.e., "gruel" and "vegetables" at breakfast, and "rice," "soup," and "vegetables" at lunch. The anja also announces when servers enter to provide second helpings, to collect lunch spirit offerings, *saba*, to distribute water for cleaning bowls, and to provide buckets for collecting the water. *102n. 15, 105n. 33*

kata (掛搭) Literally, "hang one's belongings" (for a monk their robes and bowls) at a particular temple and practice there as a resident monk for some period. *54n. 30*

kata (方) Direction, side, method, or person. *196n. 113*

katatan (掛搭單) Literally, "the tan where you hang your belongings," at the back of which is hung a nameplate for the monk assigned to that place. In modern Sōtō Zen, a black lacquer plaque is used with white ink that is easily erasable. *102n. 13*

katsu (喝) An exclamatory shout or roar, literally "to yell," used especially in the Linji tradition to induce or express awakening. *190n. 59*

keiko (稽古) Diligent practice, literally, "contemplating the ancients," an important term for Dōgen referring to practice modeled on study of and reflection on the ancient sages and their standards. In modern Japanese it is a common term for practice of arts and sports, as in practicing tea ceremony, practicing the piano, or practicing karate. *193n. 84*

keshin (化身) Nirmanakaya, a historically appearing transformation body of buddha; one of the three bodies of buddha. See also *hōshin*, *hosshin*. *104n. 27*

kie (帰依) To take refuge, as in taking refuge in buddha. *195n. 100*

ko (更) The five watches into which the time between sunset and sunrise are divided in monasteries. Traditionally, they vary seasonally with the length of the nighttime. Each of these is also divided into five shorter periods called *ten*. *Koten* time signals are given at the end of evening zazen, and the beginning and end of morning zazen, with a drum for *ko* and bell or chime for *ten*. In American training centers, and some Japanese monasteries, these signals are now given to indicate the clock hour for *ko*, and the third of the hour (first, middle, or last twenty minutes within the hour) for *ten*. *77n. 12*

kōan (公案) A story or dialogue from the former masters used as an object of meditation or study. With the spread of Zen in the West, the word "koan" has entered English usage. Koans are not nonsensical riddles to be solved and discarded. Rather they are subtle teachings about one's own life. Based in the dialectic and logic of awakening, koans challenge our limiting, conditioned viewpoints and refine our alignment with our deeper nature. *13–14, 76n. 4*

kōka (後架) Literally, "back shelves." Refers to the washroom and separate toilet room at the back of the sōdō, off the passageway around the *naidō* and *gaidō* (see *shōdō*). *78n. 19*

kokugō (黒業) Bad karma, literally "black conduct;" activity that produces suffering. *191n. 72*

kōshu (好手) Skillfulness; also connotes attention to the whole field of activity, appropriateness, wholesome attitude. *55n. 36*

kōso (高祖) High Ancestor, usually used only for great founders, e.g.

GLOSSARY OF JAPANESE TERMS 221

Mahakashyapa, Dongshan Liangjie, and Dōgen himself. *55n. 41*

kudō (庫堂) Another name for *kuri* or *kuin*. *192n. 76*

kuin (庫院) Also called the *kuri* or *kudō*, this is the building to the right of the dharma hall, which houses the temple administrators' offices and the kitchen and food storage areas. *50n. 4, 192n. 76*

kunshi (君子) Noble person, implying a wise, respected person of honor. *197n. 117*

kunsu (鎖子) All the other eating bowls after the *zuhatsu*, the largest being the *zukun*. *103n. 19*

kuri (庫裡) Also called the *kuin* or *kudō*, this is the building to the right of the dharma hall. It houses the temple administrators' offices and the kitchen and food storage areas. *50n. 4, 192n. 76*

kusu (庫司) Director; the same as *kan'in* or *inju*. It refers to the previous director position, now divided into the first three of the modern six temple administrators. *183n. 18*

kyōsaku (警策) Long flat stick carried in the meditation hall and used to strike the shoulders of sleeping monks or at the request of monks for releasing stiffness. It is not mentioned in Dōgen's writing, and probably was not used by him. In modern times it is sometimes carried by the jikidō, the shuso, or the abbot, or by a rotation of other monks. Its use has been discarded in a number of modern Sōtō temples, both in Japan and the West. *200n. 133*

majū (磨頭) Old term for a monastery's mill manager. Other terms for this position are *mage*, *ma'in* and *masa*. *147–48, 193n. 79*

mappō (末法) The Latter Age of the Dharma, when only the teaching, and not the enlightenment and practice of the True and Semblance Ages [*shōbō* and *zōhō*] remain. According to this theory, which was popular in Dōgen's time, in the Semblance Age only practice and teaching are available, and in the Latter Age (considered to have already arrived) only the teaching still exists. Although Dōgen sometimes uses this theory of Buddhist history in exhortations, elsewhere he discounts its validity, affirming that the whole of buddha's practice and enlightenment is always available. *117n. 13 mato* (魔黨) Demonic inclination, literally "the demons' faction"; those who are possessed by the demons of ego and so are blind to reality. *194n. 89*

meifuku (冥福) Blessing in the unknown realms after death, dedicated to the well-being of spirits of the departed, a term used in association with memorial ceremonies. *Fuku* is blessing; *mei* means dark, unknown, or unseen. *195n. 104*

metsudo (滅度) Parinirvana, literally extinction and crossing over, referring to a buddha's passing into the ultimate state of nirvana upon death. *198n. 124*

mintan (眠單) The word Dōgen uses for a sleeping mat, called futon in modern Japan. *78n. 18*

mokugyō (木魚) Literally, "wooden fish"; in Dōgen's time the name for the long, hollow, wooden, fish-shaped drum hanging in the outer hall. It is now called the *hou*, "fish drum." This is used during the meal ritual, struck by a long wooden pole. *Mokugyō* currently refers to a spherical, wooden drum used during chanting. It is struck by a wooden striker with a large, padded head. Often painted red, it has the stylized image of two fishes with dragon heads, together holding a round jewel in their mouths. This spherical mokugyō was introduced to Japan in the seventeenth century by the Chinese monk Yinyuan, founder of the Japanese Ōbaku school. *86, 102n. 12*

monjin (問訊) A standing bow in *gasshō*. *76n. 8*

nahen (那辺) Literally, "over there," sometimes indicating absolute reality, as opposed to *shahen*, "right here." *52n. 16*

naidō (內堂) [also *naitan*] The main or inner hall. Both inner and outer halls are arranged with assigned places based on monks' positions and seniority. Generally, the monks with more important functions have their places closer to the altar, i.e., to the center of the hall. *78n. 14*

natō (那頭) "That" signifying universal interdependence; contrasted with *shatō* "this," or individual, concrete phenomena. *54n. 35*

GLOSSARY OF JAPANESE TERMS 223

nen (念) Mindfulness, determination, or remembrance; as in nembutsu [chanting homage to a buddha's name] or nenju. *193n. 85*

nenju (念誦) Literally, "remembrance chanting," a ceremony on afternoons of days ending with a three or eight in the date, still held in modern times in Sōtō monasteries. In this ceremony the names of buddha are chanted, and then all the monks circumambulate the sōdō [*jundō*] to reenact their entry into the monastery and refresh their intention. In Dōgen's time evening meeting was held after *nenju*, but commonly today this is followed by the *hōsan* procedure releasing the monks from evening meeting and signaling the somewhat relaxed four, nine day schedule. *134, 146, 184n. 25*

nichiri jikitotsu (日裏直裰) One-piece robe (*jikitotsu*) used during day. *79n. 27*

nyohō (如法) "According to the dharma," i.e., in appropriate manner, respectful, upright, dedicated. *54n. 28*

odayaka (穏やか) Peaceful, calm, quiet; sometimes referring to nirvana. *191n. 69*

okesa (御袈裟) A monk's robe—a large, rectangular wrap, since the time of Shakyamuni traditionally sewed together by monks following a particular pattern and ritual sewing practice. Originally the okesa was made from discarded rags, dyed uniformly. *39, 53n. 22, 70*

on (恩) Generosity, kindness, blessing; a traditional Japanese social concept that implies some benefaction or kindness from which one incurs a natural response of obligation. *191n. 65*

ōryōki (応量器) Literally, "container for the appropriate amount," another name for *hatsu-u*, the set of five eating bowls with wrapping cloth, wiping cloth, lap cloth, utensil bag with utensils, and lacquered paper place mat. The word *ōryōki* is used for the whole set or just for the largest bowl, and is much more commonly used today than the word *hatsu-u* (although Dōgen does not use the word *ōryōki* in "The Dharma for Taking Food"). In modern Sōtō practice, in Japan and the West, the traditional style of ōryōki is used only by priests, and a slightly simplified version with three bowls is used by laypeople. *103n. 19 oshō* (和尚) High priest; originally used for the Sanskrit *upadhyaya*, ordination master. Today in China and Japan it refers to all fully trained, ordained monks. *116n. 5*

ri (理) Principle, a technical term in Buddhism contrasted to phenomena *ji*, and referring to the fundamental nature of universal reality beyond discrimination. These terms derive from Huayan Buddhist philosophy and dialectics, derived from the *Avatamsaka Sutra*, which were the intellectual background for much of early Chan. Later in Japanese Buddhism, including Zen, ri and ji were used less philosophically, with ri as the ideal, abstract, or logical, contrasted with ji as the actual, concrete, or practical. *100n. 3*

rō (老) Literally, "elders" or short for "grandmotherly"; as *rōshin*, used for the tenzo's "nurturing mind." *56n. 48*

rōhatsu (臘八) The December eighth commemoration of Shakyamuni Buddha's enlightenment, in the modern era the culmination of the year's most intense seven days *sesshin*, commonly called rōhatsu sesshin. *192n. 74*

ryō (寮) Refers to spaces to study or take breaks (e.g., the shuryō) for monks who sleep in the sōdō; to work spaces or offices for various positions and their staffs (e.g., the tenzo ryō or inō ryō); and sometimes to dormitory spaces where senior monks sleep as well as study. Sometimes ryō also refers to the staff itself of a certain position rather than to a work space. Thus sometimes the tenzo ryō refers to the kitchen workers. *199n. 126*

ryōshu (寮主) The shuryō manager, a separate position rotated at weekly to monthly intervals between all of the monks. The ryōshu cleans and cares for the study hall, requests supplies when needed, and pacifies disputes within the shuryō. *81n. 39*

ryūten (龍天) "Dragon heavenly being," a nature spirit who helps control weather to avoid natural disasters. Traditionally, all monks in training keep a scroll dedicated to the guardians Ryūten and *Dōji*, a protector spirit of grounds and buildings, and honor it in their personal services. The scroll is opened, hung, and given offerings the first three days of the new year. *146, 190n. 61*

GLOSSARY OF JAPANESE TERMS

saba (生飯) "Beings' food." These offerings are for beings in the unfortunate realms, especially the hungry ghosts or spirits. At lunchtime, the offerings are put on the end of the monks' bowl-cleaning sticks before eating, and then later collected by the meal servers. After lunch they are usually put outside for animal "spirits" to eat. *106n. 42*

samu (作務) Community work, also called *fushin*, during which everyone in the monastery, without exception, is expected to work. This tradition derives from Baizhang. *184n. 26*

san (参) To study thoroughly. Also diversity or multiplicity. Also the community dharma meeting with the teacher to receive instruction, sometimes with questions and responses. There are various different kinds of *san* meetings, depending on where and when it is held, e.g., *chōsan* in the morning, *bansan* in the evening, *shōsan* in the abbot's room, and *daisan* in the dharma hall. *52n. 17*

san'e (三会) Three roll-downs on a han or bell, a common signal in the monastery with seven, then five, then three slowly and evenly spaced hits, or sometimes seven, five, and then three minutes of such hits, each followed by a series of rapidly accelerating hits which culminate with one, two, and then three hits, respectively. *101n. 6*

sangō (山号) Mountain name of a temple. East Asian Buddhist temples traditionally have both a mountain name, after the name of the mountain where they are located, and a temple name, *jigō*. *108n. 64*

sankun (衫裙) The Chinese style robes, with separate pieces for top and bottom, respectively, worn beneath the okesa. In use until replaced by the one-piece *jikitotsu* in the twelfth century. *78n. 17*

sashu kyaku (做手脚) Everyday activities; literally, "using your arms and legs." *191n. 69*

seidō (西堂) Literally, "west hall," named for the person's seat at the head (beginning) of the platform inside the front (west) entrance of the monks' hall, toward the south, left "lower" side. This refers to a visiting teacher participating in the monastic practice period. Originally it was a former abbot of another temple, but now it is used for any highly respected visiting teacher. *105n. 34 sejikige* (施食偈) A meal-offering verse; chanted after the homages to the ten names of buddha. *104n. 29*

sendai (闡提) Lacking the requisite faith for entering practice. It is short for *issendai*, which is the standard Japanese transliteration of the Sanskrit word *icchantika*. This is a traditional Indian Buddhist term for beings initially understood as completely devoid of buddha nature and therefore incapable of enlightenment, but later interpreted as those completely lacking in faith but who might possibly later develop some capacity for practice. *194n. 89*

seshu (施主) Patron or donor; generally, laypeople supporters of a temple. *53n. 21*

sesshin (接心) Seven days (or at some times three or five days) of concentrated zazen practice. Although a common practice in all of modern Zen, it is not mentioned by Dōgen. In Dōgen's time there was apparently sufficient daily zazen to make such special sesshin periods unnecessary. *192n. 74*

setsu (刷) Also called *hassetsu*, a wooden stick about seven inches long with a changeable cloth tip, used for wiping the eating bowls after meals. *104n. 23*

sezoku (世俗) Worldly people, also called *zoku*. It often refers to laypeople as opposed to monks. *195n. 101*

shahen (這辺) Literally, "here," which sometimes indicates the concrete reality here and now, as opposed to *nahen*. *52n. 16*

shashu (叉手) The hand position when standing or walking in the monks' hall or in other formal contexts in the monastery, i.e., when not working or carrying objects. In modern Sōtō Zen, hands are folded at chest height with forearms parallel to the floor. The right hand covers the left hand, which is closed in a fist with thumb inside. There are various slightly different styles of shashu. In Dōgen's time and previously, shashu sometimes referred to the above position, and sometimes to holding the hands flat against the chest (not in a fist) with thumbs interlaced. *See isshu. 64, 77n. 9*

shatō (這頭) "This," signifying individual, concrete phenomena; con-

GLOSSARY OF JAPANESE TERMS 227

trasted with *natō*, "that" or universal interdependence. *54n. 35*

shika (知客) The guest manager of a monastery. See *chōshū*. *52n. 18*

shinenju (四念住) The four abodes of mindfulness: remembrance of the impurity of the body; of the suffering inherent in sensation; of the impermanence of mind; and of the insubstantiality of all entities. *117n. 8*

Shingi (清規) Pure standards, as in *Eihei Shingi*. *Gi* is standard or measure. This *shin* means pure. This could also be interpreted as "standards for purity," so that Dōgen's work might also imply standards for a pure community. *115n. 1*

shingi (箴規) Regulations, as in "Shuryō Shingi"; pronounced the same as the *Shingi* [pure standards] of *Eihei Shingi*. *Gi* [standard or measure] is the same in both terms. This *shin* means accupuncture needle or admonition, as in Dōgen's essay "Zazenshin" in *Shōbōgenzō*. *115n. 1*

shinjutsu (心術) Arts, techniques, or skillfulness of mind; generally, all helpful mental attitudes. *195n. 96*

shinnyo (眞如) Used for the Sanskrit *tathata*, suchness or thusness, i.e., ultimate reality. *194n. 93*

shishin (至信) Persevering, sincere, or complete faith that reaches the ultimate. *194n. 92*

shissui (直歳) The monastery work leader responsible for maintenance of the physical facilities; one of the six temple administrators. See *chiji*. 34, *50n. 4*, 143, 179–81

shō (證) Actualized or awakened, one of the characters used to mean enlightenment, it implies to certify, verify, or authenticate enlightenment. *75n. 4*

shōbō (正法) The Age of True Dharma, in which enlightenment, practice, and teaching all exist. According to this theory, which was popular in Dōgen's time, in the Semblance Age, *zōhō* only practice and teaching are available, and in the Latter Age, *mappō* (considered to have already arrived), only the teaching persists. Dōgen sometimes uses this theory of Buddhist history as an exhortation, but elsewhere discounts it, affirming that the whole of buddha's practice and enlightenment is always available. *118n. 13*

Shōbōgenzō (正法眼蔵) True Dharma Eye Treasury; the name of Dōgen's masterwork. Also the description of what was transmitted between Shakyamuni and Mahakashyapa. *ix, 1–2, 19, 21, 22, 25*

shōdō (照堂) The back passageway between the sōdō and the washrooms; literally, "illuminated hall," so-named because it had a space in the roof for light to enter. *79n. 21*

shōgo (省悟) A Rinzai term referring to enlightenment opening experiences. Sometimes contrasted with *daigo*, great enlightenment, shōgo literally means "see, examine, or reflect" [*shō*], "awakening" [*go*]. *183n. 17*

shōju (醬頭) Manager of miso in a monastery kitchen. *193n. 79*

shōken (正見) Right view, one of the practices of the noble eightfold path, taught by Shakyamuni as the fourth Noble Truth, the way to the end of dissatisfaction or suffering. *196n. 109*

shoki (書記) The head scribe/secretary, who always sits next to the shuso in the sōdō, and otherwise assists the head monk. See *chōshū*. *52n. 18, 90, 105n. 32*

shoku (食) Food; also, to eat, subsistence, or livelihood. *196n. 112*

shōmyo (正命) Right livelihood, one practice of the noble eightfold path of Shakyamuni. *197n. 116*

shōnen (正念) Right mindfulness, one of the practices of the noble eightfold path, taught by Shakyamuni as the fourth Noble Truth. *194n. 92*

shōryō (商量) "Carefully determine," used both for merchants settling on a price and, in Zen dialogues, for investigating understanding of dharma. *52n. 19*

shōsan (小参) Dharma meeting of the community in the abbot's room. See *san*. *52n. 17*

shosō (聖僧) Literally, "holy monk," this refers to the figure on the central altar. In the *sōdō* this is Manjushri, the bodhisattva of wisdom, evoking the penetrating insight of meditation cutting through

GLOSSARY OF JAPANESE TERMS 229

delusion. In the *shuryō* study hall the shosō is Avalokiteshvara, the bodhisattva of compassion, who studies the causes and conditions of suffering and the skillful teachings to alleviate it. *76n. 6, 81n. 40*

shōtai chōyō (聖胎長養) Literally, "sustained development of a womb of sages." This term is used for practice after enlightenment. *53n. 23*

shōtōkaku (正等覺) Japanese pronunciation for the usual Chinese translation of the Sanskrit *anuttara samyak sambodhi*, the unsurpassed, complete perfect enlightenment of a buddha. *100n. 4*

shu (衆) One of four terms for a monk that Dōgen commonly uses in *Eihei Shingi*, along with *sō*, *unsui*, and *biku*. *Shu* also means assembly, or the community of monks. *53n. 22*

shukin (手巾) A long piece of material, traditionally cotton or linen and off-white or gray colored, about fifteen inches by four yards. It is used while washing in order to tie up the long sleeves of a monk's sitting robe and also dry the face and hands. *78n. 20*

shukuhanjū (粥飯頭) A name for abbot that means, literally, "provider of food," referring to the abbot's responsibility to monks in his temple. *55n. 37*

shukujū (粥頭) Manager of gruel in a monastery kitchen. *193n. 79*

shuryō (衆寮) The monks' study hall (or, literally, "assembly hall") behind the sōdō, where monks study, rest, or drink tea at assigned places during breaks. It is structured like the sōdō in terms of seating assignments and configuration. The seats are on narrower platforms than in the sōdō, since they are not for sleeping, and instead of cabinets for bedding, at the end of each monk's platform is a small desk for study materials. Instead of Manjushri, the shuryō has Avalokiteshvara enshrined on the central altar. *70, 80n. 30, 109–15, 116n. 1*

shushō (修証) Practice-certification, authentification, or enlightenment. Used by Dōgen to express the nonduality of practice and true awakening. Practice is the expression and celebration of enlightenment, rather than a means to attain some later, resultant experience identified as enlightenment. *75n. 4 shuso* (首座) The head monk of a practice period, who shares the teaching responsibilities of the abbot, sits facing the center of the sōdō, and leads and encourages the monks' practice as an exemplary monk. The shuso's seat in the sōdō is at the head of the platform immediately next to the abbot's seat, inside the front door on the right "upper" side of the hall. See *chōshū*. 52*n*. 18, 76*n*. 6, 105*n*. 34

sō (僧) As in *sōdō*, one of four terms for a monk that Dōgen commonly uses in *Eihei Shingi*. The others are *shu*, *unsui*, and *biku*. 53*n*. 22

sōdō (僧堂) The monks' hall, where monks meditate, eat, and sleep. 53*n*. 22, 76*n*. 5

sōjō (僧正) Traditionally the highest rank in the hierarchy of monks' supervisors in Japanese temples. 108*n*. 64

sokurei (触禮) An informal full prostration, done with the *zagu* folded up and placed horizontally on the ground in front of the bowing monk, rather than spread out on the ground. 118*n*. 16

sonshuku (尊宿) Venerable elders; abbots or other honored masters. 126*n*. 4

soseki (叢席) Monastic practice; literally, "monastic seats or places." 195*n*. 97

sōshu (莊主) Property manager; the manager of the fields and minor temple buildings. A term no longer in use. 191*n*. 67, 193*n*. 79

suijū (水頭) The water manager, responsible for carrying and supplying water throughout the temple. 193*n*. 79

taiho henshō (退步返照) Another expression for *ekō henshō*, "Take the backward step of inner illumination," or "learn to withdraw, turning the light inwards, illuminating the Self," which is described in Dōgen's "Fukanzazengi," "The Way of Zazen Recommended to Everyone." 52*n*. 14

taiko (大己) A senior (greater than oneself), described in "The Dharma when Meeting Senior Instructors," where they are defined as those who have completed five monastic training periods. 126*n*. 1

takuhatsu (托鉢) "Entrust or hold up bowls" at nose height with the thumb and first two fingers of both hands. Takuhatsu also refers to the customary monks' begging rounds, in which the bowls are also held in this way to receive donations. *103n. 18, 105n. 36*

tamin jikitotsu (打眠直裰) One-piece robe worn during nighttime. *79n. 27*

tan (單) Platforms in the sōdō on which monks sit, eat, and sleep. Zazen is done facing the wall, while meals are taken facing the center of the room. The tan is also wide enough for monks to sleep at their places; cabinets with bedding are along the wall. *Tan* could also refer to the sitting platforms in the shuryō. *77n. 10*

tanbutsu (歎仏) "Praising the Buddha;" used for verses giving homage to buddha (and the three treasures), such as the one chanted as a dedication for donors of meals: "We give homage to the Bhagavat,/ the perfect sutras,/ and the Mahayana bodhisattva sangha,/ with merit and virtue inconceivable." *104n. 28*

tangaryō (旦過寮) The room where traveling monks stay when visiting or before they are accepted into the sōdō. Traditionally, for about a week before admittance to a monastery, Zen monks must sit still in zazen all day inside the tangaryō, intermittently also receiving instructions in the procedures and customs of the particular temple and region. *187n. 44*

tanjū (炭頭) The fire and fuel, or charcoal manager, responsible for tending the fire for warmth and maintaining fuel supplies. *102n. 11, 193n. 79*

tantō (單頭) Literally, "head of the tan," referring to the person who assists the *godō* as head of training. The tantō sits at the head of the platform opposite the *seidō*, by the back entrance of the south, lower side of the monks' hall. *105n. 34*

tasuki (絆) A sash or cord used for tying up robe sleeves. *79n. 22*

ten (点) The five shorter periods into which *ko* are divided. The *ten* in the *koten* time signals are signaled by striking a bell or small flat chime. *77n. 12*

tenzo (典座) The chief cook of a monastery. Dōgen discusses this position in detail in the first essay, "Instructions for the Tenzo," and in a later section of "Pure Standards for the Temple Administrators." This is one of the six temple administrator positions. *See chiji.* 33–49, *50n. 4*, 136–43, 170–79

tōju (灯頭) The lamp manager, who takes care of lamps and lamp oil. *193n. 79*

tōkin (等均) Parity, or the equivalence of two separate things. *100n. 4*

tokudo (得度) Literally, "attain the Way;" used for home-leaving monk ordination. *See jukai. 182n. 3*

tōryō (等量) Equality, or the equal measure of two different quantities. *100n. 4*

tsui chin (槌砧) A wooden sounding block used in rituals. It usually consists of a thin, eight-sided block a few feet high, with a small block a few inches high set on top of it to be used as a mallet. It stays to the left of the Manjushri altar, and when not in use the smaller block is covered by a cloth (in modern times usually purple). 87, 89, *103n. 16*, 135, 136

tsūsu (都寺) The director of a monastery, one of the six temple administrators. *See chiji.* 34, *50n. 4, 102n. 11*

undō (雲堂) Another name for *sōdō*, the monks' hall. *76n. 5*

unpan (雲版) A cloud-shaped flat metal gong in front of the kitchen. It is struck with a wooden mallet. *80n. 29*

unsui (雲水) One of four terms for a monk that Dōgen commonly uses in *Eihei Shingi*. (The others are *sō, shu*, and *biku*.) Unsui, literally, "clouds and water," refers particularly to trainee monks, who as home-leavers wander freely through the mountains like clouds and rain. *53n. 22, 188n. 46*

watō (話頭) "Words and stories," also "turning word" or "head word." In the formal practice of meditative concentration on koans, especially in the Linji tradition, a brief phrase or single "head word" from a dialogue is the object of concentration. *54n. 32*

yakuseki (薬石) Optional evening food served informally, not in the monks' hall, and considered medicine, not a meal. Literally, "medicine stone," its name comes from the ancient monastic practice of

GLOSSARY OF JAPANESE TERMS   233

  warming rocks and placing them on the belly to stave off hunger.
  From Dōgen's time to the present, Sōtō monasteries have served
  food instead. *100n. 1*

yōji (楊枝) Tooth stick; a willow twig whose end was chewed and
  softened so as to be used like a modern toothbrush for ritual teeth
  care. Its length was between four and sixteen fingers' width. *79n. 23*

yokusu (浴司) The bath attendant. One of the six *chōshū*. *52n. 18, 193n. 79*

yusan (遊山) Literally, "playing or wandering out in the mountains," a
  common Chinese and Japanese expression for going out to enjoy
  oneself. *184n. 23*

zabuton (坐蒲団) Literally "sitting futon," this word is usually used in
  the West for the square, flat mat the zafu is placed on during
  zazen. In Japan this is called *zaniku*, and the word zabuton is used
  for smaller, everyday sitting mats. *78n. 18*

zafu (坐蒲) The modern word for the round sitting cushion used in
  zazen. Dōgen instead usually uses the word *futon* for what we now
  call a zafu; the *ton* of futon means "round." In contemporary Rinzai
  Zen flat cushions are used instead of zafus. *78n. 18*

zagen (坐蒲) Another term for shuso [head monk], or for someone who
  has been a shuso. *190n. 62*

zagu (坐具) A bowing cloth, sewn ritually along with the okesa. It is
  spread out on the ground to protect the okesa when monks bow.
  53n. 22, 139

zaike (在家) Householder; used for lay ordination. See *jukai*. *182n. 3*

zaniku (坐褥) In Japan, the word for the square, flat mat upon which a
  zafu is sometimes placed during zazen, often called *zabuton* in the
  West. In Japan the word zabuton is used for smaller, everyday
  sitting mats. *78n. 18*

zōhō (像法) The Semblance Age, in which only practice and teaching
  are available, said to follow the initial Age of True Dharma, *shōbō*,
  in which enlightenment, practice, and teaching all exist. According
  to this theory, in the Final Age, *mappō*, only the teaching remains.
  See *mappō*. *117n. 13*

zōsu (蔵主) The librarian of a monastery. *See chōshū*. *52n. 18*

zuda (頭陀) Wandering ascetic, from the Sanskrit *dhuta*, referring to ascetic practitioners. Originally the term referred to a set of twelve specific purifying practices, including always remaining outdoors, only taking one meal daily before noon, and never lying down. *186n. 36*

zuhatsu (頭鉢) "Head bowl," the largest eating bowl of the hatsu-u. It has rounded edges. Currently referred to in the West as the "buddha bowl." *103n. 19*

zuiki (随喜) To feel appropriate delight and enjoyment when participating in practice; a Buddhist term for the joy of engaging in beneficial activity, including ceremonies and other formal practice activities. It is derived from the *Lotus Sutra*, chapter 18 "The Merit of Appropriate Joy," which describes the zuiki of the bodhisattva upon hearing the Dharma or upon seeing others' good deeds or resultant happiness. In the sutra, the bodhisattva Maitreya says in a gatha, "After the World-Honored One's passage into extinction, / If there is one who hears this scripture / And if he can rejoice appropriately [*zuiki*], / How much happiness shall he obtain?" *203n. 151*

zukun (頭䤵) The largest *hatsu-u* eating bowl after the *zuhatsu*; largest of the *kunsu*. *103n. 19*

zun'an (童行) Novice monks or children raised in the monastery, in some cases preparatory to full monk ordination. *192n. 75*

Glossary and Index of Names

Names of Chinese persons in *Dōgen's Pure Standards for the Zen Community* are given in alphabetical order by their Chinese Pinyin transliteration, followed by dates, alternate Wade-Giles Chinese transliteration in brackets, Chinese characters, and Japanese pronunciation. Japanese and Indian persons are listed alphabetically by their Japanese and Indian names without Chinese pronunciation, although with characters included for Japanese names. The names and dates are followed by biographical information and all the page numbers where they appear in the text or notes. Persons included without page citation are figures not in Dōgen's text (or mentioned in the notes), but who are important as teachers or students of persons mentioned.

Ananda [Indian] (6th century B.C.E.) Shakyamuni Buddha's cousin, close disciple, and personal attendant. Ananda was known for his perfect recall, and the sutras were all said to be dictated by him after Shakyamuni's passing into parinirvana, each with Ananda's opening, "Thus have I heard." Ananda did not awaken until after the Buddha's death, but he became the second ancestor after Mahakashyapa in the Zen lineage. 128, 130, 165

Aniruddha [I.] (6th cent. B.C.E.) Blind disciple of Shakyamuni. Once he fell asleep during Shakyamuni's lecture, then vowed never to sleep again. Fulfilling this vow, he ruined his eyesight but also developed the heavenly eye with the supernatural power to see past and future. *117n. 12*

Ashoka [I.] (d. ca. 232 B.C.E.) A powerful warrior king who unified India and then became a devout patron of Buddhism, building many temples. He is considered the model of an awakened Buddhist political leader. 44, *55n. 39, 56n. 47*

Ashvaghosha [I.] (1st–2nd cent.?) Buddhist poet and teacher, considered the twelfth Indian ancestor in the Zen tradition, two generations before Nagarjuna. Amongst texts uncertainly, though traditionally, attributed to him are the early Mahayana classic, *The Awakening of Faith*, and "The Dharma of Serving your Teacher." *126n. 3*

Baizhang Huaihai (749–814) [Pai-chang Huai-hai] (百丈懷海) Hyakujō Ekai. A Dharma successor of Mazu, he compiled the first regulations for a Zen community, and insisted, "A day of no work is a day of no food." Teacher of Huangbo and Guishan, he was also famous for giving a monk's funeral to a fox. See *Book of Serenity* [*Shōyōroku*] case eight, and *Gateless Gate* [*Mumonkan*] case two. 20, 45, *55n. 41, 57n. 56*, 109, *116n. 1*, 136–38, 140–41, *184n. 26, 186nn. 32, 36, 187n. 38*, 205

Baizhao Zhiyuan (9th cent.) [Pai-chao Chih-yüan] (白兆志圓) Hakuchō Shien. Possibly the former teacher of Baoen Xuanze before Fayan. *183n. 14*

Baoen Xuanze (9th–10th cent.) [Pao-ên Hsüan-tsê] (報恩玄則) Hōon Gensoku. A Dharma heir of Fayan. 132–33, 135, *183nn. 14, 16*

Baofu Benquan (n.d.) [Pao-fu Pên-ch'üan] (保福本權) Hofuku Hongon. A Dharma heir of [Huanglong] Huitang Zuxin. 143

Baoji [Huayan] Xiujing (9th cent.) [Pao-chi Hua-yen Hsiu-ching] (寶智

[華嚴] 休靜) Hōji [Kegon] Kyujo. A Dharma heir of Dongshan Liangjie, the founder of Caodong/Sōtō Zen. 135

Baoming Renyong (11th century) [Pao-ming Jên-yung] (保寧仁勇) Honei Ninyu. A Dharma successor of Yangqi Fanghui, the founder of one of the two main branches of Rinzai Zen. 34, 173

Bimbisara [I.] (6th cent. B.C.E.) King of Magadha who was a follower of Shakyamuni and donated land for the first Buddhist monastery. 113

Bodhidharma [I.] (d. 532) Legendary Indian monk who came to China and became founder of Chan Buddhism. He is considered twenty-eighth in the Indian lineage from Shakyamuni. 75n. 3

Butsuju Myōzen [Japanese] (1184–1225) (仏樹明全) Dharma successor of Eisai, he was Dōgen's Japanese teacher and friend, who accompanied Dōgen to China and died there while staying at the Tiantong Monastery. Dōgen praised him highly. 43, 54n. 26, 55n. 42

Caoshan Benji (840–901) [Ts'ao-shan Pên-chi] (曹山本寂) Sōzan Honjaku. Dharma heir of Dongshan Liangjie, and sometimes considered the cofounder of the Caodong (Sōtō) School, he developed the five ranks philosophical teachings. 132

Cavampati [I.] (6th cent. B.C.E.) Shakyamuni Buddha's disciple. In a past life he had ridiculed a monk, so in this life he was always moving his mouth like a cow chewing its cud. However, he became foremost in understanding of the Vinaya. 117n. 12

Changlu Zongze (d. 12th cent.) [Ch'ang-lu Tsung-tsê] (長蘆宗賾) Chōro Sōsaku. A master in the Yunmen lineage, in 1103 he compiled the *Zen'en Shingi* [*Pure Standards for the Zen Garden; Chanyuan Qinggui* in Chinese], which was the model for Dōgen's *Eihei Shingi*, and which Dōgen quotes extensively. 20, 50n. 2

Chengjin (2d cent.) [Ch'êng-chin] (成縉) Seishin. Governor of Nanyang during the reign of the Later Han dynasty eleventh emperor (147–67). 164

Chen Xiuwen (441–513) [Ch'ên Hsiu-wên] (沈休文) Chin Kyūbun. A Liang dynasty poet. 164

Chuanzi Decheng (n.d.) [Ch'uan-tzu Tê-ch'êng] (船子德誠) Sensu Tokujō. A Dharma heir of Yaoshan nicknamed "the boatman," he lived in the world as a ferryman after the persecution of Buddhism in 842. After transmitting the Dharma to Jiashan Shanhui, he overturned the boat and disappeared in the water. 142, *188n. 47*

Ciming [Shishuang] Quyuan (986–1039) [Tz'u-ming Shih-shuang Ch'ü-yüan] (慈明 [石霜] 楚圓) Jimyō [Sekisō] Soen. Student of Fenyang Shanzhao, and teacher of both Yangqi and Huanglong, founders of the two main branches of Linji/Rinzai Zen, Ciming taught at Shishuang Mountain, the temple established by Shishuang Qingzhu. 133–34, *183n. 19, 184nn. 22–24*

Dahui Zonggao (1089–1163) [Ta-hui Tsung-kao] (大慧宗杲) Daie Sōkō. Dharma successor of Yuanwu Keqin, he was famous as a proponent of intent koan introspection and *watō* koan practice, and critic of silent illumination meditation. He is a key figure in the Linji/Rinzai lineage. In some writings Dōgen strongly criticized him. *54n. 30, 196n. 105*

Daixiao Lingtao (666–760) [Tai-hsiao Ling-t'ao] (大曉令韜) Daigyō Reitō. A disciple of the Sixth Ancestor who later cared for the Sixth Ancestor's memorial stupa and mummy. When someone who had tried to cut off and steal the head of the mummy was apprehended, Daixiao encouraged forgiveness and leniency by the authorities. 114, *118n. 18*

Daixue Huailian (1009–90) [Tai-hsüeh Huai-lien] (大覺懷璉) Daigaku Eren. A Dharma successor in the Yunmen lineage. 159–60

Dajian Huineng (638–713) [Ta-chien Hui-nêng] (大鑑慧能) Daikan Enō. The famous Sixth Ancestor of Chan (five generations after the founder Bodhidharma), whose biography and teachings were expounded in the *Platform Sutra*. The Sixth Ancestor is a primary example in Zen of a humble, illiterate person who realizes complete awakening. *53n. 20, 118nn. 14, 18, 202n. 147*

Danxia Tianran (739–824) [Tan-hsia T'ien-jan] (丹霞天然) Tanka Tennen. A student of Shitou, Danxia is famous for burning a buddha statue to warm himself. His second-generation successor was Touzi Datong.

GLOSSARY AND INDEX OF NAMES 239

Daokai Dayang. See Furong Daokai.

Daowu Yuanzhi (769–835) [Tao-wu Yüan-chih] (道吾圓智) Dōgo Enchi. Daowu was a student of Baizhang, then became Dharma heir of Yaoshan Weiyan, along with Daowu's biological and Dharma brother Yunyan, the teacher of Dongshan, founder of the Caodong/ Sōtō Lineage. A number of dialogues between Daowu and Yunyan remain as koans. 138–39, *187n. 41*

Daoxuan (596–667) [Tao-hsüan] (道璿) Dōsen. Founder of the Chinese Risshu [Precept] School. *126n. 3*

Dayang Qingxuan (d. 1027) [Ta-yang Ch'ing-hsüan] (太陽警玄) Taiyō Kyōgen. Caodong/Sōtō master who outlived his Dharma successors. His friend Fushan Fayuan transmitted Dayang's Caodong lineage to his own student Touzi in Dayang's name after Dayang's death. *187n. 43*

Deshan Xuanjian (780–865) [Tê-shan Hsüan-chien] (德山宣鑑) Tokusan Senkan. Teacher of Xuefeng, he is famous for his animated style of teaching by shouts and striking his students. Previously a lecturer on the *Diamond Sutra*, he burnt his books after being awakened to Chan by an old woman selling tea cakes. *51n. 7*, 144, *190n. 56*

Devadatta [I.] (6th cent. B.C.E.) Shakyamuni Buddha's cousin, who after joining his order tried to become his rival and even tried to have the Buddha killed. 156, *194n. 86*

Dhrtaka [I.; Daitaka in Japanese] (n.d.) The fifth ancestor in India, according to the lineage accepted in Zen. 137, *186n. 35*

Dōgen. See Eihei Dōgen.

Dongkeng Yanjun (882–966) [Tung-k'êng Yen-chün] (東京巖俊) Tonkin Genshun. A successor of Touzi Datong, who was two generations after Danxia Tianran, a student of Shitou. 159

Dongshan Liangjie (807–69) [Tung-shan Liang-chieh] (洞山良价) Tōzan Ryōkai. Founder of the Caodong (Sōtō) lineage, the branch of Chan later transmitted by Dōgen to Japan. He is author of the "Song of the Jewel-Mirror Samadhi" ["Hōkyō-Zammai" in Japanese], which initiated the five ranks or degrees teaching as a dialectical underpinning to Caodong practice. Dongshan was Dharma successor of Yunyan, although he also studied with Nanquan and Guishan. 13, 35, *50nn. 3, 6, 51n. 7, 55n. 41*, 135, 144, 174–75, *194n. 87*

Dongshan Shouchu (910–90) [Tung-shan Shou-ch'u] (洞山守初) Tōzan Shusho. A disciple of Yunmen cited by Dōgen as a model tenzo. 33, 47, 49, *50n. 3, 56n. 46*

Eihei Dōgen [J.] (1200–1253) (永平道元) Founder of the Japanese Sōtō Zen lineage. Founder of Eiheiji monastery. Author of the *Shōbōgenzō* and *Eihei Shingi*.

Eisai. See Myōan Eisai.

Fayan Wenyi (885–958) [Fa-yen Wên-yi] (法眼文益) Hōgen Mon'eki. Three generations after Xuefeng and the student of Luohan Guichen, Fayan is considered the founder of the Fayan lineage, one of the five houses or "schools" of classical Zen. 132–33, *204n. 155*

Fengxue Yanzhao (896–973) [Fêng-hsüeh Yen-chao] (風穴延沼) Fūketsu Enshō. Three generations after Linji and a successor of Nanyuan Huiyong. All the subsequent Rinzai tradition descends from his lineage, as supposedly predicted by Yangshan. Teacher of Shoushan Xingnian. *190n. 64*

Fenyang Shanzhao (947–1024) [Fên-yang Shan-chao] (汾陽善昭) Funyō Zenshō. Teacher of Ciming Quyuan's, and thus ancestor of all surviving Linji lineages, Fenyang was the first master to add verse commentaries to the old stories or koans. A student of the Caodong/Sōtō lineage before receiving the Linji/Rinzai transmission from his teacher Shoushan Xingnian, Fenyang introduced the Caodong five ranks teaching into the Linji tradition. 134, 156, *184n. 24*, *194n. 87*

Foyan Qingyuan (1067–1120) [Fo-yen Ch'ing-yüan] (佛眼清遠) Butsugen Seion. Student of Wuzu Fayan, and teacher of Zhu'an Shigui. 135–36

Furong (Dayang) Daokai (1043–1118) [Fu-jung Tao-k'ai] (芙蓉 [太陽] 道楷) Fuyō [Taiyō] Dōkai. Dayang and later Furong are both places he taught. Although Dōgen refers to him as Dayang, he is more commonly known by the name Furong. The Dharma heir of Touzi

GLOSSARY AND INDEX OF NAMES 241

Yiqing, Furong was particularly known for revitalizing the monastic standards of the Caodong/Sōtō lineage. He is particularly praised by Dōgen for vehemently refusing the offer of fancy robes and imperial honors, which caused him a period of exile. 13, 142, 189n. 50

Fushan Fayuan (991–1067) [Fu-shan Fa-yüan] (浮山法遠) Fusan Hōen. Dharma heir of Shexian Guisheng, despite having been previously expelled from his assembly. He also saved the Caodong/Sōtō lineage from extinction when Dayang Qingxuan was going to die without a Dharma heir. Fushan was in complete Dharma accord with Dayang, but was unwilling to take on the responsibility of publicly proclaiming the Sōtō style in addition to his Rinzai lineage from Guisheng. However, he was able later to transmit the Sōtō lineage from Dayang to his own student, Touzi Yiqing. 12, 139–40, 141, 166, 187n. 43, 188n. 49

Gaoan Dayu (n.d.) [Kao-an Ta-yü] (高安大愚) Kō'an Daigu. Two generations after Mazu Dao-i, he was teacher of Moshan and also was one of Linji's teachers.

Gentō Sokuchū [J.] (1729–1807) (玄透即中) Fiftieth abbot of Eiheiji, he published the popular Rufubon edition of the *Eihei Shingi* in 1794. Also compiled a major edition of the *Shōbōgenzō*. 22, 77n. 11

Gesshū Sōko [J.] (1618–96) (月舟宗胡) Sōtō Zen reformer who brought attention to Dōgen's writings. 22

Guanzhi Zhixian (d. 895) [Kuan-chih Chih-Hsien] (灌溪志閑) Kankei Shikan. Considered a Dharma heir of Linji, Guanzhi also studied under, and venerated, the nun Moshan Laoran. 145

Guishan Huaixiu (11th cent.) [Kuei-shan Huai-hsiu] (潙山懷秀) Isan Eshū. Became a successor of Huanglong Huinan. 150

Guishan Lingyou (771–853) [Kuei-shan Ling-yu] (潙山靈祐) Isan Reiyū. A disciple of Baizhang Huaihai, Guishan was the founder, along with his disciple Yangshan Huiji, of one of the five lineages of classical Chinese Zen Buddhism, the Guiyang house (Igyō in Japanese). Guishan's "Admonitions" is an early warning against laxity in the Zen community. Praised by Dōgen as a former tenzo, he is referred to frequently in the *Eihei Shingi*. 33, 39, 47, 49, 51n. 8, 53n. 20, 57n. 56, 131–32, 136–38, 140–43, 144, 149, 172, 176, 178, 185n. 31, 186n. 32, 187n. 40, 188nn. 47, 49, 201n. 145, 202nn. 147, 149

Guyun Daoquan (13th cent.) [Ku-yün Tao-ch'üan] (孤雲道權) Koun Dōgon. Disciple of Zhuoan Deguang. 41, 54n. 30

Haihui [Baiyun] Shouduan (1025–1072) [Hai-hui Pai-yün Shou-tuan] (海會 [白雲] 守端) Kai'e [Haku'un] Shutan. Main successor of Yangqi Fanghui and teacher of Wuzu Fayan. 147

Hongzhi Zhengjue (1091–1157) [Hung-chih Chêng-chüeh] (宏智正覺) Wanshi Shōgaku. Also called Tiantong Hongzhi, having been abbot at the Tiantong monastery where Dōgen's master Tiantong Rujing later taught, Hongzhi was the most influential Chinese Sōtō teacher in the century before Dōgen. Hongzhi poetically articulated the Caodong/Sōtō tradition's meditation praxis, known as silent or serene illumination, and he also selected the cases and wrote the verse commentaries that were later compiled into the important koan collection called the *Book of Serenity* [*Shōyōroku* in Japanese]. 13, 16

Hualin Shanjue (n.d.) [Hua-lin Shan-chüeh] (華林善覺) Karin Zenkaku. A Dharma heir of Mazu, defeated in dharma combat by Guishan while they served in Baizhang's assembly. Later he became abbot at Hualin (his name after that). He once was asked by Prime Minister Pei Xiugong if he had any attendants. Hualin called out the names "Large Emptiness" and "Small Emptiness," and two tigers appeared. When Pei Xiugong became frightened, Hualin asked the tigers to leave for a while. They roared and departed. 137–38, 187n. 38

Huangbo Xiyun (d. 850) [Huang-po Hsi-yün] (黃檗希運) Ōbaku Kiun. Dharma heir of Baizhang and teacher of Linji, Huangbo was a tall, imposing figure, known for dynamic teaching, including beating students with a stick. *See also* Pei Xiugong. 149

Huanglong Huinan (1002–69) [Huang-lung Hui-nan] (黃龍慧南) Ōryu E'nan. Dharma heir of Ciming Quyuan and teacher of Huitang Zuxin, Huanglong is considered founder of one of the main branches of Rinzai Zen, from which Dōgen's first Zen teacher, Myōzen, was descended. 110, 150–151, 158

[Huanglong] Huitang Zuxin (1025–1100) [Hui-t'ang Tsu-hsin] ([黃龍] 晦堂祖心) [Ōryu] Maidō Soshin. Dharma heir of Huanglong Huinan. Huitang taught by raising a fist and saying, "If you call this a fist you've said too much. If you say it's not a fist you do not hit the mark." 143, 150, *189n. 52*

Huizhao. See Linji Yixuan. Huizhao, a posthumous name, is *Eshō* in Japanese.

Jeta [I.] (6th cent. B.C.E.) Prince Jeta, the son of King Prasenajit of Shravasti. His grove was donated to the Buddha's order by Anthapindika. See Sudatta. 161

Jianzhi Sengcan (d. 606) [Chien-shih Sêng-ts'an] (鑑智僧璨) Kanchi Sōsan. The Third Ancestor of Chan, a leper who was later cured, he is said to have died standing up. The still-popular long teaching poem "Inscription on Faith in Mind" ("Shinjinmei" in Japanese), is attributed to him. 176, *202n. 147*

Jianyuan Zhongxing (n.d.) [Chien-yüan Chung-hsing] (漸源仲興) Zengen Chūkō. Considered a Dharma heir of Daowu Yuanzhi. 138–39, 141, 172, *187n. 41*

Jiashan Shanhui (805–881) [Chia-shan Shan-hui] (夾山善會) Kassan Zenne. Dharma heir of Chuanzi Dechung, who was nicknamed "the boatman" because he lived in the world as a ferryman after the persecution of Buddhism in 842. After transmitting the Dharma to Jiashan, he overturned the boat and disappeared in the water. 141–43, 172, *188nn. 47–79*

Keizan Jōkin [J.] (1264–1325) (瑩山紹瑾) Dharma heir of Tettsu Gikai and founder of Sōjiji Monastery, Keizan extended Sōtō Zen widely into the Japanese lay populace. Author of the *Keizan Shingi*, he is considered the second founder of Japanese Sōtō Zen. 23, *188n. 50*

Kōshō Chidō [J.] (d. 1670) (光紹智堂) Thirtieth abbot of Eiheiji, in 1667 he first published all six essays of the *Eihei Shingi* together in the Shohon edition. 21–2, *77n. 11*, 205–06

Kōshū [J.] (1424–1502?) (光周) Fifteenth abbot of Eiheiji, he first collected and copied "Tenzokyōkun" and "Chiji Shingi." 21, *51n. 13*

Koun Ejō [J.] (1198–1280) (孤雲懷奘) Dōgen's senior student and Dharma heir, and second abbot of Eiheiji. He edited many of Dōgen's writings and talks. x

Li Jingrang (n.d.) [Li Ching-jang] (李景讓) Ri Keijō. A government official who was a student and benefactor of Guishan. 138

Lingyuan Weiqing (d. 1117) [Ling-yüan Wei-ch'ing] (靈源惟清) Reigen Isei. A successor of Huitang Zuxin. 150

Linji Yixuan (d. 867) [Lin-chi Yi-hsüan] (臨濟義玄) Rinzai Gigen. Successor to Huangbo, he was the great, dynamic founder of the Linji/Rinzai branch of Zen. 14, 145, 149–50, *187n. 39, 191nn. 64–65*

Luohan Guichen (867–928) [Lo-han Kuei-ch'ên] (羅漢桂琛) Rakan Keishin. Second generation successor after Xuefeng, he was the teacher of Fayan Wenyi, founder of the Fayan lineage of Chan. Dōgen praises Luohan for his saying, "The tenzo enters the kitchen." *204n. 155*

Mahakashyapa [I.] (6th cent. B.C.E.) The disciple of Shakyamuni considered to be the first Indian ancestor of Zen. He said to have received transmission of the true Dharma eye treasury when he smiled at Shakyamuni's twirling of a flower before the assembly at Vulture Peak. He was known as foremost amongst the disciples in ascetic practice, and is said to be waiting in a Himalayan cave to transmit Shakyamuni's robe to the future Buddha Maitreya. *55n. 41*, 113, 173, *201n. 142*

Maudgalyayana [I.] (6th cent. B.C.E.) One of Shakyamuni's ten great disciples, foremost in the manifestation of supernatural powers. He was inō at Veluvana vihara, the monastery donated by King Bimbisara. 170

Mazu Dao-i (709–88) [Ma-tsu Tao-i] (馬祖道一) Baso Dōitsu. Two generations after the Sixth Ancestor Huineng, he was the great master of his time along with Shitou, and had 139 awakened disciples, including Baizhang and Nanquan. Mazu was an instigator of dynamic, animated Chan style. 83–84, *100n. 3, 186n. 36, 187n. 38*

GLOSSARY AND INDEX OF NAMES 245

Mingzhao Qisong (1007–72) [Ming-chao Ch'i-sung] (明教契嵩) Myōkyō Kaisū. A noted scholar-monk who compiled a history of the Chan transmission, he was an heir of Dongshan Xiaocong (Tōzan Gyōsō in Japanese) in the Yunmen lineage. 159

Moshan Laoran (n.d.) [Mo-shan Lao-jan] (末山了然) Massan Ryōnen. A nun who was Dharma heir of Gaoan Dayu, one of Linji's teachers, she was a teacher of Linji's disciple Guanzhi Zhixian. 145, *190n. 58–59*

Mozi (5th cent. B.C.E.) [Mo-tzu] (墨子) Bokushi. Founded a school of philosophy named after him in China's Warring States Period (403–221 B.C.E.) 165

Myōan [Yōjō] Eisai [J.] (1141–1215) (明庵 [葉上] 栄西) Travelled to China and became successor in the Huanglong (Ōryu) branch of Rinzai Zen, which he introduced to Japan. He founded the Kenninji Temple in Kyoto, where Dōgen practiced before, and just after, going to China. Dōgen may have met him as a young monk, and later spoke of Eisai with great respect. *55n. 42,* 98, *108n. 64*

Myōzen. See Butsuju Myōzen.

Nagarjuna [I.] (2d–3d cent.) A great early exponent of Mahayana Buddhism in India and especially of the Madhyamika teaching, which minutely analyzed the implications of sunyata [relativity or emptiness] doctrine. Nagarjuna's teaching is so universally acclaimed that virtually all later Mahayana movements claim him as an ancestor; he is considered the fourteenth ancestor in the Zen lineage. 162, *196n. 112, 201n. 143*

Nanda [I.] (6th cent. B.C.E.) Half-brother of Shakyamuni; they were both sons of King Suddhodana. After Shakyamuni left home Nanda became the heir to the throne, but later joined the Buddhist order and became an awakened arhat. 127–31, *181n. 1, 182n. 5*

Nanquan Puyuan (748–835) [Nan-ch'üan P'u-yüan] (南泉普願) Nansen Fugan. A Dharma heir of Mazu and teacher of the great Zhaozhou, Nanquan is featured in many koans; he is known for his sickle, his love of cows, and for cutting a cat. 144

Nanyuan Huiyong (d.930) [Nan-yüan Hui-yung] (南院慧顒) Nan'in Egyō. Teacher of Fengxue Yenzhao. *191n. 64*

Nanyue Cikan (n.d.) [Nan-yüeh Tz'u-k'an] (南嶽慈感) Nangaku Jikan. Also known as Tiemien, "Iron Face," because of his strictness, he was a successor of Huanglong Huinan. 150

Pangyun (d. 808) [P'ang-yün] (龐蘊) Hōun. This famous lay adept, known as Layman Pang, was a student of Mazu, Shitou, and Yaoshan, among others. His whole family were practitioners, and his daughter also is especially noted as an adept. *189n. 51*

Pei Xiugong (797–870) [P'ei Hsiu-kung] (裴公休) Hai Kōkyu. Prime minister and governor of several provinces, he was also a lay Zen adept who studied with many masters, including Guishan and Huangbo. Pei Xiugong compiled Huangbo's *Record* (see translation by John Blofeld, *The Zen Teaching of Huang Po*), arranged the building of Huangbo's temple, and also met Hualin's tigers. 138, *187n. 38*

Qingfeng Zhuanchu (9th cent.) [Ch'ing-fêng Chuan-ch'u] (青峰傳楚) Seihō Denso. Student of Yaopu Yuan'an, he was probably the teacher of Baoen Xuanze before Fayan. 132, *183n. 14*

Qingyuan Xingsi (d. 740) [Ch'ing-yüan Hsing-ssu] (青原行思) Seigen Gyōshi. One of the two main disciples of the Sixth Ancestor along with Nanyue Huairang. Qingyuan was the teacher of Shitou. *53n. 20*

Sanghanandi [I.; Sōgyanandai in Japanese] (d. 74 B.C.E.) A prince who abandoned kingship to become a monk, he is recognized as the seventeenth Indian ancestor in the Zen lineage. 158, *194n. 92*

Shanku Huang (1045–1105) [Shan-k'u Huang] (山谷黃) Sankoku Ō. A noted poet and government official who was a lay disciple of Huitang Zuxin. 143, *189n. 53*

Shariputra [I.] (6th cent. B.C.E.) One of the ten great disciples of Shakyamuni. He was especially noted for wisdom. 173, *201n. 143*

Shexian Guisheng (10th cent.) [Shê-hsien Kuei-shêng] (葉縣歸省) Sekken Kishō or Kissei. A Dharma successor of Shoushan Xingian in the fifth generation after Linji, he was known for his strictness. 139–40, *187n. 43*

GLOSSARY AND INDEX OF NAMES 247

Shishuang Qingzhu (807–888) [Shih-shuang Ch'ing-chu] (石霜慶諸) Sekisō Keisho. Dharma heir of Daowu Yuanzhi, who had been tenzo for Guishan, Shishuang Qingzhu's assembly was noted for always sleeping sitting up, and so was called the "Dead Tree Hall." 139, 144, 178, *187n. 41*, 202*n. 149*

Shishuang Quyuan. See Ciming.

Shitou Xiqian (700–790) [Shih-t'ou Hsi-ch'ien] (石頭希遷) Sekitō Kisen. Shitou was two generations after the Sixth Ancestor and three generations before Dongshan Liangjie, founder of the Sōtō lineage which Dōgen brought back to Japan from China. Shitou and Mazu, the two great teachers of their time, regularly sent students to each other. Shitou authored the long poem "Sandōkai" ["Unifying of Sameness and Difference"; "Cantongqi" in Chinese], which is still important in the Sōtō tradition. It is chanted daily in Sōtō training temples. He also wrote "Song of the Grass Hut." xvii, 13, 112, *117n. 11*

Shoushan Xingnian (926–93) [Shou-shan Shêng-nien] (首山省念) Shusan Shōnen. Student of Fengxue Yanzhao; teacher of Fenyang and of Shexian Guisheng.

Shuangling Hua (n.d.) [Shuang-ling Hua] (雙嶺化) Sōrei Ke. A Dharma successor of Huitang Zuxin. 150

Shukan (3d cent. B.C.E.) [Shu-k'an] (疎広) Sōkō. A prince of the Early Han dynasty, famous for his straightforwardness and honesty. 160

Sima Chengzheng (n.d.) [Ssu-ma Ch'êng-chêng] (司馬承禎) Shiba Shōtei. A lay disciple of Mazu Dao-i, Sima was noted for geomantic skill, which he used to help find sites for temples, including Guishan. 137, *186n. 36*

Sudatta [J.] (6th cent. B.C.E.) Also known as Anthapindika ["Giver of Food to the Unprotected"]. He was a wealthy patron of Shakyamuni Buddha in Shravasti who built the Jetavana vihara (monastery) in the Jeta garden for the order of monks. 161

Taiyuan Fu (9th cent.) [T'ai-yuan Fu] (太原孚) Taigen Fu. A disciple of Xuefeng who was awakened by a tenzo. 49, *57n. 55*

Tettsū Gikai [J.] (1219–1309) (徹通義介) Student of Dōgen who later

248 GLOSSARY AND INDEX OF NAMES

became Dharma heir of Koun Ejō and third abbot of Eiheiji. He traveled to China to study Chinese monastic architecture and forms. Teacher of Keizan Jōkin. x

Tiantong Rujing (1163–1228) [T'ien-t'ung Ju-ching] (天童如淨) Tendō Nyojō. Dōgen's teacher. Dōgen practiced with him for three years at Mt. Tiantong in China and received from him the Caodong/Sōtō transmission. 54n. 25, 109, 146

Tianyi Yihuai (993–1064) [T'ien-yi Yi-huai] (天衣義懷) Tenne Gikai. A Dharma heir of Xuedou, he also studied with Shexian Guisheng together with Fushan Fayuan. Tianyi was teacher of Yuantong Faxiu. 139–40, *187n. 43*

Touzi Datong (819–914) [T'ou-tzu Ta-t'ung] (投子大同) Tōsu Daidō. Teacher of Dongkeng Yanjun. Touzi was in the lineage two generations after Danxia Tianran, the student of Shitou famous for burning a buddha statue to warm himself. 159

Touzi Yiqing (1032–83) [T'ou-tzu Yi-ch'ing] (投子義青) Tōsu Gisei. Student of Fushan Fayuan who received from him the Sōtō lineage of Dayang and maintained that tradition, incorporating his prior Huayan studies. Teacher of Furong Daokai. 142, *187n. 43*, *188n. 49*, *189n. 50*

Wuliang Congzhou (13th cent.) [Wu-liang Ts'ung-shou] (無量宗壽) Muryō Sōju. Compiled "The Daily Life in the Assembly" in 1209 as a procedural handbook for daily monks' practice, using many of the same sources as *Eihei Shingi*. *79n. 26*

Wuzhuo Wenxi (821–900) [Wu-cho Wên-hsi] (無著文喜) Mujaku Bunki. Dharma heir of Yangshan, he was known for his conversations with Manjushri, the bodhisattva of wisdom. 139, 141, 172, *187n. 42*

Wuzu Fayan (1024–1104) [Wu-tsu Fa-yen] (五祖法演) Goso Hōen. Named for his temple site on Wuzu [Fifth Ancestor] Mountain, where the Fifth Ancestor had taught, Wuzu was a successor of Haihui Shouduan, who was a successor of Yangqi. Known for his straight-forward style, Wuzu was the teacher of Yuanwu Keqin (the compiler of the *Blue Cliff Records*) and of Foyan Qingyuan. 12, 136, 147–48, 151–52, 166, *184n. 29*

GLOSSARY AND INDEX OF NAMES 249

Xuanze. See Baoen Xuanze

Xuedou Chongxian (980–1052) [Hsüeh-tou Ch'ung-hsien] (雪寶重顯) Setchō Jūken. A master in the Yunmen lineage and noted poet, his selection of one hundred cases with verse commentaries was the basis for the famous *Blue Cliff Record* [*Hekigan Roku*] koan anthology. 43, *54n. 34*, *187n. 43*

Xuefeng Yicun (822–908) [Hsüeh-fêng I-tsun] (雪峰義存) Seppō Gison. After serving as tenzo at many temples, he finally became the heir of Deshan Xuanjian. Xuefeng was the teacher of Yunmen and was the third-generation ancestor of Fayan, founders of two of the five classical Chan lineages. 12, 35, *51n. 7*, *56n. 44*, 144, 174–75, *190n. 56*

Yangqi Fanghui (992–1049) [Yang-ch'i Fang-hui] (楊岐方會) Yōgi Hōe. The founder of one of the two main branches of Linji (Rinzai) Zen. All modern Japanese Rinzai Zen derives from his lineage. Student of Ciming [or Shishuang] Quyuan. 133–35, 151, *183n. 20*, *184n. 29*

Yangshan Huiji (807–83) [Yang-shan Hui-chi] (仰山慧寂) Gyōsan Ejaku. Student of Guishan, he is considered cofounder of the Guiyang (Igyō) lineage, one of the classical five houses of Chan. Yangshan is nicknamed "Little Shakyamuni," and is sometimes said to have had prophetic talents. He used symbolic diagrams in his teaching. *51n. 8*, 149, *187n. 42*, *191n. 64*, *201n. 145*

Yaopu [Yaopo] Yuan'an (834–98) [Yao-p'u Yüan-an] (洛浦 [樂普] 元安) Rakufu [Rakuho] Gen'an. The teacher of Qingfeng Zhuanchu. 135

Yaoshan Weiyan (745–828) [Yao-shan Wei-yen] (藥山惟儼) Yakusan Igen. Dharma heir of Shitou, he also studied with Mazu. He was the teacher of Dongshan Liangjie's teacher Yunyan. His description of zazen as "beyond-thinking," *hishiryo*, is much quoted by Dōgen. *80n. 36*, 142, 156, *188n. 47*, *194n. 87*

Yinyuan Longqi (1592–1673) [Yin-yüan Lung-ch'i] (隱元隆琦) Ingen Ryūki. Chinese master who founded the Japanese Ōbaku School in 1654, importing the style and forms of Ming dynasty Chinese Buddhism. 22, *102n. 12*

Yōjō. See Myōan Eisai.

Yongjia Xuanjie (675–713) [Yung-chia Hsüan-chieh] (永嘉玄覺) Yōka Genkaku. Famous for becoming a successor to the Sixth Ancestor after spending only one night at his temple. Yongjia's "Song of Enlightenment [or Verification] of the Way," "Shōdōka" in Japanese, remains a popular Zen text. 176, 202*n*. 147

Yuantong Faxiu (1027–90) [Yüan-t'ung Fa-hsiu] (圓通法秀) Entsū Hōshu. A Dharma heir of Tianyi Yihuai, he also was head monk under Haihui Shouduan and supported Wuzu Fayan, as well as Touzi Yiqing. 147–48

Yuanwu Keqin (1063–1135) [Yüan-wu Kê-ch'in] (圜悟克勤) Engo Kokugon. Dharma heir of Wuzu Fayan and compiler of the *Blue Cliff Record* [*Hekigan Roku*] koan collection based on Xuedou's verse comments. He was the teacher of Dahui. 184*n*. 29

Yunmen Wenyan (864–949) [Yun-mên Wên-yen] (雲門文偃) Unmon Bun'en. Dharma successor of Xuefeng and founder of one of the five houses of Chan, he is famous for pithy response to questions and is featured in many of the classical koans. 50*n*. 3, 55*n*. 40, 56*n*. 46

Yunyan Tansheng (781–841) [Yün-yen T'an-shêng] (雲巖曇晟) Ungan Donjō. Dharma heir of Yaoshan after serving twenty years as Baizhang's jisha without having realization (unlike his older biological brother Daowu, who was also a student of Baizhang and Yaoshan). Yunyan later was the teacher of Dongshan Liangjie, who honored Yunyan as his master before other, more famous teachers only because Yunyan "Never explained anything to him directly." 194*n*. 87

Zhaozhou Congshen (778–897) [Chao-chou Ts'ung-shên] (趙州從諗) Jōshū Jushin. Dharma successor of Nanquan Puyuan, he is considered one of the all-time great Zen masters, and is source of many of the classic koans, such as his response to the question, "Does a dog have Buddha Nature?" His dharma was so strong that no students were capable of matching and succeeding him, and his own lineage did not long survive, but he is revered in all subsequent Zen lineages. 75*n*. 2, 144, 156

Zhu'an Shigui of Longxiang (1083–1146) [Chu-an Shih-kuei of Lung-hsiang] (竹菴 [能翔] 士珪) Chikuan Shikei of Ryūshō. A Dharma heir of Foyan Qingyuan, who was a student of Wuzu Fayan. Zhu'an is also known as Kushan [Drum Mountain], where he later taught and which was a center of Buddhist studies in Dōgen's time. Zhu'an, who is praised by Dōgen for his literary expression of Dharma, compiled a collection of stories, "Zen Gate Jeweled Instructions," together with Dahui. 135–36, *185n. 30, 196n. 105*

Zhuangzi (4th cent. B.C.E.) [Chuang-tzu] (莊子) Sōshi. Highly venerated early Taoist philosopher and writer, known for his wit, colorful parables, and deep insight. 163–64, *197n. 117*

Zhuoan Deguang (1121–1203) [Cho-an Tê-kuang] (拙菴德光) Setsuan Tokkō. A disciple of Dahui Zonggao; an abbot of Ayuwang Monastery. *54n. 30*

Lineage Charts

The following lineage charts show the Dharma relationships of the persons in *Dōgen's Pure Standards for the Zen Community*, and may help clarify the interrelationships of teachers and students. However, as is clear in some of the stories in "The Pure Standards for Temple Administrators," many of these figures studied intently with other teachers besides the ones formally identified as their primary Dharma teachers. The actuality of the lineage of Zen teaching and experience is the interweaving of these lineages and the tangled causes and conditions of awakening. These charts include names of some significant persons in the lineages who are not mentioned in the Glossary of Names or elsewhere in *Dōgen's Pure Standards for the Zen Community*. Also, a few less important figures who are mentioned by Dōgen are not included in these charts. The Chinese names are given, followed by Japanese pronunciations (in parentheses) and dates when available.

Chart I

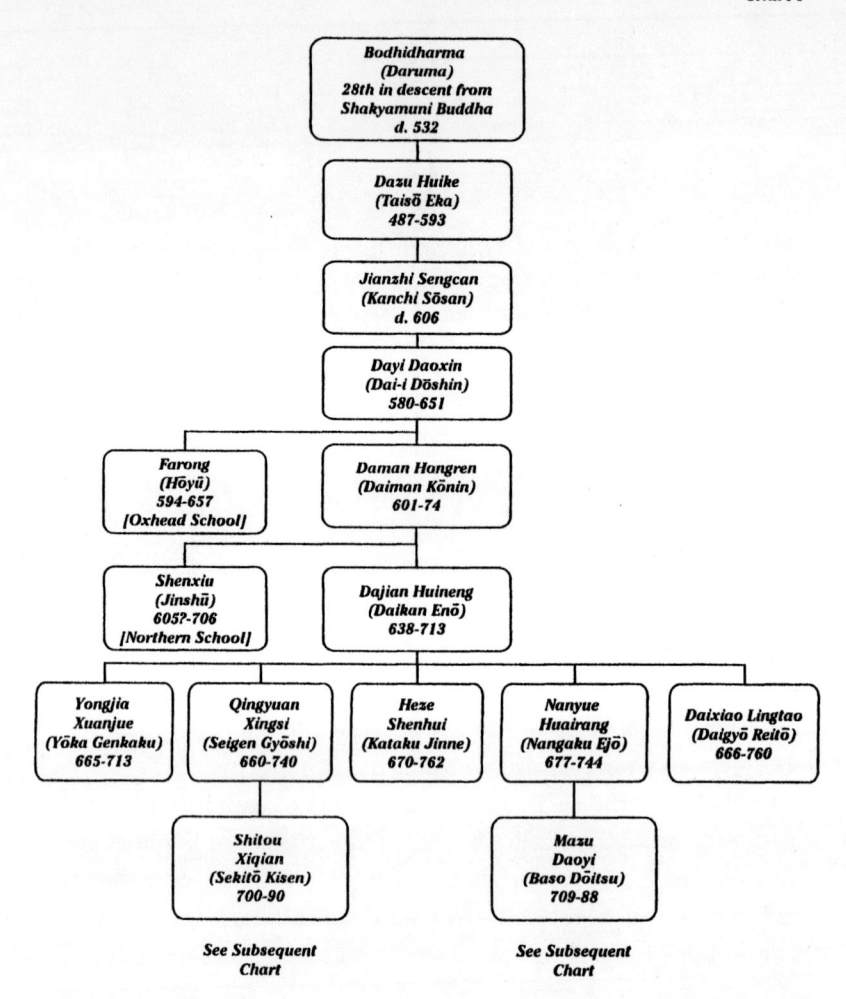

```
                    Bodhidharma
                     (Daruma)
                28th in descent from
                Shakyamuni Buddha
                      d. 532
                        |
                    Dazu Huike
                    (Taisō Eka)
                     487-593
                        |
                  Jianzhi Sengcan
                  (Kanchi Sōsan)
                      d. 606
                        |
                    Dayi Daoxin
                   (Dai-i Dōshin)
                     580-651
                   ___|_____
                  |               |
               Farong        Daman Hongren
               (Hōyū)        (Daiman Kōnin)
              594-657            601-74
           [Oxhead School]          |
                        _____|
                       |          |
                    Shenxiu   Dajian Huineng
                   (Jinshū)   (Daikan Enō)
                   605?-706      638-713
              [Northern School]
```

| Yongjia Xuanjue (Yōka Genkaku) 665-713 | Qingyuan Xingsi (Seigen Gyōshi) 660-740 | Heze Shenhui (Kataku Jinne) 670-762 | Nanyue Huairang (Nangaku Ejō) 677-744 | Daixiao Lingtao (Daigyō Reitō) 666-760 |

Shitou Xiqian (Sekitō Kisen) 700-90

Mazu Daoyi (Baso Dōitsu) 709-88

See Subsequent Chart

See Subsequent Chart

Bodhidharma to Shitou and Mazu.

Chart II

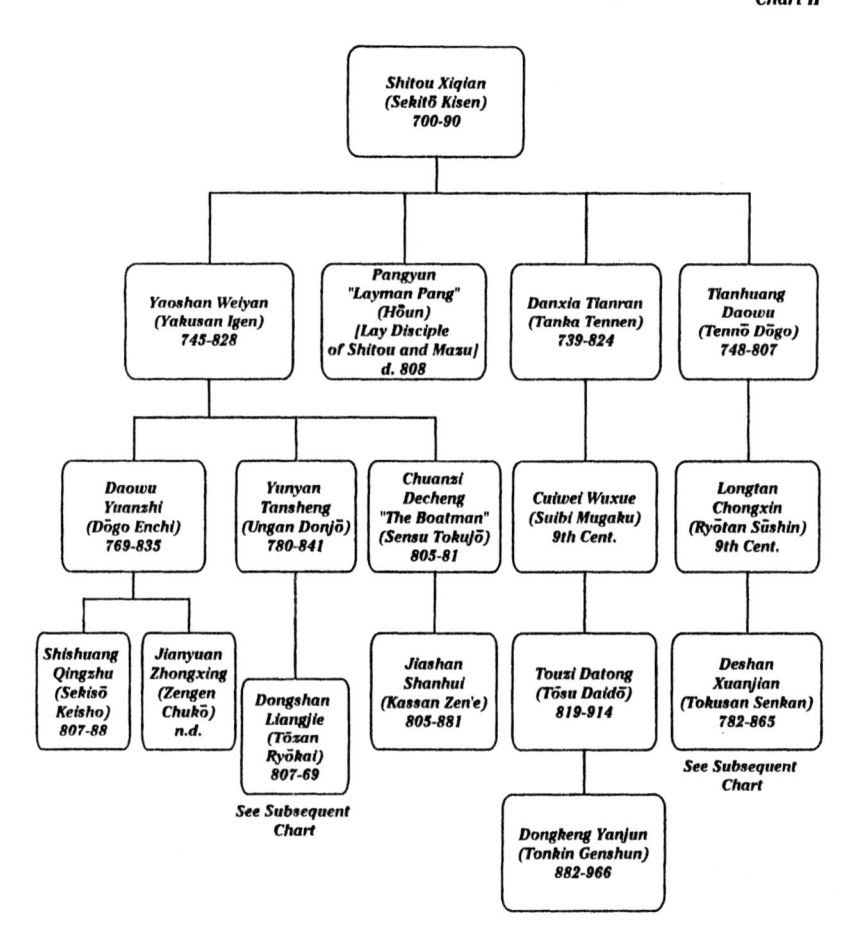

```
                          ┌─────────────────────┐
                          │   Shitou Xiqian     │
                          │   (Sekitō Kisen)    │
                          │      700-90         │
                          └─────────────────────┘
```

- **Yaoshan Weiyan** (Yakusan Igen) 745-828
- **Pangyun "Layman Pang"** (Hōun) [Lay Disciple of Shitou and Mazu] d. 808
- **Danxia Tianran** (Tanka Tennen) 739-824
- **Tianhuang Daowu** (Tennō Dōgo) 748-807

Under Yaoshan Weiyan:
- **Daowu Yuanzhi** (Dōgo Enchi) 769-835
  - **Shishuang Qingzhu** (Sekisō Keisho) 807-88
  - **Jianyuan Zhongxing** (Zengen Chukō) n.d.
- **Yunyan Tansheng** (Ungan Donjō) 780-841
  - **Dongshan Liangjie** (Tōzan Ryōkai) 807-69
  - *See Subsequent Chart*
- **Chuanzi Decheng "The Boatman"** (Sensu Tokujō) 805-81
  - **Jiashan Shanhui** (Kassan Zen'e) 805-881

Under Danxia Tianran:
- **Cuiwei Wuxue** (Suibi Mugaku) 9th Cent.
  - **Touzi Datong** (Tōsu Daidō) 819-914
    - **Dongkeng Yanjun** (Tonkin Genshun) 882-966

Under Tianhuang Daowu:
- **Longtan Chongxin** (Ryōtan Sūshin) 9th Cent.
  - **Deshan Xuanjian** (Tokusan Senkan) 782-865
  - *See Subsequent Chart*

Shitou to Dongshan Liangjie and Deshan Xuanjian.

Chart III

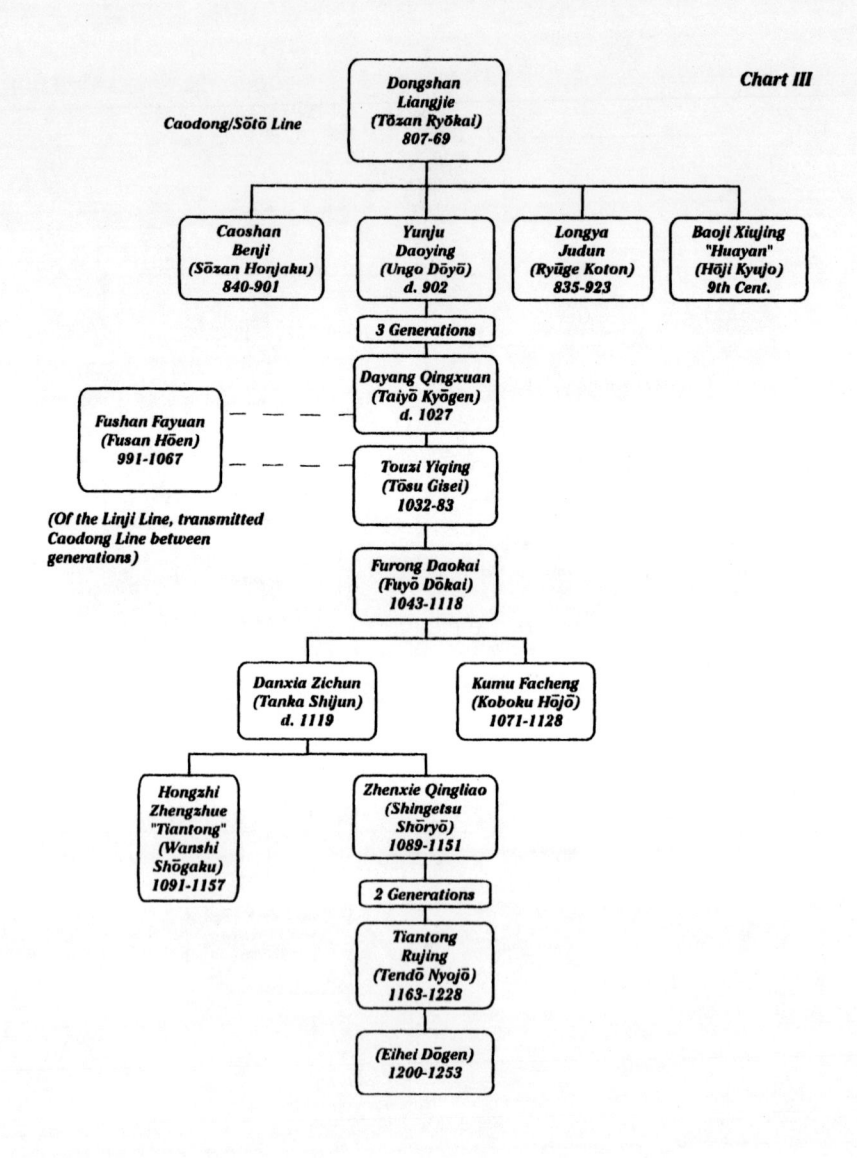

Caodong/Sōtō Line

- Dongshan Liangjie (Tōzan Ryōkai) 807-69
  - Caoshan Benji (Sōzan Honjaku) 840-901
  - Yunju Daoying (Ungo Dōyō) d. 902
    - *3 Generations*
    - Dayang Qingxuan (Taiyō Kyōgen) d. 1027
      - Touzi Yiqing (Tōsu Gisei) 1032-83
        - Furong Daokai (Fuyō Dōkai) 1043-1118
          - Danxia Zichun (Tanka Shijun) d. 1119
            - Hongzhi Zhengzhue "Tiantong" (Wanshi Shōgaku) 1091-1157
            - Zhenxie Qingliao (Shingetsu Shōryō) 1089-1151
              - *2 Generations*
              - Tiantong Rujing (Tendō Nyojō) 1163-1228
                - (Eihei Dōgen) 1200-1253
          - Kumu Facheng (Koboku Hōjō) 1071-1128
  - Longya Judun (Ryūge Koton) 835-923
  - Baoji Xiujing "Huayan" (Hōji Kyujo) 9th Cent.

Fushan Fayuan (Fusan Hōen) 991-1067

(Of the Linji Line, transmitted Caodong Line between generations)

Dongshan to Dōgen; the Caodong/Sōtō lineage.

Chart IV

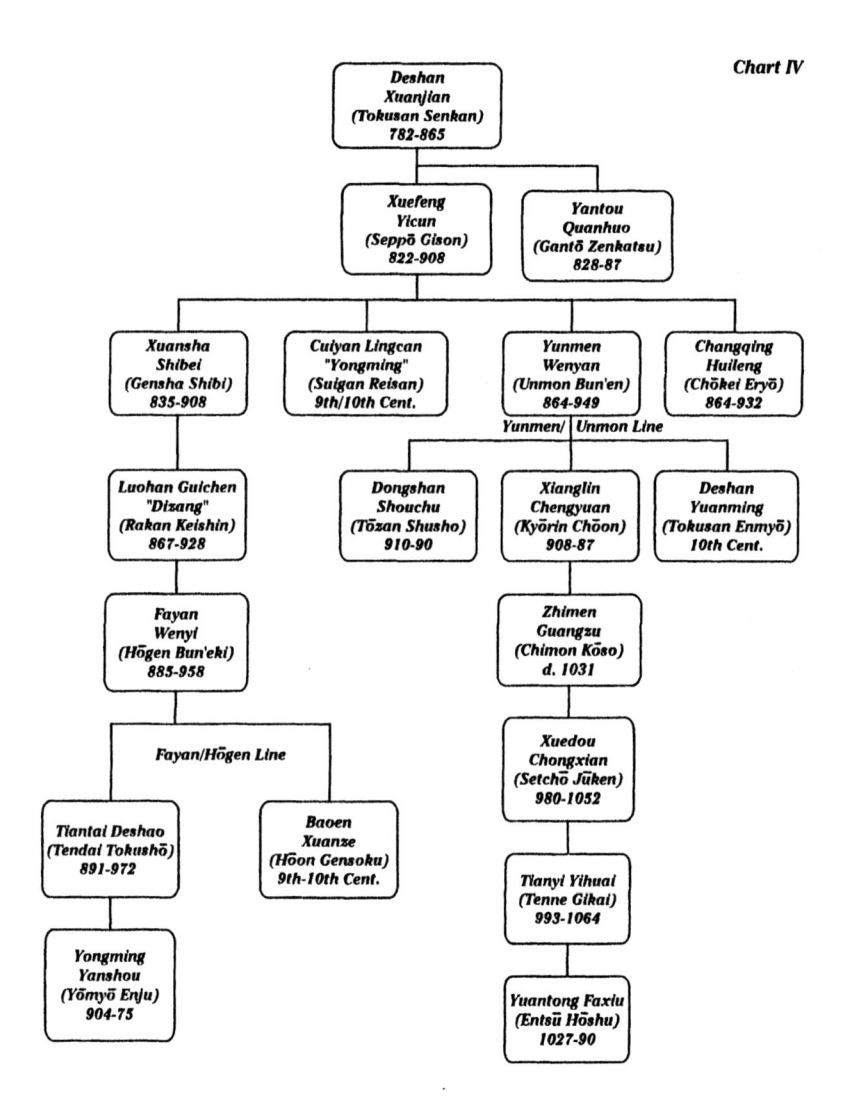

```
                    Deshan
                    Xuanjian
                (Tokusan Senkan)
                    782-865
                    /        \
              Xuefeng          Yantou
               Yicun          Quanhuo
            (Seppō Gison)  (Gantō Zenkatsu)
              822-908          828-87
```

Xuefeng Yicun branches to:
- Xuansha Shibei (Gensha Shibi) 835-908
- Cuiyan Lingcan "Yongming" (Suigan Reisan) 9th/10th Cent.
- Yunmen Wenyan (Unmon Bun'en) 864-949
- Changqing Huileng (Chōkei Eryō) 864-932

Yunmen/Unmon Line

Yunmen Wenyan branches to:
- Dongshan Shouchu (Tōzan Shusho) 910-90
- Xianglin Chengyuan (Kyōrin Chōon) 908-87
- Deshan Yuanming (Tokusan Enmyō) 10th Cent.

Xuansha Shibei → Luohan Guichen "Dizang" (Rakan Keishin) 867-928 → Fayan Wenyi (Hōgen Bun'eki) 885-958

Fayan/Hōgen Line

Fayan Wenyi branches to:
- Tiantai Deshao (Tendai Tokushō) 891-972 → Yongming Yanshou (Yōmyō Enju) 904-75
- Baoen Xuanze (Hōon Gensoku) 9th-10th Cent.

Xianglin Chengyuan → Zhimen Guangzu (Chimon Kōso) d. 1031 → Xuedou Chongxian (Setchō Jūken) 980-1052 → Tianyi Yihuai (Tenne Gikai) 993-1064 → Yuantong Faxiu (Entsū Hōshu) 1027-90

Deshan to the Fayan and Yunmen lineages.

Chart V

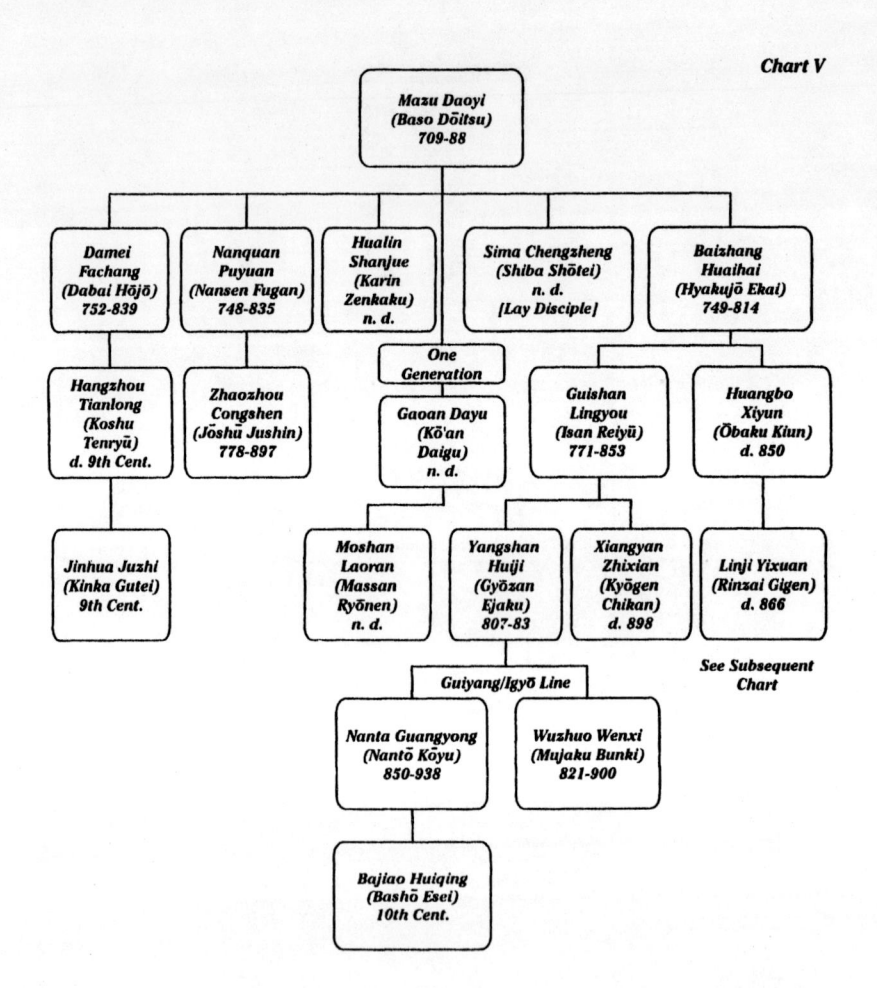

```
                          Mazu Daoyi
                          (Baso Dōitsu)
                            709-88
    ┌───────────┬──────────┬─────┴─────┬───────────┬───────────┐
  Damei      Nanquan      Hualin      Sima        Baizhang
  Fachang    Puyuan       Shanjue     Chengzheng  Huaihai
 (Dabai Hōjō)(Nansen      (Karin     (Shiba Shōtei)(Hyakujō Ekai)
  752-839    Fugan)        Zenkaku)   n. d.        749-814
             748-835       n. d.     [Lay Disciple]
    │           │            │                        │
    │           │         One Generation              │
    │           │            │                        │
 Hangzhou   Zhaozhou      Gaoan Dayu              ┌───┴────┐
 Tianlong   Congshen      (Kō'an                Guishan   Huangbo
 (Koshu    (Jōshū Jūshin)  Daigu)               Lingyou   Xiyun
 Tenryū)    778-897        n. d.               (Isan Reiyū)(Ōbaku Kiun)
 d. 9th Cent.                                   771-853   d. 850
    │                         │                    │        │
 Jinhua Juzhi         ┌───────┼──────┐         ┌───┴───┐  Linji Yixuan
 (Kinka Gutei)      Moshan  Yangshan Xiangyan          (Rinzai Gigen)
 9th Cent.          Laoran  Huiji    Zhixian           d. 866
                   (Massan (Gyōzan  (Kyōgen
                    Ryōnen) Ejaku)   Chikan)         See Subsequent
                    n. d.  807-83    d. 898            Chart
                         Guiyang/Igyō Line
                    ┌────────┴────────┐
              Nanta Guangyong     Wuzhuo Wenxi
              (Nantō Kōyu)        (Mujaku Bunki)
              850-938             821-900
                    │
              Bajiao Huiqing
              (Bashō Esei)
              10th Cent.
```

Mazu to Linji and to the Guiyang lineage.

Chart VI

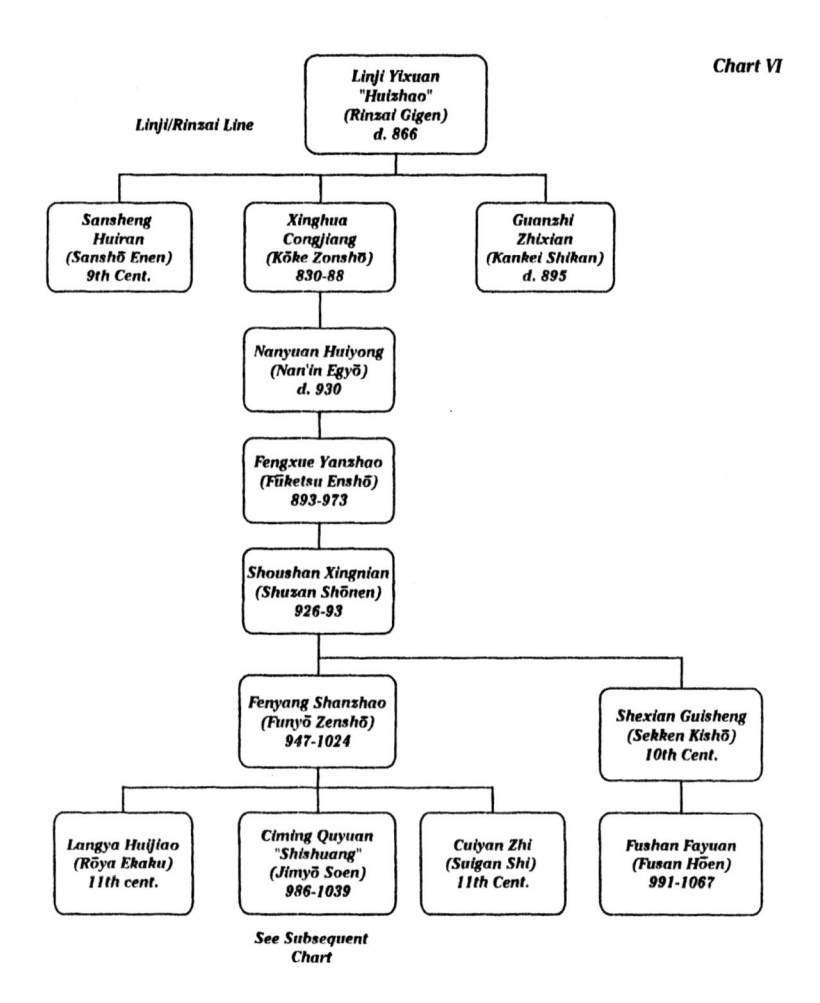

Linji/Rinzai Line

- Linji Yixuan "Huizhao" (Rinzai Gigen) d. 866
  - Sansheng Huiran (Senshō Enen) 9th Cent.
  - Xinghua Congjiang (Kōke Zonshō) 830-88
    - Nanyuan Huiyong (Nan'in Egyō) d. 930
      - Fengxue Yanzhao (Fūketsu Enshō) 893-973
        - Shoushan Xingnian (Shuzan Shōnen) 926-93
          - Fenyang Shanzhao (Funyō Zenshō) 947-1024
            - Langya Huijiao (Rōya Ekaku) 11th cent.
            - Ciming Quyuan "Shishuang" (Jimyō Soen) 986-1039
              See Subsequent Chart
            - Cuiyan Zhi (Suigan Shi) 11th Cent.
          - Shexian Guisheng (Sekken Kishō) 10th Cent.
            - Fushan Fayuan (Fusan Hōen) 991-1067
  - Guanzhi Zhixian (Kankei Shikan) d. 895

Linji to Ciming Quyuan; the Linji/Rinzai lineage.

Chart VII

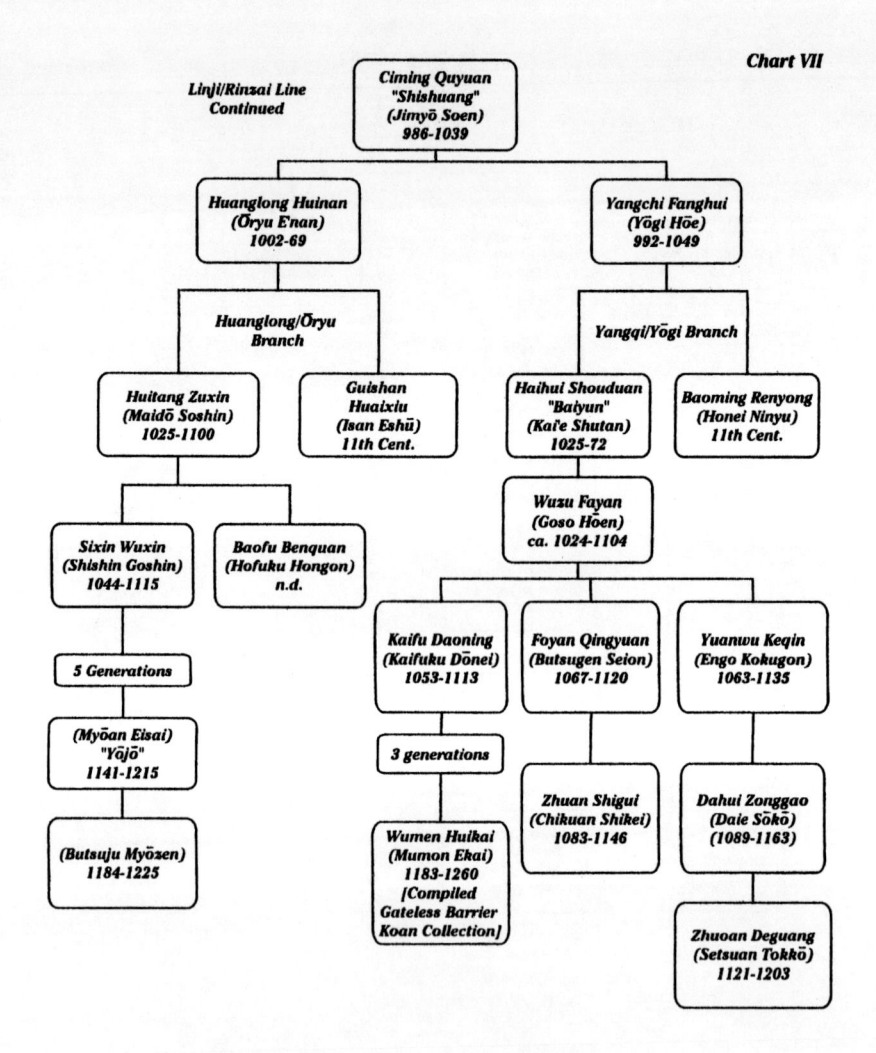

Linji/Rinzai Line Continued

- **Ciming Quyuan "Shishuang" (Jimyō Soen) 986-1039**
  - **Huanglong Huinan (Ōryu E'nan) 1002-69** — *Huanglong/Ōryu Branch*
    - **Huitang Zuxin (Maidō Soshin) 1025-1100**
      - **Sixin Wuxin (Shishin Goshin) 1044-1115**
        - 5 Generations
          - **(Myōan Eisai) "Yōjō" 1141-1215**
            - **(Butsuju Myōzen) 1184-1225**
      - **Baofu Benquan (Hofuku Hongon) n.d.**
    - **Guishan Huaixiu (Isan Eshū) 11th Cent.**
  - **Yangchi Fanghui (Yōgi Hōe) 992-1049** — *Yangqi/Yōgi Branch*
    - **Haihui Shouduan "Baiyun" (Kai'e Shutan) 1025-72**
      - **Wuzu Fayan (Goso Hōen) ca. 1024-1104**
        - **Kaifu Daoning (Kaifuku Dōnei) 1053-1113**
          - 3 generations
            - **Wumen Huikai (Mumon Ekai) 1183-1260 [Compiled Gateless Barrier Koan Collection]**
        - **Foyan Qingyuan (Butsugen Seion) 1067-1120**
          - **Zhuan Shigui (Chikuan Shikei) 1083-1146**
        - **Yuanwu Keqin (Engo Kokugon) 1063-1135**
          - **Dahui Zonggao (Daie Sōkō) (1089-1163)**
          - **Zhuoan Deguang (Setsuan Tokkō) 1121-1203**
    - **Baoming Renyong (Honei Ninyu) 11th Cent.**

Ciming to the Huanglong and Yangqi branches of the Linji lineage.

Selected Bibliography

WORKS IN CHINESE OR JAPANESE

The base text for this translation of Eihei Shingi *is from:*
Kosaka Kiyū and Suzuki Kakuzen, eds. *Dōgen Zenji Zenshū*. Vol. 6. Tokyo: Shunjūsha, 1989.

Other Eihei Shingi *texts consulted*

Ōkubo Dōshū, ed. *Dōgen Zenji Shingi*. Tokyo: Iwanami Shoten, 1941.
———. *Dōgen Zenji Zenshū*. Vol. 2. Tokyo: Chikuma Shobō, 1970.
Sōtō Shū Shūmuchō. *Eihei Gen Zenji Shingi*. Tokyo: Sōtō Shū Shūmuchō.

Consulted for other works by Dōgen

Kosaka Kiyū and Suzuki Kakuzen, eds. *Dōgen Zenji Zenshū*. 7 vols. Tokyo: Shunjūsha, 1989.
Ōkubo Dōshū, ed. *Dōgen Zenji Zenshū*. 2 vols. Tokyo: Chikuma Shobō, 1970.

Commentaries on Eihei Shingi

Akizuki Ryūmin. *Dōgen Zenji no Tenzo Kyōkun o Yomu*. Tokyo: Daihōrinkaku.

Ando Bun'ei. *Eihei Daishingi Tsūkai*. 1936. Revised and enlarged edition. Edited by Itō Shunkō. 1969. Reprint. Tokyo: Kōmeisha, 1981.
Aoyama Shuntō. *Tenzo Kyōkun: Suzuyaka ni Ikiru*. Tokyo: Daizō Shuppan.
Menzan Zuihō. *Tenzo Kyōkun Monge*. 1767. Kyoto: Baiyō Shoin.
Shinohara Hisao. *Eihei Daishingi: Dōgen no Shūdō Kihan*. Tokyo: Daitō Shuppansha, 1980.
———. *Tenzo Kyōkun: Zenshin no Seikatsu*. Tokyo: Daizō Shuppan, 1969.
Uchiyama Kōshō. *Inochi no Hataraki: Chiji Shingi o Ajiwau*. Tokyo: Hakujusha, 1972.
———. *Jinseiryōri no Hon: Tenzo Kyōkun o Ajiwau*. Tokyo: Sōtō Shū Shūmuchō, 1970. Original text for *Refining Your Life*.
Ueda Sohō. *Shinshaku Tenzo Kyōkun: Chōri to Zen no Kokoro*. Tokyo: Keibunsha.

Related Primary Texts

Dachuan Puji, ed. *Gotō Egen* [*Wudeng Huiyuan* in Chinese]. 1252. In *Dai-Nihon zoku-zōkyō*. 2, B, 11. Kyoto, 1905–12.
Daoyuan, ed. *Keitoku Dentōroku* [*Jingde Chuandeng Lu* in Chinese]. 1004. In *Taishō Shinshū Daizōkyō*, 51:196–467. Tokyo: Taishō Issaikyō Kankokai, 1924–33.
Kagamishima Genryū, Satō Tatsugen, and Kosaka Kiyū, eds. *Yakuchū Zen'en Shingi*. Tokyo: Sōtō Shū Shūmuchō, 1972.
Sōtō Shū Shūmuchō Kyōgakubu. *Sōtōshū Gyōji Kihan*. Tokyo: Sōtō Shū Shūmuchō, 1967.

Dictionaries

Iriya Yoshitaka. *Zengo Jiten*. Kyoto: Shibunkaku Shuppan, 1991.
Nakamura Hajime. *Bukkyōgo Daijiten*. Tokyo: Tokyo Shoseki, 1981.
Tōdō Akiyasu. *Gakken Kanwa Daijiten*. Tokyo: Gakushū Kenkyūsha, 1978.
Zengaku Daijiten Hensansho. *Zengaku Daijiten*. Tokyo: Daishūkan Shoten, 1978.

WORKS IN ENGLISH

Abe, Masao. *A Study of Dōgen: His Philosophy and Religion*. Albany: State University of New York Press, 1992.

---. *Zen and Western Thought*. Honolulu: University of Hawaii Press, 1985.

Aitken, Robert. *The Dragon Who Never Sleeps: Verses for Zen Buddhist Practice*. Berkeley: Parallax Press, 1992.

---. *The Mind of Clover: Essays in Zen Buddhist Ethics*. San Francisco: North Point Press, 1984.

---, trans. *The Gateless Barrier: The Wu-men Kuan (Mumonkan)*. San Francisco: North Point Press, 1990.

App, Urs, trans. and ed. *Master Yunmen: From the Record of the Chan Master "Gate of the Clouds."* New York: Kodansha International, 1994.

Bielefeldt, Carl. *Dōgen's Manuals of Zen Meditation*. Berkeley: University of California Press, 1988.

Blofeld, John, trans. *The Zen Teaching of Huang Po: On the Transmission of Mind*. New York: Grove Press, 1958.

Bodiford, William M. *Sōtō Zen in Medieval Japan*. Honolulu: Kuroda Institute, University of Hawaii Press, 1993.

Buddhist Text Translation Society. *Buddha Speaks the Brahma Net Sutra: The Ten Major and Forty-eight Minor Bodhisattva Precepts*. Translated by Bhikshuni Heng Tao. Talmage, Calif.: Dharma Realm Buddhist University, 1982.

Buswell, Robert E., Jr. *The Zen Monastic Experience*. Princeton: Princeton University Press, 1992.

Chang Chung-Yuan, trans. *Original Teachings of Ch'an Buddhism: Selected from "Transmission of the Lamp."* New York: Vintage Books, 1971.

Chang, Garma C. C. *The Buddhist Teaching of Totality: The Philosophy of Hwa Yen Buddhism*. University Park: Pennsylvania State University Press, 1971.

---. *The Practice of Zen*. New York: Harper & Row, 1975.

---, ed. *A Treasury of Mahayana Sutras: Selections from the Maharatnakuta Sutra*. University Park: Pennsylvania State University Press, 1983.

Chien, Bhikshu Cheng, trans. *Manifestation of the Tathagata: Buddhahood According to the Avatamsaka Sutra*. Boston: Wisdom Publications, 1993.

---, trans. *Sun-Face Buddha: The Teachings of Ma-tsu and the Hung-chou School of Ch'an*. Berkeley: Asian Humanities Press, 1992.

Cleary, J. C., trans. *Swampland Flowers: The Letters and Lectures of Zen Master Ta Hui*. New York: Grove Press, 1977.

———, trans. and ed. *Zen Dawn: Early Zen Texts from Tun Huang*. Boston: Shambhala, 1986.

Cleary, Thomas, trans. *The Book of Serenity*. Hudson, N.Y.: Lindisfarne Press, 1990.

———, trans. *Entry into the Inconceivable: An Introduction to Hua Yen Buddhism*. Honolulu: University of Hawaii Press, 1983.

———, trans. *Entry into the Realm of Reality, the Guide: A Commentary on the "Gandhavyuha" by Li Tongxuan*. Boston: Shambhala, 1989.

———, trans. *The Flower Ornament Scripture: A Translation of the Avatamsaka Sutra*. 3 vols. Boston: Shambhala, 1983–86.

———, trans. *Instant Zen: Waking Up in the Present*. Berkeley: North Atlantic Books, 1994.

———, trans. and ed. *Minding Mind: A Course in Basic Meditation*. Boston: Shambhala, 1995.

———, trans. and commentary. *No Barrier: Unlocking the Zen Koan, A New Translation of the Mumonkan*. New York: Bantam Books, 1993.

———, trans. and ed. *The Original Face: An Anthology of Rinzai Zen*. New York: Grove Press, 1978.

———, ed. and trans. *Rational Zen: The Mind of Dōgen Zenji*. Boston: Shambhala, 1993.

———, trans. *Record of Things Heard: The "Shōbōgenzō Zuimonki," Talks of Zen Master Dōgen as Recorded by Zen Master Ejō*. Boulder, Colo.: Prajna Press, 1980.

———, trans. *Sayings and Doings of Pai-Chang*. Los Angeles: Center Publications, 1978.

———, trans. *"Shōbōgenzō": Zen Essays by Dōgen*. Honolulu: University of Hawaii Press, 1986.

———, ed. and trans. *Timeless Spring: A Soto Zen Anthology*. Tokyo: Weatherhill, 1980.

———, trans. *Transmission of Light: Zen in the Art of Enlightenment by Zen Master Keizan*. San Francisco: North Point Press, 1990.

———, trans. *Zen Essence: The Science of Freedom*. Boston: Shambhala, 1989.

SELECTED BIBLIOGRAPHY 265

———, trans. *Zen Lessons: The Art of Leadership*. Boston: Shambhala, 1989.

Cleary, Thomas, and J. C. Cleary, trans. *The Blue Cliff Record*. 3 vols. Boulder, Colo.: Shambhala, 1977.

Collcutt, Martin. "The Early Ch'an Monastic Rule: *Ch'ing kuei* and the Shaping of Ch'an Community Life." In Whalen Lai and Lewis Lancaster, eds., *Early Ch'an in China and Tibet*. Berkeley: Asian Humanities Press, 1983.

———. *Five Mountains: The Rinzai Zen Monastic Institution in Medieval Japan*. Cambridge: Council on East Asian Studies, Harvard University Press, 1981.

Conze, Edward, trans. *The Perfection of Wisdom in Eight Thousand Lines & Its Verse Summary*. Bolinas, Calif.: Four Seasons Foundation, 1973.

Cook, Francis. *How to Raise an Ox: Zen Practice as Taught in Zen Master Dōgen's "Shōbōgenzō."* Los Angeles: Center Publications, 1978.

———, trans. *The Record of Transmitting the Light: Zen Master Keizan's Denkōroku*. Los Angeles: Center Publications, 1991.

———. *Sounds of Valley Streams: Enlightenment in Dōgen's Zen*. Albany: State University of New York Press, 1989.

Dumoulin, Heinrich. *Zen Buddhism: A History*. Translated by James W. Heisig and Paul Knitter. 2 vols. New York: Macmillan, 1990.

Eidmann, Phillip Karl, trans. *The Sutra of the Teachings Left by the Buddha*. Osaka: Koyata Yamamoto, 1952.

Faure, Bernard. "The Daruma-shū, Dōgen, and Sōtō Zen." *Monumenta Nipponica* 42, no. 1 (Spring, 1987).

———. *The Rhetoric of Immediacy: A Cultural Critique of Chan/Zen Buddhism*. Princeton: Princeton University Press, 1991.

Foulk, Griffith, trans. "The Daily Life in the Assembly." *Ten Directions* (Los Angeles) 12, no. 1 (1991).

Gimello, Robert M., and Peter N. Gregory, eds. *Studies in Ch'an and Hua Yen*. Honolulu: Kuroda Institute, University of Hawaii Press, 1983.

Hakeda, Yoshito S., trans. with commentary. *The Awakening of Faith; Attributed to Asvaghosha*. New York: Columbia University Press, 1967.

Heine, Steven. *A Blade of Grass: Japanese Poetry and Aesthetics in Dōgen Zen*. New York: Peter Lang, 1989.

———. *Dōgen and the Koan Tradition: A Tale of Two "Shōbōgenzō" Texts.* Albany: State University of New York Press, 1994.

———. "Dōgen Casts off 'What': An Analysis of *Shinjin Datsuraku*," *Journal of the International Association of Buddhist Studies* 9, no. 1 (1986).

———. *Existential and Ontological Dimensions of Time in Heidegger and Dōgen.* Albany: State University of New York Press, 1985.

———. "Truth and Method in Dōgen Scholarship: A Review of Recent Works." *Eastern Buddhist* 10, no. 2 (1978).

Hirakawa Akira. *A History of Indian Buddhism: From Sakyamuni to Early Mahayana.* Translated and edited by Paul Groner. Honolulu: University of Hawaii Press, 1990.

Hurvitz, Leon, trans. *Scripture of the Lotus Blossom of the Fine Dharma.* New York: Columbia University Press, 1976.

Inagaki, Hisao. *A Dictionary of Japanese Buddhist Terms.* Kyoto: Nagata Bunshōdō, 1984.

———. *A Glossary of Zen Terms.* Kyoto: Nagata Bunshōdō, 1991.

Ishida Hōyū. "Dōgen's Change of Attitude Toward the Laity's Attainment of Enlightenment." *Asian Pacific Cultural Center* XVII, no. 3 (1989).

———. "Genjōkōan: Some Literary and Interpretive Problems of its Translation." *Scientific Reports of Shiga Prefectural Junior College* 34 (1988).

———, trans. "Zazenshin, Admonitions Concerning Seated Meditation." *Scientific Reports of Shiga Prefectural Junior College* 35 (1989).

Ishigami, Zennō, ed. *Disciples of the Buddha.* Translated by Richard L. Gage and Paul McCarthy. Tokyo: Kōsei Publishing Co., 1989.

Kasulis, T. P. *Zen Action/Zen Person.* Honolulu: University of Hawaii Press, 1981.

Katagiri, Dainin. *Returning to Silence: Zen Practice in Daily Life.* Boston: Shambhala, 1988.

Katagiri, Tomoe, trans. "Continuous Practice in the Monks' Hall" by Tsugen Narasaki Rōshi. Unpublished translation of *Sōdō no Gyōji*, available from the Minnesota Zen Meditation Center.

Kawai, Hayao. *The Buddhist Priest Myōe: A Life of Dreams.* Translated and edited by Mark Unno. Venice, Calif.: The Lapis Press, 1992.

Kim, Hee Jin. *Dōgen Kigen: Mystical Realist*. Tucson: University of Arizona Press, 1975.

———, trans. *Flowers of Emptiness: Selections from Dōgen's "Shōbōgenzō."* Lewiston, N.Y.: Edwin Mellen Press, 1985.

King, Sallie B. *Buddha Nature*. Albany: State University of New York Press, 1991.

Kodera, Takashi James. *Dōgen's Formative Years in China: An Historical Study and Annotated Translation of the Hōkyō-ki*. Boulder, Colo.: Prajna Press, 1980.

LaFleur, William R., ed. *Dōgen Studies*. Honolulu: Kuroda Institute, University of Hawaii Press, 1985.

Leighton, Taigen Daniel. "Being Time through Deep Time." *Kyoto Journal* 20 (1992).

———, and Yi Wu, trans. *Cultivating the Empty Field: The Silent Illumination of Zen Master Hongzhi*. San Francisco: North Point Press, 1991.

Mathews, R. H. *Chinese-English Dictionary*. Shanghai: China Inland Mission and Presbyterian Mission Press, 1931.

Matsunaga, Alicia. *The Buddhist Philosophy of Assimilation: The Historical Development of the Honji-Suijaku Theory*. Tokyo: Tuttle, 1969.

Matsunaga, Daigan, and Alicia Matsunaga. *Foundations of Japanese Buddhism*. 2 vols. Los Angeles: Buddhist Books International, 1976.

Miura, Isshū, and Ruth Fuller Sasaki. *Zen Dust: The History of the Kōan and Kōan Study in Rinzai (Lin-chi) Zen*. New York: Harcourt, Brace & World, 1966.

Mizuno, Kōgen. *Buddhist Sutras: Origin, Development, Transmission*. Tokyo: Kōsei Publishing Co., 1982.

Morrell, Robert E. *Early Kamakura Buddhism: A Minority Report*. Berkeley: Asian Humanities Press, 1987.

Nhat Hanh, Thich. *The Miracle of Mindfulness*. Boston: Beacon Press, 1976.

———. *Present Moment, Wonderful Moment: Mindfulness Verses for Daily Living*. Berkeley: Parallax Press, 1990.

Nishijima, Gudo Wafu, and Chodo Cross, trans. *Master Dogen's Shobogenzo*. Book 1. Woods Hole, Mass.: Windbell Publications, 1994.

Okumura, Shohaku, and Taigen Leighton, trans. *Bendōwa: Talk on Wholehearted Practice of the Way*. Kyoto: Kyoto Sōtō Zen Center, 1993.

Okumura, Shohaku, and Thomas Wright, trans. *Opening the Hand of Thought*. New York: Penguin, 1994.

Okumura, Shohaku, trans. and ed. *Dōgen Zen*. Kyoto: Kyoto Sōtō Zen Center, 1988.

———. *Shikantaza: An Introduction to Zazen*. Kyoto: Kyoto Sōtō Zen Center, 1985.

———, trans. *"Shōbōgenzō Zuimonki": Sayings of Eihei Dōgen Zenji, Recorded by Koun Ejō*. Kyoto: Kyoto Sōtō Zen Center, 1987.

Powell, William F., trans. *The Record of Tung-shan*. Honolulu: Kuroda Institute, University of Hawaii Press, 1986.

Price, A. F., and Mou-Lam Wong, trans. *The Diamond Sutra and the Sutra of Hui Neng*. Berkeley: Shambhala, 1969.

Reps, Paul, and Nyogen Senzaki. *Zen Flesh, Zen Bones: A Collection of Zen and Pre-Zen Writings*. Garden City, N.Y.: Doubleday Anchor.

Sangharakshita. *The Eternal Legacy: An Introduction to the Canonical Literature of Buddhism*. London: Tharpa Publications, 1985.

Sasaki, Ruth Fuller, trans. *The Recorded Sayings of Ch'an Master Lin-chi Hui-chao of Chen Prefecture*. Kyoto: The Institute for Zen Studies, 1975.

Sasaki, Ruth Fuller, Yoshitaka Iriya, and Dana R. Fraser, trans. *The Recorded Sayings of Layman P'ang: A Ninth-Century Zen Classic*. New York: Weatherhill, 1971.

Satō, Shunmyo. *Two Moons: Short Zen Stories*. Translated by Rev. and Mrs. Shugen Komagata and Daniel Itto Bailey. Honolulu: The Hawaii Hochi, Ltd., 1981.

Saunders, E. Dale. *Mudra: A Study of Symbolic Gesture in Japanese Buddhist Sculpture*. Princeton: Princeton University Press, 1960.

Schloegl, Irmgard, trans. *The Zen Teaching of Rinzai*. Berkeley: Shambhala, 1976.

Sheng-Yen, Master. *Getting the Buddha Mind: On the Practice of Ch'an Retreat*. Elmhurst, N.Y.: Dharma Drum Publications, 1982.

———. *The Poetry of Enlightenment: Poems by Ancient Ch'an Masters*. Elmhurst, N.Y.: Dharma Drum Publications, 1987.

———. *The Sword of Wisdom: Lectures on "The Song of Enlightenment."* Elmhurst, N.Y.: Dharma Drum Publications, 1990.

Snyder, Gary. *The Practice of the Wild*. San Francisco: North Point Press, 1990.

Soothill, William Edward, and Lewis Hodous. *A Dictionary of Chinese Buddhist Terms*. Delhi: Motilal Banarsidass, 1937.

Stambaugh, Joan. *Impermanence is Buddha-Nature: Dōgen's Understanding of Temporality*. Honolulu: University of Hawaii Press, 1990.

Suzuki, D. T., trans. *The Lankavatara Sutra: A Mahayana Text*. London: Routledge & Kegan Paul, 1932.

———. *Manual of Zen Buddhism*. New York: Grove Press, 1960.

———. *The Training of the Zen Buddhist Monk*. New York: Grove Press, 1934.

———. *Zen and Japanese Culture*. Princeton: Princeton University Press, 1959.

Suzuki, Shunryū. *Zen Mind, Beginner's Mind*. New York: Weatherhill, 1970.

Tanahashi, Kazuaki, ed. and trans. *Moon in a Dewdrop: Writings of Zen Master Dōgen*. San Francisco: North Point Press, 1985.

Tanahashi, Kazuaki, and Tensho David Schneider, eds. *Essential Zen*. San Francisco: Harper, 1994.

Thurman, Robert A. F. "Buddhist Monasticism: A Spiritual and Social Perspective." Unpublished manuscript for Vinaya Conference, San Francisco, 1990.

———, trans. *The Holy Teachings of Vimalakirti: A Mahayana Scripture*. University Park: Pennsylvania State University Press, 1976.

Uchiyama, Kōshō. *The Zen Teaching of "Homeless" Kōdō*. Trans. by Kōshi Ichida and Shohaku Okumura. Kyoto: Kyoto Sōtō Zen Center, 1990.

Waddell, Norman, trans. "Being Time: Dōgen's Shōbōgenzō Uji." *Eastern Buddhist* 12, no.1 (1979).

———. "Dōgen's Hōkyō-ki." *Eastern Buddhist* 10, no. 2 (1977); 11, no. 1 (1978).

———. *The Essential Teachings of Zen Master Hakuin*. Boston: Shambhala, 1994.

Waddell, Norman, and Masao Abe, trans. "Dōgen's Bendōwa." *Eastern Buddhist* 4, no. 2 (1973).

---. "Fukanzazengi and Shōbōgenzō Zazengi." *Eastern Buddhist* 4, no. 2 (1973).

---. "The King of Samadhi's Samadhi: Dōgen's Shōbōgenzō Sammai O Zammai." *Eastern Buddhist* 7, no. 1 (1974).

---. "One Bright Pearl: Dōgen's Shōbōgenzō Ikka Myōju." *Eastern Buddhist* 5, no. 2 (1971).

---. "Shōbōgenzō Buddha Nature." *Eastern Buddhist* 8, no. 2 (1975); 9, nos. 1 & 2 (1976).

---. "Shōbōgenzō Genjōkōan." *Eastern Buddhist* 5, no. 2 (1972).

---. "Shōbōgenzō Zenki and Shōji." *Eastern Buddhist* 5, no. 1 (1972).

Watson, Burton, trans. *The Complete Works of Chuang Tzu*. New York: Columbia University Press, 1968.

---, trans. *Ryōkan: Zen Monk-Poet of Japan*. New York: Columbia University Press, 1977.

---. *The Zen Teachings of Master Lin-Chi*. Boston: Shambhala, 1993.

Welch, Holmes. *The Practice of Chinese Buddhism: 1900–1950*. Cambridge: Harvard University Press, 1967.

Wright, Thomas, trans. *Refining Your Life: From Zen Kitchen to Enlightenment, by Zen Master Dōgen and Kōshō Uchiyama*. New York: Weatherhill, 1983.

Wu, John C. H. *The Golden Age of Zen*. Taipei: United Publishing Center, 1975.

Wu, Yi. *Chinese Philosophical Terms*. Lanham, Md.: University Press of America, 1986.

---. *The Mind of Chinese Ch'an (Zen): The Ch'an School Masters and their Kung-ans*. San Francisco: Great Learning Publishing Company, 1989.

Yamada, Kōun, trans. *Gateless Gate*. Los Angeles: Center Publications, 1979.

Yampolsky, Philip B., ed. and trans. *The Platform Sutra of the Sixth Patriarch*. New York: Columbia University Press, 1967.

Yokoi, Yūhō, trans. *Regulations for Monastic Life: Eihei-Genzenji-Shingi*. Tokyo: Sankibō Buddhist Bookstore, 1973.

---. *The Shōbōgenzō*. Tokyo: Sankibō Buddhist Bookstore, 1986.

Yokoi, Yūhō, with Daizen Victoria. *Zen Master Dōgen: An Introduction with Selected Writings*. New York: Weatherhill, 1976.

The Translators

TAIGEN DANIEL LEIGHTON is an ordained priest and disciple of Tenshin Anderson Rōshi in the lineage of Shunryū Suzuki Rōshi. He is a graduate of Columbia University and has an M.A. in Philosophy and Religion from the California Institute of Integral Studies in San Francisco. He practiced at the New York and San Francisco Zen Centers; was head monk at Tassajara Zen Mountain Center; and practiced for two years in Japan. He is cotranslator of *Moon in a Dewdrop: Writings of Zen Master Dōgen; Cultivating the Empty Field: The Silent Illumination of Zen Master Hongzhi; Bendōwa: Talk on Wholehearted Practice of the Way;* and *Essential Zen.* Leighton currently teaches at the Green Gulch Farm Zen Center in Muir Beach, California, and at the Institute of Buddhist Studies of the Berkeley Graduate Theological Union.

SHOHAKU OKUMURA is an ordained priest and Dharma successor of Kōshō Uchiyama Rōshi in the lineage of Kōdō Sawaki Rōshi. He is a graduate of Komazawa University and has practiced at Antaiji and Zuiōji in Japan; the Pioneer Valley Zendo in Massachusetts; and most recently the Kyoto Sōtō Zen Center. His six previously published books of translations are *Shikan Taza: An Introduction to Zazen*; *"Shōbōgenzō Zuimonki": Sayings of Eihei Dōgen Zenji*; *Dōgen Zen*; *Zen Teaching of 'Homeless' Kōdō*; *Opening the Hand of Thought*; and *Bendōwa: Talk on Wholehearted Practice of the Way*. Okumura Sensei currently is head teacher of the Minnesota Zen Meditation Center.

Printed in the United States
940600003B